FROM THE CAPE TO KASSERINE

Ten Years of African Hunting
2007—2016

FROM THE CAPE TO KASSERINE

Ten Years of African Hunting 2007—2016

Craig T. Boddington

Essex, Connecticut

An imprint of The Globe Pequot Publishing Group, Inc.
64 South Main Street
Essex, CT 06426
www.globepequot.com

Distributed by NATIONAL BOOK NETWORK

Library of Congress Catalog Card Number: 2017940431

ISBN 978-1-57157-526-5

First edition

Printed in India

DEDICATED

To the memory of my father
Lt. Edward M. "Bud" Boddington Jr. USNR
1922–2000
World War II (Pacific Theater)

and

To the memory of my father-in-law
Pfc. Robert T. "Bob" Lurvey 1925–2016
Korean War (during the worst of it)

Table Of Contents

Author's Note: ...... The Lights of Luanda vii

Chapter One: .... The Cape Mountains 1
Chapter Two: .... Eden, Erindi, and Etosha 7
Chapter Three: .... In the Valley 24
Chapter Four: .... An Ending in Botswana 42
Chapter Five: .... Across from Ol Doinyo Lengai 55
Chapter Six: .... Mayo N'Duel 63
Chapter Seven:. .... A New Beginning in Mozambique 72
Chapter Eight: .... Fisher's Corner 83
Chapter Nine:. .... First Hunt in Coutada 11 89
Chapter Ten: .... Secrets of the Eastern Cape 96
Chapter Eleven: .... By Foot in Coutada 14 103
Chapter Twelve: .... Kigosi and Kilombero 110
Chapter Thirteen: ..... Rungwa 119
Chapter Fourteen: ..... Ghana 127
Chapter Fifteen: ...... The Pearl of Africa 133
Chapter Sixteen: .... The Kasserine Pass 143
Chapter Seventeen: .... The Liberian Forest 151
Chapter Eighteen: ..... Natal, Cape, and Karoo 161
Chapter Nineteen: ..... Namibia's Escarpment 173
Chapter Twenty: .... Kalahari Lion 183
Chapter Twenty-one:. ... Arly 191
Chapter Twenty-two: ... Back to the Valley 201
Chapter Twenty-three: .. The Golden Oryx 210
Chapter Twenty-four: ... Horses, Dogs, and Cats 218
Chapter Twenty-five: ... Blaauwkrantz . . . Thirty Years Later 230
Chapter Twenty-six: .... Rhino at Otjiwa 239
Chapter Twenty-seven: .. On the Frontier 249
Chapter Twenty-eight: .. At Long Last, Caprivi 263
Chapter Twenty-nine: ... The Bella Forest 271
Chapter Thirty: .... Caprivi Buffalo 283
Chapter Thirty-one: .... The Zambezi Delta 293

Author's Note

The Lights of Luanda

Long-suffering readers will be aware that this is my fourth "ten-years-of-African-hunting" book, commemorating the last quarter of fully forty years of, initially, near-annual and, in recent years, more frequent African sojourns. This was not planned—not the first book, nor any since. As I've written before, I was still quite young when I worked extra jobs and saved my pennies so that I could get to Africa *just once* . . . and get it out of my system once and for all.

That plan hasn't worked particularly well. I am no longer young; in fact, I'm reaching a point where the wonderfully flexible euphemism "middle-aged" may be a bit of a stretch. Even so, I can honestly say that my fascination with Africa has not lessened over time. We who have been there know what that's all about: Africa is a seductive, addictive place. I cannot predict and certainly don't promise that there will be another such volume in another ten years, but I can positively assert that I'm not done yet. Or at least I hope I'm not. In the fall of 2016, however, I can say that this volume and this part of the journey are both complete, and I hope you enjoy my ramblings about a place that I love and filled with wildlife that I love.

As we have different motivations to be hunters, I suppose we have different reasons for being drawn to Africa . . . and, undoubtedly, different reasons for our compulsion to return. It is not impossible that some of you may have caught the African virus from my previous writings, and some of you may catch it from this book. I'm not sure whether I should envy you or pity you. The former because a first African sojourn is a magnificent and life-changing experience, and the latter because, once Africa gets hold of you, she is most reluctant to let go. Forty years into my own journey, I thought I would share three events that led me inextricably to Africa.

The first was in 1956, when I was four years old. My mother's brother, Art Popham, embarked on a safari to Tanganyika. Although far from historic, this was an unusual event in Kansas City in those days. His Africa was quite different from mine, for in one hunt he took two lions (common in the day when lions were still considered vermin), a fantastic elephant, and, of course, a buffalo. Included in his bag was a magnificent sable antelope, but he never got his greater kudu, nor did he get a leopard. In subsequent years he hunted in many interesting places but, oddly to me, he never returned to Africa to get his kudu or to again match wits with Old

Spots. But he wanted to, and he especially lamented not going back to hunt a greater kudu. This reflection came many years later; what mattered to me in 1956 was that my uncle had gone to Africa. As a four-year-old, I swore I would do that someday.

The next event was in the early 1960s when I discovered that our grade-school library held a surprising treasure trove of Africana; regrettably for today's youth these are unlikely volumes to find on the shelves. I believe the first book I read about Africa was John Alexander "J. A." Hunter's *Hunter*, but it was quickly followed by Walter Bell, John Taylor, Ernest Hemingway, and perhaps the greatest gateway to Africa ever written, Robert Ruark's *Horn of the Hunter*. A decade would pass before I got there—"to get it out of my system once and for all"—but I was obsessed with Africa when barely a teenager . . . and I still enjoy re-reading those great old books.

The third event took place in the spring of 1975, just two years prior to my first safari in Kenya—before I was seriously considering making that dream a reality. I had almost forgotten about this until just a few weeks ago when I was in camp in Namibia's Caprivi Strip with professional hunter Dawid Muller. A couple of years younger than I, Dawid was in the South African forces during their long struggle along the Angolan border in the 1970s and 1980s.

I don't remember exactly what we were talking about. A brother of Dawid's was part of South Africa's famous Thirty-Two Battalion and was killed in the big battle on the Savuti River in 1980. Maybe that brought it up, but Dawid mentioned that, in early 1975, he'd been with South African recce forces deep in Angola. They were on high ground and had the lights of Luanda in sight. Their officers had told them American assistance was forthcoming . . . and then, inexplicably, they were ordered to withdraw. For more than forty years he'd wondered what that was all about, why they'd pulled back when the majority of the fight had been won . . . and the seeming fantasy that American forces were coming to support them.

That was an odd moment for me. In early 1975, I was a rifle platoon commander with Second Battalion, First Marine Regiment, First Marine Division at Camp Pendleton, California. The duty rotated, but that particular month we were the designated Air Contingency Battalion, subject to four-hour recall. So, one sunny afternoon, we were trucked to the airstrip. Ammunition was issued, C-130s were on the strip, and we were told we were on our way to Angola. I don't remember specific orders about actions to be taken once on the ground—those probably would have trickled down during the long transit. I do remember clearly that we were told South African reconnaissance units had "the lights of Luanda" in view, and we were going in. I also recall that, as we waited, one of my Samoan troops—I think it was Lance

Corporal Manelelelua—was diligently sharpening his entrenching tool, a time-honored pastime for Marine grunts preparing for battle. As I checked my platoon's gear, he looked up at me with a grin and said, "Lieutenant, we go kill Cubans, yes?"

It didn't happen. I will never know exactly what political maneuver prevented us from going in, or exactly how close we came, but we were ordered to stand down. For Dawid Muller, our conversation was the first time since he saw the lights of Luanda that he knew American intervention was that close, and his officers had told him the truth as they knew it.

So I came close to seeing Africa for the first time that day . . . or a couple days later, after a very long journey in a C-130. The larger politics were lost on me, but even then I knew an opportunity had slipped past, and I've long pondered how different the face of Africa might be today if our paltry eight-hundred-man battalion had gone in to secure the airfield. Perhaps another fifteen years of bush war in that region might have been averted. Or, perhaps not. I know that I nearly got to Africa that time, and it made me more determined than ever to see her on my own terms. Which I did, but instead of getting her out of my system once and for all, I became enthralled, seemingly forever.

I certainly don't promise another book in this series, but I can also promise that I'm not done with Africa. I've got some plans for the next couple of years, and there

Here I am with PH Mark Haldane planning an afternoon hunt in Mozambique. After forty years, the best advice I can still offer is to "listen to your professional hunter."

are potential opportunities I've waited a long time for. Sudan is not currently open, and while much of it has been ravaged, it's known that East Equatoria holds one of the continent's greatest remaining reservoirs of wildlife. I'd like to see it. Also, aside from my aborted "safari" there in 1975, I remember when Angola was open, and I've known a lot of people who hunted there, most of them gone now. During the last decade there have been many rumors about Angola reopening. It hasn't happened, but the potential remains. So, just maybe, after all these years it's possible that I might yet see the lights of Luanda.

In recent years I've had a wonderful time sharing my African habit. In my previous volume, *Tracks across Africa*, both elder daughter Brittany and wife and partner Donna were introduced to Africa, and both have become addicted. In this volume my younger daughter, Caroline, is introduced to Africa, a wonderful thrill for her dad. Here and there in this book I share a first African safari with several other hunters. That's also a wonderful experience . . . and perhaps sharing a first safari is the only way a jaded old hack like me can recapture the wonder of that initial African experience.

That brings me to a couple of people I wish I could have shared Africa with, the two gentlemen to whom I dedicated this book. Bud Boddington was by definition a member of "the greatest generation." He and his lifelong best friend, my godfather, Pleasant B. "Plez" Miller, tried to sign up immediately after Pearl Harbor. However, like a lot of kids from landlocked Kansas, they wanted to join the navy, and they both wanted to fly. So they went back to KU to finish the spring semester of 1942, joined up, and went on to fly in the Pacific. By all accounts Dad did a good job as an F6F Hellcat pilot, but fighter training took a lot longer than training to fly a torpedo bomber, especially after Midway, when two entire torpedo squadrons were practically annihilated. So Plez, itching to get into the war, became a TBF pilot and got to the Pacific first, eventually winning the Navy Cross for sinking a Japanese cruiser in Manila Harbor. Both came home in 1945, went back to school, started careers and families, and lived good lives.

But let's not forget that, just five years later, all too many World War II vets and a huge group of Americans too young for "the big war" were thrown into a cauldron on the Korean Peninsula, America's most forgotten conflict—and one of our most brutal. Bob Lurvey came home from Korea, went back to school, started a great career, and fathered six children. He shared only glimpses of his Korean experience with his kids, but it wasn't pleasant. He got through it, as did the vast majority of his fellows. From a distance of nearly sixty-five years, it seems more than appropriate to include our Korean War vets and their families as part of Tom Brokaw's "greatest generation."

Dad was a lifelong bird hunter, but from the 1960s on we did some great hunts together as far away as Canada. Into his seventies, Pop was still one of the fastest and surest hands I ever saw with a shotgun; it's no surprise that he was a good fighter pilot. The rifle was an unfamiliar tool to him and he was never confident, but he was actually a fine marksman, far more competent than he ever gave himself credit for. Interestingly, one thing Bud Boddington and Bob Lurvey had in common, although they never met, is toward the end they both wanted to see Africa.

Over the years I tried several times to talk Dad into going to Africa with me. He was always interested—he once asked me for a really good wall map of Africa, annotated with the places I'd been. After he retired he had the map on the wall in the basement, where he worked on his saddlery. He would have loved Africa, and I wish we could have shared it, but Pop had a problem. He was carrier-based in the Pacific, flying off the USS *San Jacinto,* time and again having to find the postage stamp of the carrier by dead reckoning and kneepad calculations. In 1945, when he turned off the switch for the last time, he swore he would never again fly over blue water . . . and he never did. Every time we brought it up he'd consider it seriously, and then come back to the same conclusion: "Nope, I'm not going to cross an ocean."

Dad fought cancer for a long time. His horses were his therapy, and he rode nearly every day no matter how bad he must have felt. When the battle was lost, he accepted it. I understood that later, because after he went for his last ride he put his saddle away, removing cinches and breast collar . . . placing them in storage, not awaiting ready use. My sister and I weren't allowed to see him at the end—he didn't want to be remembered that way. But we talked on the phone, and here's one of the last things he said to me: "Son, we had a lot of good times and some great hunts, but I wish we'd gone to Africa. That's one thing I was wrong about."

Bob Lurvey hunted a bit, but he wasn't really a hunter. He was definitely an adventurer, and he instilled that love of adventure in Donna, and to varying degrees in all his children. He was also a pilot; he loved his airplanes like my Dad loved his horses. Quite unlike my dad, however, he loved to travel. He retired relatively early and had a good life for a long time, enjoying flying his airplane and riding his Harley when he was in his mid-eighties. By that time, his daughter, Donna, had been to Africa several times. Bob Lurvey wanted to go, just to see it, and we wanted him to go, but his downhill slide was abrupt and steep, and mercifully short. We didn't get it done. Dad would have loved Africa, and Bob would have, too.

Maybe there's a message there. None of us knows how much time we're allotted, so we must use what we have as well as we can. Despite the best-laid plans, I don't really know if I'll get back to Africa—but I'm glad I've been there. If Africa is on *your* bucket list, don't wait too long.

Craig Boddington
Elk City, Kansas
October 2016

Chapter One

The Cape Mountains

Africa is a very big place. Nobody will see it all, but Lord knows, for forty years now I've tried to see as much of it as I could. Of course, that's only one game plan regarding African hunting, and I'll never say mine is the best. My buddy Dwight van Brunt has now been to Africa a couple dozen times, but always in the same country with the same outfitter. Neither approach is right nor wrong, better nor best, but clearly my approach has been a lot more eclectic. I've hit a lot of nooks and crannies (and missed a few more), but even without consciously planning, sometimes I find myself drawn back to special places.

I remember my old boss Ken Elliott's Two Rules of Life: First, don't sweat the small stuff. Second, it's *all* small stuff! Africa is the opposite of that in that *all places are special*. Regrettably, there are many places in Africa that I won't return to, but not because I wouldn't like to. Some are hot; a few are cold; some are thick; some are open. All have been special, and I can't recall an African hunting area I've been to that I wouldn't be grateful to return to. Having been at this for a long time, in some cases "not returning" means either hunting has closed or it's a place I can no longer afford; in other cases it means that, as good as it was, I can't find a proper excuse to do it again. That said, I felt it was appropriate to begin my fourth decade of African hunting with a return to the Cape Mountains.

It was not just a return to the Cape Mountains, but it was also a hunt for South Africa's most exclusive specialty, the Vaal rhebok. My fourth decade of African hunting began at Noel Ross's place up in the Cape's high country. The "vaalie" is one of South Africa's several indigenous rarities, but to me it's South Africa's greatest prize. Why? The vaalie is found only in the highest mountains, and it is resistant to all efforts at game ranching. The males (locally called "rams") are just too aggressive; they tend to kill each other if any attempt is made at confining them in a breeding program.

Noel Ross, Donna, and Russell Lovemore with a very fine Vaal rhebok, to my thinking South Africa's top trophy. Noel Ross has spent much of his life studying and trying to conserve the Vaal rhebok; he's one of the top authorities on this unique mountain antelope.

In the mid-1980s I took a fine ram with Lew Tonks, but it wasn't received in shipment, so a few years later he took me to the source, Noel Ross, and I took a monster. Noel's farm rides the crest of the Cape Mountains, and although he's avoided the international limelight, he's an icon in South African hunting. His lifelong project has been to "manage the unmanageable"—to propagate Vaal rheboks.

Understand, I didn't need another, and will almost certainly never take another, but Donna had neither hunted Vaal rheboks nor seen their country, so I had an excuse and a "surrogate shooter." My friend and frequent Eastern Cape outfitter Russell Lovemore set the hunt up, and he didn't actually tell me we were going to Noel's place until we were nearly there. Cool! Maybe too cool—it was brutally cold and windy up there, with amazing snow drifts down in the valleys. When we arrived however, Noel had a big fire going, and it was great to catch up after so many years.

As I said, nobody has successfully "game-farmed" Vaal rheboks, so for that animal it didn't matter much, but Noel's farm was now part of an unfenced conservancy, a growing trend in Southern Africa where neighbors join together to extend habitat and both conserve and properly utilize their wildlife. Sure, I had an agenda. Donna would hunt Vaal rheboks and, with luck, mountain reedbucks, and in the valleys below rhebok habitat, I could hunt lechwes and fallow deer, both species non-native to South Africa, both relatively widespread, but neither especially easy to find in a free-range situation.

Most difficult would be the Vaal rhebok . . . but it was even more difficult than we expected. We caught a period with blowing snow and gusty winds—terrible conditions to hunt an animal that is never easy prey anyway. The cold wind kept them down in the cuts, so on the first day we climbed and glassed—and saw nothing. On the second day, from the top, we saw a fine ram working up a valley at extreme distance. Scrambling hard against the wind, we got in on him, sort of. Donna got a shot, which went off to the right—was it wind, wobble, or rifle? The group stopped somewhere past three hundred yards, and she had another chance. It was a long poke for a .30-06, but this shot, too, was off to the right. It was probably the rifle, so we checked it again at dawn the next morning when the wind was finally dropping.

It was just three inches to the right at one hundred yards . . . thus nine inches right at 300. No way could anyone hit a Vaal rhebok that way. So we re-zeroed the rifle, and on a cold, calm morning we tried again. With the wind down, the vaalies were moving. A nice male and several females were working their way up a ridge, so we scrambled and got ahead of them to a point where Donna could set up on a bipod. When they reached the crest, the male's straight, black horns showed clear—but he was masked by a ewe. Then she stepped clear, and we all took a deep breath as Donna took the shot. This time the rifle was on, and so was the bullet. A really fine animal went down on the spot.

The lechwes and fallow deer were in scattered pockets well off the tops. We had glassed some fallow deer at distance—no obvious bucks—and were working our way to them when we ran into a huge mass of mountain reedbucks in a brushy valley to the right of the road. How many I don't know, but I've never seen so many in one place, so there surely were twenty and maybe thirty. It was my turn, but who cares? Donna's

This excellent southern mountain reedbuck was a huge bonus, taken from an unusually large group while we were looking for fallow deer.

.30-06 was in camp, so she took my .375 Ruger and made a slow stalk up the road with Russell as the reedbucks, spooked by the vehicle, made their way uphill.

Twenty yards is not a normal shot at a mountain reedbuck, but I suppose that made up for our challenges with the vaalies. Russell set up the sticks as the reedbucks filed past, and when a good buck showed, he whistled. Perfect shot . . . and now it really was my turn.

Fallow deer have been present in South Africa since the middle of the nineteenth century, but apparently neither genetics nor conditions especially favor this introduced deer because they tend to be modest in antler and have relatively poor paddles. This I understood, but I'd never taken one in South Africa, and this was a free-range opportunity. So we looked fairly hard and turned down a number of bucks, knowing we might not find better. And then we found a fallow deer working his way up a little cut that, well, looked like a fallow deer buck is supposed to look.

I was shooting a left-hand Hawkeye in .375 Ruger, topped with a Trijicon scope with a post and tritium triangle reticle. It's ideal for fast and close work, but this buck was pushing three hundred yards, not an easy shot off sticks, and definitely pushing the equipment I had. The buck came out of some brush and turned broadside, so I held the upper point of the triangle just on the backline, or as near as I could. The buck dropped to the shot, flattened. I breathed a sigh of relief.

That was in the morning of a pretty fine day. In the afternoon, we caught a group of lechwes in a little valley, managed to get the wind right, stalked in to about two hundred yards, and took a fine male, very big for a South African lechwe. Understand, these are not native; their ancestors came from warmer, lower country. I'm surprised that they do so well in this high, cold climate.

There are numerous stories about how lechwes got started in South Africa—too many to be sure of the truth—but in South Africa they are big-bodied, often with quite a bit of black on the chest and shoulders. Thus, they are unlikely to be the smaller black lechwes from Bangweulu, and equally unlikely to be red lechwes from western Zambia, Botswana, and Caprivi.

Legend has it, and is probably correct, that they are Kafue lechwes from the floodplains south of Lusaka. Horns in South Africa don't get as big as the best Zambian heads, but they are large in the body and often have black streaking on the chest. This seems to be consistent, and although few properties have large herds,

Donna and Russell Lovemore join me to hunt a South African fallow deer. Fallow deer were introduced to South Africa no later than the mid-nineteenth century and are widespread, but antler development is generally modest. For free-range fallow deer, this is a pretty good one.

they are extremely widespread. I hunted red lechwes in Botswana, and black and Kafue lechwes in Zambia. Maybe if I live long enough and the politics allow, I might have a chance to hunt Nile lechwes in Sudan. Until then, I'm glad I added the South African lechwe to the set.

At that time, blithely oblivious to what would transpire with elephants, lions, and rhinos (regarding hunting circumstances, importation, and management), a number of us were trying to raise awareness of the need to target older, hard-bossed, post-breeding buffalo bulls. Dr. Kevin Robertson—"Doctari"—lived in reasonable proximity to Noel Ross, so on our last evening he was good enough to drive over and allow me to get on video his views on the necessity to "hunt old buffalo." The interview was excellent; Kevin is a good guy and remains extremely outspoken in the effort to promote hunting mature buffaloes and to leave soft-boss bulls alone so that they can grow up to breed.

This remains extremely important for proper buffalo management, but, realistically, it's no longer a front-burner issue in African hunting. The buffalo is not threatened in any way and is unlikely to be. For sure there are issues in some countries, as you'll see as this book progresses, but buffaloes have recovered fully in parts

These gorgeous lechwes were found in the high country. Although the lechwe is now widespread in South Africa, most herds are quite small.

of Mozambique, and numbers are coming up fast in Namibia and South Africa. As Doctari has been championing, it is important to shoot older buffalo bulls, but buffalo hunting remains secure; it's the rest of the Big Five that's in turmoil.

Anyway, we got a great interview from Kevin, but maybe the timing wasn't exactly right. He was leaving soon for what would be a short-lived stint in Mozambique's Coutada 12. It turned out to be an environment that's quite a bit different from the Zimbabwe hunting he is more familiar with, and the season didn't end well. At that time I'd only hunted in Mozambique a couple of times, and all I could tell him was it was a whole lot different from the buffalo hunting he was used to.

Today, after spending many weeks in the Marromeu complex, I know a lot more. There are plenty of buffaloes, better every year, but both the timing and the hunting differ from elsewhere. Of course, one doesn't know what one doesn't know. So, full of confidence, Kevin went off to Coutada 12 much too early in the season, and it was a disaster. I've never forgotten that conversation because today I could probably have offered some meaningful suggestions. Back then I could not.

CHAPTER TWO

EDEN, ERINDI, AND ETOSHA

In my time I've seen South-West Africa become Namibia, and a quiet little backwater of Africa that no one (at least, no Americans) cared about has turned into Africa's second-largest safari destination. That's after South Africa, which didn't even have a safari industry when I started hunting in Africa back in the 1970s. The antihunters can say what they like, but the safari market has helped the wildlife. When I first hunted in South-West Africa in 1979 the numbers were good, but today I am convinced the wildlife has increased

Dirk de Bod and his Jack Russell, Jack, with Donna and me and her leopard, dead under the tree after just a couple hours in the blind. This was a very easy leopard, but she earned it elsewhere . . . having tried for a leopard a couple times before.

twentyfold. As a country, Namibia is a place that you never get enough of, with its clear skies, big horizons, and lots of game.

In the summer of 2007 several opportunities arose in successively awesome places. In previous years I'd gotten lucky with leopards both in Zimbabwe's Zambezi Valley and at Erindi, a huge private conservancy in central Namibia. Donna hadn't had the chance, and it was clearly her turn, so we planned a hunt with our friend Dirk de Bod, with Donna's leopard as the sole object (remember that). Then we'd join the Remington folks at Erindi for a few days of plains-game hunting with Corné and Nic Kruger of Omujeve Safaris. Finally, we'd cap our safari off with a hunt at Eden, east of Etosha National Park, with our friend Dwight van Brunt of Kimber and his PH buddy, Jamy Traut. Ambitious? You bet! Daughter Brittany would join us for the first part of the trip, and then head off and do her own thing when we went up to Jamy's.

Dirk's home territory is just an hour or so northwest of Windhoek, a particularly beautiful farm with rocky hills that overlook deep valleys. Jointly owned by Dirk and our old friend Joe Bishop, the place teems with a wide variety of antelopes. With plentiful prey, there are always a few leopards cruising the ridges, so that's where we started. Finding leopard tracks wasn't a problem, and the zebra quarters we hung are normally irresistible to a leopard. After a couple of days, it was clear that we had at least two leopards, a female and a big male, walking right past our baits. In this area these

While baiting for Donna's leopard we'd seen a lot of lion tracks, including this huge track, an obvious male. When the permit fell into our hands, this is the lion we were after.

Photographed three years earlier by Danny Bartlett, we believe this to be same lion, probably seven years old when this photo was taken. His mane was fuller, but the mane color, dark body color, and darker stripe down his back are distinctive.

Here Dirk and I pose with what is almost certainly my last lion. This wonderful old warrior had apparently just been kicked out of the pride and was bitten clear through the nose to the palate. Even so, he answered Dirk's roaring and came in looking for a fight.

are "ranch leopards," shy and clever and not easy to get on bait—and that's with Dirk only hunting a leopard there every couple of years.

We knew an outbreak of Namibia's periodic rabies epidemics, a disease that seems to primarily impact kudus and elands, was taking place. About the third day we tracked a leopard past one of the baits to a fresh kudu carcass, leading us to the immediate conclusion that there might be too much food lying around to get a leopard on bait. Thorough PH that he is, Dirk usually has backup plans, so he started calling around. Danny Bartlett, managing the Onguma property on the southeast edge of Etosha National Park, told us to get on the road. He'd had a tom leopard feeding just a few days earlier, and was certain he could get it back on bait in a short time.

"Certain" is not a word I like to hear in any hunting context, and most certainly *not* with leopard. But we packed up and made the long drive north, pitching up at Onguma's tented camp just at dark. This property had been developed as a private reserve adjoining Etosha (for both hunting and photography), and we found the game sparse and skittish. As we dug around looking for impalas and/or warthogs for leopard baits, the reason became clear: Onguma was overrun with lions! Most roads had lion spoor in the sandy soil, and although many were lionesses, we saw several tracks of big males.

Stephen Bindon and Corné Kruger with Bindon's sable, taken in another area a couple hours' drive from Erindi.

We eventually scratched up an impala and a warthog and got some baits hung, and that night after dark we went out looking for jackals and perhaps a hyena for Britt. I don't think we saw any canines that night, but we ran into lions three times, including one group of several young males. Even then, concerns were escalating about Africa's dwindling lion population, so the situation begged serious questions. The Etosha fence line looks like the antitank obstacles at Normandy, an intimidating affair of steel girders and cable. Apparently it works pretty well for elephants and rhinos, but is very porous as far as lions are concerned.

Because there are lots of lions in Etosha, the pride system there is fairly full, so many lions wander out . . . including young males in search of prides and older outcast males. Some of the adjoining properties are private game areas, but many are cattle ranches. Lions, of course, love cattle, but cattle ranchers don't love lions. By Namibian law, lions that endanger livestock are *fair game for the landowner*. However, there is no established lion quota for sport hunting.

The reason is simple and understandable: The authorities don't want operators baiting lions out of the park. (In 2015 this practice, common in many areas, would become a key issue in the *cause célèbre* over the death of Cecil the lion in Zimbabwe.) The downside then and to this day is that more than a hundred lions are shot annually by landowners along the Etosha boundary, with no economic benefit whatsoever. If landowners refrain from shooting lions and take their lumps and losses—and pester the game department enough—the occasional "problem lion permit" is issued. A lion taken on a formal problem-animal permit becomes exportable, and methods normally illegal in Namibia, such as night hunting and calling, are allowed, but such permits cannot be counted on and have relatively short shelf lives.

At any rate, Onguma was clearly infested with lions, and I immediately understood the near-certainty of getting a leopard on bait: With so many lions around, the leopards would have as difficult a time catching prey as we had finding bait.

So, no big surprise, a day or so later we had a nice tom feeding. The bait was at a distant waterhole, nicely skylined in a big tree, and a Texas-style box blind was already there for game viewing. So all we needed to do was check the rifle, clear a couple of branches, and move Dirk and Donna into the blind while Danny and I backed off a mile or so to wait. So far it seemed much too easy, and, in fact, it was, but when things work, they work. When they don't, well . . .

This was Donna's third attempt for a leopard, including a difficult three-week safari in Tanzania the year before. I don't know how many females and young males she saw on bait, or how many tracks of big toms, but she had already paid her dues. Full dark was near when we heard the shot, and then a long and nervous time passed before Dirk called. The leopard, a very nice tom, was dead under the tree.

A huge sable bull! This one is a breeder and so not up for grabs, but he's magnificent. Thanks to game ranching, Namibia is now producing some of the biggest sable antelopes in Africa.

It was late by the time we got back to camp. Brittany had gone out jackal hunting with some of

Anthony Acitelli (left), Jamy Traut, and me with Anthony's elephant. We had to shoot two young elephant bulls because they were wreaking havoc in the area. It was really a shame . . . but very exciting.

the youngsters and they'd gotten a couple, so it was a *joyful* celebration around the fire. Midnight was nigh and I think we'd broken out the Jägermeister when a vehicle rolled in. It was one of Onguma's owners. He'd come straight from the game department in Windhoek and had not one but *two* problem lion permits in his fist. It was already August and both permits had to be used by the end of the season. After a little more celebration, we struck a deal.

My situation on lions is a bit different from many. I had a terrible time getting my first lion when I started hunting in Africa even though a lion was commonly on license. After that first one, my lion luck turned. I took a couple of good ones in the 1980s, and I really never hunted lions. By the mid-2000s, it had suddenly become an extremely specialized and costly pursuit. I'd been thinking that I wanted to take one last lion. In Tanzania the previous year, Donna and I had a deal: I would take the lion, and she would take the leopard. We both failed. Now she had her leopard, and the chance for a lion had fallen into my lap.

We had seen exceptionally large tracks by a waterhole near the southern boundary of Onguma, where it joined cattle country. With some effort we got a kudu hung up there, and a warthog at another likely place. Next morning, those incredibly big tracks showed the lion had walked *past* our fresh kudu, with no apparent hesitation. "Well," we surmised, "he must have a natural kill somewhere nearby." He surely now knew the kudu was there, however. So we gathered material and returned in the late afternoon to build a blind, expecting he would visit the bait that night.

Donna and Brittany were chatting in the truck—imagine that—and we'd just about finished building a rough pole blind with camo netting and greenery. There was probably an hour of good light remaining when Donna stopped us, saying, "I just heard a lion roar."

Well, everybody knows I'm pretty deaf, and I suppose, as an occupational hazard, Dirk is a bit hard of hearing as well. (One of the advantages of being around folks with hearing loss is they tend to talk loud enough for me to hear!) Neither of us had heard anything and Dirk said, reasonably, "No, there are cattle on the next farm just a mile or so away . . . you probably heard cattle."

For once I was smart and backed Donna. I know *I'm* deaf, but she's heard plenty of lions roar in the Zambezi Valley and elsewhere. Remember, we had a legit problem-lion permit, so the gloves were off on methodology. Dirk gave a roar, and this time we all heard the lion answer, faintly. We stood for a few minutes, staring at each other, and then Dirk roared again. The answer was immediate—and a whole lot closer. This lion was on his way, and we weren't ready to receive him!

The bait was in a rectangular clearing, the almost-finished blind a few yards down a perpendicular track. Scrambling for rifles and ammo, we backed the truck into some brush fifty yards behind the blind—that was all we could do—and Danny, Dirk, and I took positions in the blind. I was standing over sticks, rifle ready, but nervous. I'd had no intention of hunting a lion on this trip, and I wasn't prepared. Brittany had her trusty Kimber

Eddie Stevenson (left), then with Remington, and Corné Kruger with an excellent old kudu bull, taken at long range with a .300 Remington Ultra Mag. A rabies outbreak had reduced the kudu population in this part of Namibia, and good bulls were hard to find.

Late in the hunt I got another chance at that big springbok, and this time I didn't mess it up. This is a really good springbok and the best one I've ever taken.

7mm-08 and Donna her Ruger .30-06. I had my double .450 3¼-inch, but the biggest *scoped* rifle we had was my .300 Remington Ultra Mag. Danny offered his CZ .375 and Dirk his .416 Mauser, but they were both right-hand rifles; my Remington was left-hand, so I figured I'd be better off with that and we'd all be a lot safer if they stood backup with right-hand rifles that they were familiar with. I was able to hedge my bet a bit: I had 200-grain Swift A-Frames.

Dirk gave one last roar before we got into the blind, and this time the thunderous reply seemed to come from just out of sight. Even so, I stood on sticks for nearly a half-hour, wondering if he would come and imagining what he might look like. He came silently, striding aggressively into the clearing. He was clearly an old lion, fairly dark in color, with a good mane. I'm sure it was surprise and shock—and maybe a little fear—because I quietly asked Dirk what he thought. He looked at me like I'd gone mad—and then the lion looked right through me, staring across forty yards of open ground. I shot him on the shoulder, then again as he reversed. I think Danny's rifle went off to my right, and I would have shot a third time but Dirk stopped me, saying, "He's pumping blood, leave it."

The lion went out of sight around the corner, back the way he'd come, but was lying just a few yards farther, breathing his last. We cannot know exactly what happened, but here's how we pieced it together: When we first saw his tracks, before Donna's leopard, there were several lionesses in the same area. It wasn't clear he was with them, although that was an assumption. Mind you, although this was only a decade ago, the recent imperative to avoid pride males wasn't yet widely known. But when he walked by the bait he was alone, and when he came into the clearing he was alone and looking for a fight. He had been bitten through the nose into the palate, so it appeared he couldn't eat, and we surmised that perhaps he had just been ejected from the pride. Danny had pictures from several years earlier of what we think is the same lion, for he had the same dark color, same distinct ridge down his back, same color mane. In the picture he is surely six, perhaps seven, with a fuller mane. Like us, some lions lose mane as they grow old, and others don't. From his body condition and teeth, we believe he was ten when he died, possibly eleven. He was a magnificent old lion, and surely my last.

We stayed at Onguma for a few more days. Brittany took a wonderful Damara dik-dik and Donna shot a fine warthog. Several times we tracked elands, but we never actually came close to getting a shot—there were lion tracks everywhere, and the game was just too spooky. From there Dirk drove us south to Erindi to meet the Omujeve guys, Eddie Stevenson, and a crew from Remington and Trijicon.

Erindi was the largest private holding in Namibia; we'd been there before and it was truly a wonderful place. Shortly thereafter the owners took it primarily into phototourism, but at that time it was loaded with game—in fact, probably seriously overstocked, which was a problem we were happy to help with.

We took some old gemsboks with worn horns and both Donna and Brittany took ostriches. I got lucky on a couple of good warthogs, but most of my hunting wasn't serious. That was when Remington had the Model 798 on a Serbian Mauser action . . . and they had a prototype *left-hand* .375 in camp. That was serious! I broke it in on a nice blue wildebeest, but I really wanted to take an eland with it. They had an elevated blind overlooking a waterhole, and they were

Because of the lions, most of the plains game at Onguma were scarce and extremely spooky, but there were lots of Damara dik-diks in the area. Brittany got this excellent ram using a little .22 rimfire that Dirk had in his truck.

sure a group of elands would come in at dusk. That seemed a little weird—I've mostly hunted elands by tracking, or at least spot-and-stalk, never by sitting—but they seemed so *positive.*

Sure enough, just at dusk a group of bulls came in, crossing our front from about a hundred and fifty yards. I picked what seemed the biggest, or at least the oldest, and shot him on the shoulder—then twice more as he vanished into the gloom. It was full dark when we found him, but fortunately he hadn't gone far. He was a beautiful eland bull. As we liked to say around the campfire when an animal was taken with the 798, we "Mausered" him! This far south in Namibia these elands are probably Cape elands, but the distinctions are blurry; although very muted, this bull definitely had white side-stripes.

At that time Remington wasn't involved in the *Tracks across Africa* TV show I was hosting, but Trijicon definitely was, so I spent several days hunting with Trijicon's president, Stephen Bindon, while the girls went elsewhere. I was with him when he got an eland, gemsbok, mountain zebra, and a Damara dik-dik on Erindi, and I went with Stephen and Corné Kruger when we went "down the road" to a ranch that had some special animals.

That was quite a day: Bindon took a tsessebe, a good sable, and a gorgeous southern roan. Consistently, he shot extremely well. Eddie Stevenson, then working PR for Remington, is also an old friend. I hunted with Eddie a few days, and was with him when he shot a beautiful old kudu bull.

Jamy's fly camp in Bushmanland. There wasn't much game in this wild, arid country—but it was a very good spot for leopard.

After that, as I recall, Brittany was off to Cape Town to visit friends, and Donna and I went up to Eden to hunt with Jamy Traut, joining Kimber's Dwight van Brunt and Federal's Anthony Acitelli. Eden was another incredible place, a standalone conservancy off to the northeast of Etosha, just before you get to Bushmanland. There I kept my

A really beautiful eland bull with heavy, worn horns and an exceptionally thick forehead brush, taken at Eden. This far north in Namibia these should be Livingstone eland, but the body stripes on this bull are extremely muted, more like a Cape eland to the south.

own rifles cased, for the point was to try out Kimber's brand-new Caprivi in .375, along with the lightweight Montana in .30-06. I don't remember exactly how it went down, but it seems to me another writer was supposed to be there but had to cancel, which meant there was a lot of quota available. (And we used it very well!)

I also don't recall why I got tagged, but we had one leopard available in an adjacent Bushmanland concession. Mind you, I didn't resist—that sounded interesting. Eden had a small herd of elephants, all fairly young, but two young bulls had apparently turned juvenile delinquents and were breaking out and terrorizing neighboring farms, so we had problem-animal permits for their removal. Eden held the full complement of northern Namibian plains game, with specialties being excellent kudus and a lot of elands.

We checked zero at midday, and in the late afternoon Donna and I went out with Jamy for eland while Anthony and Dwight went in separate directions. Donna drew first blood. Jamy spotted a lone eland bull slipping through a tree line, so we hustled to get ahead. Although a lovely rifle, the Caprivi was too long and too heavy for her, so she was carrying one of the little Montana rifles stoked with Federal's then-new (and untried) Trophy Tip Bonded bullet. The bull was just coming out of the trees and into

This old gemsbok with worn horns was exactly what we were looking for.

an opening when we got into position. Donna got on the sticks and shot quickly, and the bull made a short run and was down. It was a pretty good start, and the bullet performance was impressive—as it would prove to be throughout the hunt.

The next day Jamy and I left at midday to check on the leopard situation. It was about a two-and-a-half-hour drive, but the country changed dramatically. As I'd heard, Bushmanland is extremely open, with rolling grassy hills and few trees. It was in Bushmanland where Kai-Uwe Denker made his reputation with big elephants, but it didn't look much like elephant country—or leopard country either. Jamy had a fly camp along a dry watercourse, with the bait maybe a twenty-minute walk away. I had written my book *Leopard* a couple of years previously, but that doesn't mean I know everything about leopards, and I learned something that afternoon.

The bait hadn't been hit in a while and had turned rancid. We thought that might be the case, so we were prepared to either stay if the signs were good, or fix things up and leave it for a couple more days. The latter course was appropriate, so we replaced the bait and checked out the blind—and this was the new wrinkle: Jamy had built a little waterhole next to the bait, something I'd not seen before. That's a good idea under a lot of circumstances, but in really dry country like Bushmanland, it's brilliant. With things all ready for our spotted guests, we drove back to camp.

Donna had gone out with a tracker that afternoon and shot a nice zebra, and Dwight and Anthony both had animals in the skinning shed, so everything was looking good. Jamy's camp overlooked a waterhole, and from midmorning on a constant flow of animals came in—lots of kudus, waterbucks, springboks, impalas, and more. It was a kaleidoscopic hunt, with so much going on that I can't remember the exact sequence, but I do remember that, a couple days later, Jamy and I got onto a huge springbok, easily the biggest I'd ever seen. He was with some females in a little grove of trees when we crawled up within a hundred and fifty yards of him. I took a careful rest over a partial wall from an abandoned watering point and . . . I missed him clean. It is probably one of the luckiest bad shots I've ever made.

Through some form of bush telegraph Jamy got word that a leopard was feeding, so we packed up and headed for Bushmanland. Before we left Eden, I had a random, sour-grapes thought about that springbok . . . and it occurred to me that we'd better check the rifle. I have no idea what could have happened, but at sixty yards, approximate blind-to-bait distance, the strike was six inches high. That's plenty enough to miss a springbok . . . and mess up a leopard. We cranked the scope down and I fired a couple shots to be sure, and off we went.

Yes, the bait had been hit . . . as had our faux waterhole, and the tracks were good, clearly a tom. Prior to our hunt Jamy had two toms feeding, one OK and one very big. The tracks I was seeing looked OK, not huge—at least by my yardstick it was a normal-size tom. We got into the blind about 3:30 and settled in for a long wait, me on the rifle, Garrick Cormack on the camera, and Jamy right behind us in the coach position.

As often happens, the leopard was suddenly there, with no warning. It was early, just a little past five o'clock, with low sun coming under the branches onto the bait and playing magically on his spotted hide. He hesitated for just a moment, and then stuck his head into the bait. Jamy whispered, "It's a nice tom, but he's not the big one. We can wait and see if you like."

Hmm. It wasn't really a dilemma at all. We had a beautiful leopard in golden light, camera rolling. As with lions back in the 1980s, in recent years I'd had pretty good luck with leopards—but historically not so hot. Jamy Traut is a great PH, and if he said there was a bigger cat working this bait then I believe him, but I wasn't willing to take the chance. The only real hesitation was in waiting for a good broadside presentation, a matter of just a few seconds.

Wild ostriches are the very devil to get a shot at. Brittany took this one at a dead run with her little 7mm-08.

When it came, the cat was facing to the right, body angling up a slanting branch. Mind you, I'd taken leopards before—and I've *tried* to take leopards since—but with special animals like this, one always has the sense that this might be the only or the last time. I really wanted to do this properly, so I remember with absolute clarity coming up the rear line of the on-foreleg, one-third up into the body, then consciously shifting the cross hairs right into the center of the shoulder.

By all rights the cat should have collapsed like a sack of cement, but upon receiving the bullet he apparently swapped ends. This I didn't see because of recoil. As I recovered I did see, with horror, the cat exiting the top left of my field of the view in a mighty leap, clearly under his own power. Not good but, fortunately, not as bad as it appeared.

With gloom gathering we organized quickly and made a line through the yellow grass. We found the leopard before we found any blood, a nice tom stretched out and dead pretty much at the end of his parabolic arc. The shot was perfect, centered on the on-shoulder and exiting the opposite. I wrote about this before in *Safari Rifles II*, and I try to avoid unnecessary duplication, but I think it's a foot-stomping point.

The obvious problem was the .375; its tough 300-grain bullets, intended for much larger game, penetrated without much expansion. I remain convinced that, with that shot, any .270, 7mm, or .30-06 with bullets intended for leopard- or deer-size game would have collapsed the cat dead under the tree. Just a couple of weeks earlier Donna accomplished this with her .30-06—with a much more difficult shot—but to this day it's a feat I have yet to manage.

Back at Eden the hunt evolved into a "take 'em as they come" plains-game safari. As one's African hunting becomes ever more specialized, this is actually a rare luxury, and I remember our time at Eden as a wonderfully *fun* safari. Sure, there were highlights. I took a beautiful kudu with a longish and tricky shot, and one, hot midday Jamy and I got a second chance at that monstrous springbok we'd missed. This time we crawled to 235 yards and I got a good prone rest over a low termite mound. On such a small antelope that's a long shot with a .375 and its typical "dangerous game" scope, so this time I was really careful, and I pasted the buck perfectly. His horns were right at 16 inches, and I doubt I'll ever beat him.

I wasn't as precise on the Day of the Eland. Once again we did no tracking. Instead we saw a big herd crossing the road in front of us. We disembarked quickly and followed, catching them feeding on the next ridge. A big bull gave me the chance for a quick quartering shot, and then was off with the herd as if nothing had happened. I was thinking this might be a long day, but our bull had stopped just over the top and I took a quick offhand shot as he tried to run. This was a gorgeous bull, with thick, deeply ridged horns and a heavy forehead brush.

Often overlooked by so many hunters, the eland is one of my favorites, not only a magnificent animal, but in my view Africa's best venison—and thus the finest in the world. This far north in Namibia, these elands are technically Livingstone elands, thus should have more prominent side stripes than the Cape elands to the south. Mine did not, nor did Donna's; although definitely present, the stripes were very muted. There are no conclusions, except that it's difficult to draw precise geographic or political boundaries between the races of elands, especially where two varieties—in this case Cape and Livingstone—collide.

Then we had two Days of the Elephant. Honestly, this was a sad business, the necessary execution of two young bulls that couldn't be allowed to persist in the middle of a district generally devoted to farming. That said, it was a tricky and dangerous undertaking since we had to penetrate the herd and winnow out correct bulls on two separate occasions. I went first, slightly flubbing a quartering brain shot

The main camp at Eden overlooked a waterhole where game constantly came to drink. We saw these waterbucks every day, but kudus, warthogs, springboks, and more made a near-constant procession.

at a bit too much distance, maybe forty yards. A short follow-up was required, and we got the bull down without incident.

Anthony followed a few days later. This was Anthony's first elephant, so the point of me going first wasn't to be hoggish, but so Anthony could observe. He must have learned well by negative example because he faced his elephant at fifteen yards and took it down with a frontal brain shot, back legs collapsing first just like it's supposed to happen. Jamy was beside him with his .458, me likewise with my double .450—but there was no need. Anthony did it perfectly.

As I've written previously, Namibia's wildlife has blossomed since I first visited there in the 1970s. This month-long sojourn was unique in that it encompassed three great hunts with three great outfitters and, very exceptional in Namibian hunting, included hunting for three of the Big Five. It also included hunting in three exceptional "E's" in Namibian hunting: Eden, Erindi, and Etosha. Unlike my three "ten-year African books" that have preceded this volume, with some exceptions I have decided that multiple hunts in certain areas must be consolidated. In part this is because there is simply too much material, but on a practical level, remember that in the early 2000s I was hosting the *Tracks across Africa* TV show. To that end I was spending several months a year in Africa, but relatively little was devoted to personal hunting. Rather, I was hosting camps and accompanying "sponsors' reps." Namibian hunts to come would include spending good times with Ruger's Mike Fifer, Hornady's Wayne Holt, and Blade Tech's Tim Wegner . . . but it's probably most appropriate that I allow them to tell their own stories if and when they desire to do so.

There would be more great hunts with the brothers Kruger of Omujeve, and with Jamy Traut, and, of course, with Dirk de Bod. Neither Eden nor Erindi would play a role. As mentioned, focus in Erindi shifted from primarily hunting to primarily photographic. Omujeve Safaris would shift to a headquarters in central Namibia, and Jamy would move on from Eden, re-establishing as Jamy Traut Safaris. Both would establish a dual focus: plains game in the south and big game in the far north and Caprivi.

Dirk would similarly concentrate on plains game on and around his "home place" in central Namibia, but with the ability to shift as requirements dictated. In 2011 we did a classic hunt with Dirk, starting at his home and then shifting to a marvelous conservancy, Etosha Heights, on the southwestern border of Etosha. Well, it was "classic" except in one sense: A primary goal was to secure both a leopard and a big kudu for a friend, but, most unusual for Dirk, we failed. We saw plenty of kudus, but never the monster we sought. We did see a really big leopard, but it's a subjective "we" because I didn't see it, and neither did our friend. I was elsewhere, sitting over a bait for the elusive brown hyena, and that afternoon our leopard hunter chose to remain in camp to catch up on phone calls. Donna, who had no leopard on her license, had an extended view in broad daylight of the monstrous leopard we were baiting. It must have been an exciting afternoon, for that same day she had a too-close view of an equally monstrous black mamba, coming straight for the truck at high speed.

We did accomplish one significant goal on that hunt. At least, it was significant to me. Up near the Etosha boundary we succeeded in taking a really good Angolan black-faced impala. I'd seen them elsewhere. In 1979 Ben Nolte was trying to breed them at Epako, near Omaruru, but ultimately the cheetahs got the better of them. On Onguma most of the impalas naturally carried the distinctive black nose stripe. Had I gotten one, I suppose that would have been an exportable "black-faced impala," since these were not officially registered as such—but we never got a shot. Here we got the real deal, a wonderful heavy-horned old ram, taken after a tense stalk along a brushy hillside. The black-faced impala is not exportable. This is regrettable because lack of value greatly hinders efforts to rebuild its numbers. The mount of this animal resides in Dirk's camp, along with the beautiful cheetah taken with Dirk and Pete Kibble a few years earlier. I hope I can continue to visit them from time to time.

Chapter Three

In the Valley

We picked up the spoor of two bulls coming up out of the riverbed, good tracks for Zambezi Valley elephants. The hunting had been difficult, and we were looking for a special elephant, but not in the conventional sense. Although never as overpopulated as Botswana's elephants are now, Zimbabwe has a longstanding elephant problem, especially to the west in the Hwange Park, and to a lesser degree in the Zambezi Valley, where we were hunting. Zimbabwe is a relatively small country, and within her borders elephant habitat is limited to the national parks, forestry areas, Designated Safari Areas (DSA), and tribal trust and communal lands on the periphery of the country. Within this limited habitat Zimbabwe's elephant population has been estimated between a low of 70,000 to well over 100,000 (this in contrast to Botswana's 2015 count of over 250,000 elephants).

With a large human population, Zimbabwe has some of the highest incidence of elephant-human conflict. The Convention on International Trade in Endangered Species (CITES) has recognized a combination of limited habitat, overpopulation, and conflict in awarding Zimbabwe the continent's highest quota for exportable sport-hunted trophy elephants: 500. This creates two problems. First, although "trophy" is a subjective term, Zimbabwe, with genetics for modest ivory, is not capable of producing 500 "trophy"—size elephant bulls that would satisfy most hunters, especially consid-

Ivan Carter and one of Chifuti's trackers working out an elephant spoor.

This big tuskless cow was the first elephant I took with Ivan Carter. We were in thick jess, *and the shot was about twelve yards. I would learn that this was a fairly long shot when hunting with Ivan.*

ering the $10,000 government trophy fee. Second, the actual harvest—combining sport-hunted elephants, self-defense shootings, and Problem Animal Control (PAC) elephants that are mostly crop-raiders—greatly exceeds 500 annually.

Despite the excesses of the Mugabe government, Zimbabwe Parks and Wildlife has soldiered on, and in the main it does a pretty good job. Over the years it has tried several creative approaches to elephant management. My first elephant, back in the 1980s, was taken on a "nontrophy bull" permit, which allowed me to take a bull with no more than twenty-five pounds of ivory per side. I was fortunate; mine was an old bull that was virtually tuskless. However, this program was quickly abandoned because it unintentionally promoted the harvest of young bulls with promise that might, in ten or fifteen years, have beautiful ivory. Also, if population control is a genuine goal, then harvesting bulls of any age does little; it is a cow harvest that is essential. Current programs include an aggressive quota on tuskless elephants since "tuskless" is viewed as an inherited and undesirable trait. Either sex is allowed, but most tuskless elephants are cows. Much more about tuskless elephant hunting later.

In other areas with serious overpopulation, there have been quotas for cows with tusks. This has never been authorized in the Lower Zambezi areas, from Mana Pools east to the Mozambique border, where I've done most of my Zambezi Valley hunting.

From the side this bull shows a lot of tusk, but he's old and the ivory is very thin with little weight. We were after a "meat elephant," and this one is a perfect candidate.

There the overpopulation isn't serious (yet), so trophy bulls and tuskless elephants are the usual targets. In the mid-2000s, they added a community meat quota: The meat had to be recovered and distributed, and the ivory went to the government. This was what Andrew Dawson and I were seeking, and although tusk size was restricted, what we wanted was an older bull with either short or thin tusks, one that was almost certain to never become a fine tusker.

We'd been looking hard, and ace tracker Mukassa was certain one of the bulls from the spoor we had picked up was older. We tracked through the thick riverine growth and up into more open gallery mopane forest. The tracks were very fresh, and it wasn't long before we had a visual. One bull was clearly young, but the other was an older bull, his hide shrinking onto his ribs and his hip bones showing. At a distance the ivory was impressively long—this bull could fool you—but lip circumference was small and the tusks tapered quickly. There was little weight there.

Andrew and I played tag with him for several minutes, maneuvering for a shot but unable to get quite close enough. By now he was nervous. Aware of a foreign presence, he was circling to get the wind. Soon he would crash off. We rushed in, cutting across the circle, and the bull instantly turned to us and charged, ears pinned back. Andrew had his famous William Evans .470; I had a new Heym .450/.400 3-inch. We planted our feet and waited, and when the bull ran straight into the two double rifles, that was that.

I started hunting in the Lower Zambezi in 2004 when, with the Safari Classics team, we did the *Boddington on Buffalo* DVD. Other DVDs morphed into the *Tracks across Africa* TV series, and the Lower Zambezi with Chifuti Safaris was our primary "studio" until I left the show in 2011. In those days the Lower Zambezi areas—Sapi, both Chewores, and Dande North—offered awesome buffalo hunting, good elephant hunting, and great hunting for lions, leopards, hippos, and crocodiles. Chifuti was a very good outfit, with a crew of fine professional hunters.

As I mentioned in the previous chapter, a lot of the "hunting" I did was accompanying sponsor reps, so I hunted with most of the Chifuti guys and was in camp with all of them. Oddly, I never hunted with Owain Lewis, who was killed by a buffalo in 2013, but I did a number of hunts with Ian Gibson, who was killed by an elephant in 2015. I watched Mark Valero progress from an eager apprentice to a truly fine PH; likewise the same can be said of young Anthony Howland, who lost an arm when a client accidentally discharged his rifle. Regrettably, he's gone to Zambia to farm and is no longer in the hunting game. I also hunted several times with Brent Leesmay, one of the most talented young PHs I've ever known. He got married and is now in a management role at the new Nuanetsi Conservancy.

Mike Payne was often there, another consummate professional hunter, now doing his own thing as a partner in Save Safaris (more about him later in this book). I hunted several times with Len Taylor—quiet, calm, efficient, effective, still in the game, and one of Zimbabwe's best. Len guided my friend John Astle to a fine tusker and a great buffalo on the first two days of their safari. On another occasion I spent a very long day with Len trying to recover a leopard another hunter had wounded. He's a guy I would hunt with again any time, as I would all of these current and former Chifuti hunters. I

Andrew Dawson and I discuss our elephant bull.

also hunted a few more times with Paul Smith, one of Chifuti's owners and a very good PH. Paddling along with these guys, I shared hunts with Steve Hornady, Dallas Safari Club's Ben Carter, Leica's Terry Moore, Ruger's Randell Pence, Texas Hunt Company's Jeff Wemmer, and other assorted characters—good guys all.

Most of my own hunting, however, was done with Andrew Dawson, Paul Smith's partner at Chifuti. Once the TV show got rolling there was never time for a full safari, but I managed to slip in a few buffaloes and some tuskless elephants, and I always enjoyed hunting with Dawson. Actually, I liked hunting with all of them, but styles varied. Dawson was careful and methodical, a style that worked very well for me. His hunters usually got their primary animals, with few wounded animals to follow and fewer that caused any problems. I mention this because our charge toward that elephant bull was one of few times I saw Andrew Dawson take such a calculated risk.

One definite way to get a shot at an elephant is to get it to charge. It's a desperate move because some elephants will simply bomb out the other way, never to be seen again, and some charges cannot be stopped . . . but most of the time, if you're aggressive, you will get a confrontation. The thing is, this should be done only if you already know for certain you're going to shoot *that* elephant if you get the chance because if the elephant commits, then *everybody* is all in. In that situation we knew we were going to take that elephant if we could. We were in relatively open mopane, not a bad place to take a charge, and a very good place to recover the elephant easily (which was a major point to the exercise). So that's what we did, and it worked perfectly. Later, when Ivan Carter came on board, I quickly understood that confrontation was his preferred tactic. To each his own, but I much preferred Dawson's approach, which was generally calmer—for both hunter and hunted—and much more methodical.

A good elephant bull track, showing plenty of wear near the heel. We don't know the size of the ivory, but the track says this is a bull we should follow up and look at.

We were able to do several more buffalo hunts together. Sometimes

Steve Hornady (left) and Paul Smith with a really nice Chewore lion. Zimbabwe isn't known for lions with especially good manes, but lions are probably overpopulated in the Lower Zambezi area and some were very good.

there were just a couple of days between clients, so we couldn't be all that picky, but in those days there were still lots of buffalo bulls in the Lower Zambezi, both in mixed herds and smaller groups of bachelor bulls. One midafternoon we walked down the Chewore, a wide sand river where *dagga* bulls were almost certain to bed. They liked to find a shady spot under overhanging branches and lie on the cool sand. Steve Hornady was with us, but it was my turn to shoot. We hadn't gone very far when we saw a dark pile of brush with something darker showing through—a nice old buffalo bull taking a nap.

Mukassa led us along the far bank, using little islands and sandbars for cover. We got to about a hundred and twenty-five yards when we found nothing but clean sand ahead. Since it was better to take the shot there than try to close and risk a moving shot, Dawson put up the sticks, and in a few seconds the bull got up and stood clear. The first shot was fine, on the shoulder, but the bull was determined to get up the steep bank, and I was determined he should not. I shot him twice more, but he won, sort of. . . . He made the top, and died right there. That was the year Hornady introduced the .375 Ruger, and I had one of the first in Ruger's new Hawkeye configuration, a really sweet-handling rifle.

Steve Hornady did several good hunts with us. His first leopard hunt was one of the rare failures for the group. Even though we hunted hard, and had several good leopards feeding, we never got a tom to come onto a bait in daylight. Undaunted, Steve came back the next year for Round Two. I think he was hunting with Ian Gibson, and I was somewhere else with Dawson. It was about the midpoint of the hunt when we heard a terrible commotion over the radio.

Hornady and "Gibbo" were having some kind of an argument, and Hornady had had enough. The hunt was over, and he was going home. I talked to Steve that night. No, he wasn't mad, he was just tired—he'd had enough. It was the same as last year, and he wanted to go home. We were somewhere in the middle of that ticklish conversation when the drums started to beat, and the staff paraded into the firelight the skin of Steve's very large leopard—dead for more than twenty-four hours and kept completely under wraps. Of several, that was probably the best practical joke I saw Steve Hornady pull.

A year or so later he took a very fine lion with Paul Smith. I wasn't there for that, but by then it was obvious there were too many lions in the area, especially in the two Chewore blocks (North and South). By 2010 we were starting to see the signs: Tracks of *dagga* bulls were much scarcer than just a couple of years previously, and although the herds were still big, a quick scan would reveal very few calves in the herds. To help with the problem, a small quota of licenses for lionesses had been instituted but unfortunately removed again when lion hunting started to come under increasing scrutiny. There's no question the African lion is in trouble in many

This group of wild dogs was photographed in Chewore South. Once extremely rare in the valley, by about 2008 sightings of wild dogs were common in the Lower Zambezi—and their impact on the smaller antelopes, especially bushbuck and nyala, was readily seen.

Andrew Dawson (left) and Anthony Acitelli with a buffalo bull, taken on the safari to test Federal's new .370 Sako Magnum cartridge.

areas—but in the Lower Zambezi there were far too many, and the buffaloes were paying the price.

Anyway, Steve Hornady came back in 2010 for a lioness hunt, this time hunting in Chewore North with Ian Gibson. It was not a difficult hunt. Ian Gibson had been stationed in Chewore with the Rhodesian Light Infantry during the war, and he never left. He went from the RLI to Parks and Wildlife, and then turned professional hunter. His home base was Chewore North. In the time that I knew him, and for many years before, he guided clients to the vast majority of the lions, three or four every year, along with plenty of buffaloes, elephants, and leopards.

On that hunt we found the spoor of a small pride and hung a bait not far from the Chewore. We quickly had them feeding, so early one morning we crawled into the blind. Just at dawn Gibbo picked out a really big lioness, and Steve shot her perfectly. Although I saw him at conventions, that was the last time I hunted with Ian Gibson. He was a careful hunter, with a wealth of experience with dangerous game—probably as much as any PH in Zimbabwe, which is saying a lot. He was quiet around the fire and quieter in the bush, and he didn't suffer fools particularly well, but he was an awesome hunter, and not a man I would have expected to die as he did. Although I didn't know him as well, I would have said the same about Owain Lewis.

In 2008 Federal teamed up with Sako to produce the .370 Sako Magnum, European designation 9.3x66mm. Essentially it is a .30-06 case necked up to take the 9.3mm (.366-inch) bullet. The cartridge is a bit faster than the old 9.3x62,

Andrew Dawson and I are all smiles over a nice buffalo I took in the bed of the Chewore River with a .375 Ruger.

but similarly fits into a .30-06-length action. It's a great little cartridge that, for whatever reason, has languished, but while the .375 caliber is often cited as the legal minimum for dangerous game, in Zimbabwe (and other jurisdictions) the actual legal minimum is the .375's European equivalent, the 9.3mm. Wanting to try out the cartridge, Federal brought a group over for a ten-day buffalo hunt. I was again paired up with Anthony Acitelli, and we were hunting with Andrew Dawson.

Despite the increase in lions, there was a small quota for buffalo cows, and the intention of this quota was to target older cows without calves. There were older biddies in every herd, ribs and hips showing and no calf at heel, but most of the time the operators didn't know exactly what to do with this quota. Buffalo hunters wanted mature bulls, naturally, and on the typical ten-day buffalo safari, PHs were reluctant to get sidetracked by any other game until the buffalo bull was in the salt. Success was fairly certain, at least back then, but it was impossible to predict exactly when. Generally the hunting was fairly easy in wet years, more difficult in dry years.

The trophy fee for a buffalo cow was much less than that for a bull, so if a bull hunter asked for a cow on the license, the "TR2," that was fine, but there weren't enough for everyone. Nor, except for buffalo bulls, was there enough of anything to go around. Those Lower Zambezi areas were primarily dangerous-game areas. A given block, for instance, might have a quota for twenty, thirty, or even forty buffalo bulls, perhaps a dozen greater kudus and, perhaps, ten buffalo cows, but only a half-dozen zebras, a handful of waterbucks, a half-dozen tuskless elephants, and three or four each of lions, leopards, and elephant bulls. Blocks that fronted the river—Sapi, Chewore North, and Dande North—would have a few hippos and crocodiles. Some blocks had a few sables and bushbucks, but not much else. Even warthogs were generally on very short quota. The only exceptions were impalas, which were plentiful and widespread, and grysboks and hyenas. Impalas were, thus, the primary bait animal for leopard hunters.

Grysboks and hyenas were plentiful, but these were quotas that were never filled, even though most hunters would have both animals on their TR2. The brush was generally so thick that it was rare to catch even a glimpse of the shy little grysbok. Two thousand and five and 2006 were dry years in the Zambezi Valley—the bush was bare, and we saw a lot of grysboks. I took two in just a couple of days, and in another year, I think 2006, Wayne Holt, then of Hornady, got a good one. Dave Fulson even filmed a pair of grysboks mating in the Chewore riverbed. Then the rains got back to normal, and in the next five years, during the period of this volume, I don't think I personally ever saw another grysbok.

Hyenas were always present, and every night their night music was a lullaby, in pretty much every camp. But in Designated Safari Areas night hunting was not allowed, so hunting them on purpose was a whole different story. After a buffalo was taken, it was always a good exercise to bait for hyenas, but it took a bit of luck to catch them on bait. In any given season quite a few were taken, but the quota was large, and almost never filled.

All this combined to make managing and properly allocating the quota a real nightmare, shared by all operators who work in Zimbabwe's Designated Safari Areas. Leopard and lion hunters simply had to have bait, so leopard hunters were always allocated a number of impalas, and lion hunters were encouraged to take a hippo. It was recommended that all cat hunters put a zebra, waterbuck, and, perhaps, a buffalo cow on their TR2. Mind you, this cost nothing until the animal was taken, but managing it was a paperwork nightmare. Since the goal for the Federal safari was to test a new cartridge, this was a perfect use for some of the buffalo cows. As I recall, we each had a buffalo bull and a couple of buffalo cows allocated.

Even at this time I was remembering the way things had been just a few years earlier when the spoor of groups of bachelor bulls could be found by cruising the

Maj. Bob Stutler took this leopard shortly before his retirement from Ruger. Stutler had an amazing Marine Corps career, a second and equally amazing career with Ruger, and now he has a gun shop in Medicine Lodge, Kansas (where he also did a couple terms as mayor).

sand rivers on almost any given day. Whether we followed or not depended on the freshness of the spoor and how many there were. One bull was almost never followed; the chance of losing just one track was too great, and since a single bull was likely to be an old-timer, there was an increased likelihood that one or both horns would be broken. Two bulls might be followed depending on the freshness of the spoor and wind direction, but we would usually follow the tracks of three or more bulls. This would reduce the chance of losing the tracks, increase the speed at which the tracks could be followed, and greatly up the odds for there being a suitable bull at the end of the tracks.

By 2008 things were starting to change, although we didn't fully recognize or appreciate the signs. Bachelor bulls were not as plentiful; we needed to cruise a lot more miles of sand river—either on foot or by vehicle—and the groups were smaller, ones and twos rather than fours and fives. In the years since, I've heard this attributed to poaching, which has surely increased in Zimbabwe (and everywhere else) since the downturn in the world economy in 2008–2009. I think that should be put to rest, and now is as good a time as any. Although Dande is a combination of communal land and DSA, Sapi and both Chewores are DSA only, meaning no human habitation is allowed. There has been an escalation of ivory poaching, especially during the rains when safaris aren't in the field, but these areas are just too roadless and remote for meat poaching to be viable.

The lions are a partial answer. Earlier in 2008 I was camped above the Angwa River with Ivan Carter and hunter Ted Jernigan, near the boundary between Chewore South and Dande South. Our neighbor from Dande South visited one evening. He'd been there through the rainy season and had identified nine prides operating along the Angwa. That's a lot of lions . . . eating a lot of game. In these areas permanent water is scarce, so plains-game populations are scattered. Buffaloes are by far the most numerous large ungulate and definitely the lions' preferred prey. So that's a lot of lions eating a lot of buffaloes.

But the economics must also be figured. Government tender—rental—for the DSAs is astronomical, even before one figures in food, fuel, and other logistics. Buffaloes are the main draw, and the only way to make these areas pay is to harvest the quota set by the government. The quota of buffalo bulls is high in these areas, but probably sustainable *absent* severe predation by lions. Add in a large population of lions, and there's trouble ahead. In the herds, calves are most vulnerable, but older bulls, on their own or in small groups, are perhaps even more vulnerable than any buffaloes in herds. In the herds, we were seeing a shortage of calves, which is purely predation. Along the sand rivers, I think we were already seeing a dual hit between an aggressive hunting quota and increasingly aggressive predation by lions.

In any case, the Federal hunt was a very good one. Working big herds is always exciting, but especially so in the thick *jess* of the Zambezi Valley. We had no real problem penetrating the herds and identifying older cows, and I was surprised at how well the little 9.3mm worked. Older African hands and many Europeans would not be surprised: With a traditional 286-grain bullet, the old 9.3x62mm is a famous and respected choice, as is the 9.3x74R for use in double rifles. As an American, however, I've generally adhered to the .375 minimum. It was fun to use the light-recoiling cartridge, and we had absolutely no issues when we hunted several buffalo cows.

Mature bulls, however, were proving hard to find, and we were well past the halfway point when we found the fresh tracks of two bulls coming up from a sand river. This time we followed them, and they led us for miles. We were well into the heat of the day, and Mukassa had long since slowed down as he expected to find the bulls resting at any moment, but still the tracks led on. Another long hour passed, and now the tracks were taking us along a well-defined elephant trail, not meandering as if searching for perfect shade, but just walking slowly, as if on a distant mission.

Intent as we were on tracks that must surely be going *somewhere*, it's amazing to me that anyone saw the bull—black animal in black shadow—tucked into dark greenery barely twenty yards to the right of the trail. Equally amazing was that it

Steve Hornady and part of the Chifuti team with a nice crocodile Steve took along the Zambezi.

stood long enough for Anthony to get his rifle up and make the shot. But he did, and the little cartridge performed perfectly.

My own bull came on tenth and last day, a good mature buffalo winnowed from a big herd. We'd played cat-and-mouse with them for an hour and, for once, knew there were a couple of good bulls in the herd. They were working their way toward a boundary river, so we cut off to circle ahead and managed a clear shot as the herd passed in front of us. Again the little 9.3mm worked just fine. Oddly, in recent years the traditional 9.3x62mm Mauser has enjoyed a considerable resurgence, but the slightly faster .370 Sako Magnum hasn't done much. Go figure. . . .

In that same period the Safari Classics folks—Tim Danklef and Dave Fulson—and I were working up to producing our *Boddington on Elephant* DVD. On Andrew Dawson's suggestion we brought Ivan Carter into the fold. Combining professional hunting with guiding experience in national parks, Ivan was a serious elephant specialist, and he also proved extremely good on camera. Chifuti donated a series of elephant safaris to SCI to be filmed for *Tracks*, with me in attendance and Ivan assigned as the PH. The latter intent was to increase Ivan's reputation—an effort that was obviously very successful!

The first of these hunts, conducted in 2007, was purchased by Jim Hall, a really great guy from Pennsylvania. Jim had never hunted an elephant; actually, this was his first African hunt. It was surely not his last—since then he's taken most everything over there, but he started at the top. We did the hunt in Sapi, sort of a buffer area between Mana Pools and the two Chewore blocks, a fantastic area, though not exclusive to any one operator. Although we were always looking for big bull tracks, the plan was to "warm up" with tuskless cows—Jim and I each had one available, but Jim had the only bull permit.

His tuskless cow hunt proved a bit ticklish in that they penetrated a cow herd in the very late afternoon, with time growing short. So I sat that one out with the trackers while Ivan and Jim went in. Using a big A-Square .416 Remington, Jim took his tuskless cow elephant with a frontal brain shot at fairly close range—perfectly and without incident. I'm sorry I missed it. However, I was there for a couple of incidents worth recounting.

We got onto a young bull in thick riverine bush, and this was the first time I observed firsthand Ivan's amazing confidence with elephant. We pushed the bull, and he didn't want to be pushed.

Ivan said, "Watch. He'll make a mock charge, head up, and he'll stop right there," motioning to a termite mound ten yards ahead. "These young bulls are usually just bullies, and they like termite mounds because it makes them look even bigger. He'll retreat, try again, try maybe a third time, and then he'll storm off."

It happened exactly as Ivan predicted, as it did on numerous other occasions.

Unfortunately it was a similar young bull that killed Ian Gibson, a far more experienced PH than Carter. But lest it appear that Ivan is a suicidal maniac, let me say that he really does know his elephants and their body language. He takes no liberties with the more unpredictable cows unless the goal is to penetrate the herd to kill a tuskless, and if a bull is in musth—usually evidenced by secretions in the tracks—he gives it a wide berth. It was a bull in musth—a mating craziness—that killed Ian.

He and his tracker knew it from the tracks, and he had no intention of pressing him. Instead, using due caution, they left the client with a young apprentice and went forward simply and only to get a visual on the elephant to see if it was worth a closer approach. They saw the elephant in open mopane at well over a hundred yards, identified it as a young bull not worth pursuing, and were just turning back when a stray swirl of breeze gave them away. The elephant instantly charged, ignoring all the waving and shouting. Ian, who characteristically never shot until he absolutely had to, kept shouting until just a second too late.

Although Sapi is an awesome elephant area, it's a long, narrow strip between Mana Pools and Chewore. So elephants (and buffaloes) cross in and out at will, and are not always present. On this hunt we had a very difficult time finding good

Ted Jernigan (left) and Ivan Carter with a nice waterbuck bull taken along the Angwa River. The Lower Zambezi is not an especially good plains-game destination, but there are concentrations of certain animals in certain areas.

bull tracks, and the hunt was complicated by Jim having issues with bad knees. So, somewhere in the middle of the hunt, we found a reasonable bull, with thick tusks in the forty-pound range, dusting right in the middle of the Chewore riverbed. The wind was right and he was facing dead away. All we had to do was walk *quietly* up to his bum, let him turn, and take the shot.

Most of the time when you are in close cover, you don't really know what gives you away, whether a stray eddy or an errant noise. You only know that, suddenly, placid elephants erupt into motion, and then they're gone. We had covered a couple hundred yards of dead-open sand and were about seventy yards out, thus just a couple dozen yards from an acceptable shot. Poor Jim stepped on one dry stick, really just a twig. Instantly, the elephant froze, still facing dead away, and in the next moment was off, straight away and into Chewore, where we could not follow. It was an object lesson in just how sensitive and aware elephants can be.

It was on that hunt that I took my first elephant with Ivan. To my thinking, Zimbabwe's tuskless program is a marvelous thing, offering an affordable opportunity to enjoy a real elephant hunt. I'm convinced tusklessness is an inherited trait because numerous times, in the riverbeds where elephants can be safely viewed from a distance, I've seen older tuskless cows with tuskless calves of different ages. As I've written elsewhere, it's really a trophy hunt in reverse. Tuskless bulls are less common and encountered only randomly, but in the Lower Zambezi (especially Sapi and the Chewores, less so in the Dande blocks) it's a common gene.

Most herds of, say, a dozen, will contain tuskless cows—but you have to penetrate the herds, locate a tuskless cow, and ensure she doesn't have a calf at heel. This makes it one of the most dangerous hunts in the world and becoming more so because, every time a herd is penetrated to winnow out a tuskless animal, that herd is educated. Over those years in the Valley I am convinced that I saw tuskless cows become less common and harder to find, which is good. Given a general overpopulation of elephants, this is the real point to the program. On the other hand, because more herds had been penetrated to find and remove a tuskless cow, I'm also sure that I saw the cow herds becoming more aggressive and paranoid . . . and who can blame them?

Anyway, when it was my turn, we had some trouble locating a tuskless cow, but we found a decent-size group feeding into some thick *jess,* and as they vanished into the mess, we were pretty sure there were a couple of tuskless cows among them. They were blissfully feeding away, so we tried from several angles. We had one big cow dead to rights at perhaps a dozen yards when we saw her calf, so we quickly backed off, but we were also pretty sure we had identified another bigger, older tuskless cow. It was really thick in there . . . call it a day or try again?

We tried again, finding a reasonably clear (and thus quiet) game trail with a quartering wind that was more or less secure. The tuskless cow we thought we wanted was in the middle of the group. We managed to slip past three or four cows to the right, for the one we wanted was straight ahead, with the bulk of the group behind her and to the left. I had my double .450, and although the shoulder was obscured, I had a side-on brain shot at maybe twelve yards. This was the first time I understood that this was not the Carter Way.

Amazingly, and much too close for any discussion, he grabbed my shirt sleeve and pulled me several steps closer. Of course, this was too much for the old biddy, so she swung her head to me and I took the frontal brain shot at six yards. Now I was shooting upward at a severe angle, so, of course, I shot a bit too high, but as the head came around, I again had the side-on brain shot clear and dumped her with the second barrel. But now my double was empty, with elephants screaming all around us. Fortunately, they crashed off the other way while Ivan covered us as I reloaded.

A wonderful old buffalo bull along the Zambezi River. At that time there were lots of bachelor bulls in groups of various sizes. We didn't always catch them, but finding tracks to follow was rarely an issue.

This was eight years ago at this writing. Today tuskless elephants are harder to find and cow herds ever more aggressive. One of the more unfortunate by-products of the tuskless hunting program is a significant increase in self-defense shootings. I can honestly say I was never present when a nontarget elephant had to be shot, but that also means I've spent a lot of time dodging aggressive cows. And I've certainly been in camp when one or another PH had to shoot an elephant in self-defense.

Regrettably, this was one of the contributors to Ian Gibson's death. As a PH, he steadfastly avoided shooting unless absolutely necessary. With a client, he always viewed any animal as the client's animal, and in the case of potentially wounded buffalo, I saw him consciously refrain from shooting when he certainly could have. However, when he was killed, he and his unarmed tracker were alone. In a self-defense shooting, the game department must be called in to investigate, and usually a game guard is on hand to verify. A shooting every few seasons may be forgiven, but with multiples in a brief time the PH is on notice, and at risk of losing his all-important license if it happens again. Also, since Ian was killed by a *bull*, he probably would have faced a hefty fine. I'm sure all these factors weighed in on his decision to wait . . . and he waited a bit too long.

Our 2008 auction hunt winner was Ted Jernigan, but scheduling was such that I came in a few days after the start of the safari, and Ted and Ivan already had their elephant. No matter. Ted's a great guy I'd always be delighted to share a camp with. We spent the remainder of his safari in Chewore South, hunting buffaloes and plains game from that scenic camp above the Angwa River.

The next year well-known gun collector Bill Jones came in, bringing a beautiful Holland & Holland .500/.465. But that was just for backup. For serious business he had both a double .600 and a double .700! I shot the .700 on the sight-in day, and that was quite enough. Even though the recoil is perhaps more of a "push" than the sharp kick of a lighter rifle, the push was very considerable—the rifle went nearly vertical. Shooting it once was plenty! Jones, wisely, chose not to shoot the .700 at the range, but he used it on both a tuskless cow and his bull, and with some adrenaline working, he shot it very well, effectively using both barrels on both occasions.

His bull was maybe the twentieth bull we had tracked and looked at, and it was a really interesting stalk. When we caught up, the bull was giving a big baobab hell, just his back end exposed on the right side of the tree and his front end covered by the huge tree trunk. Ivan took them in a ring-around-the-rosy maneuver to the left, so as they stepped around the tree, the massive head was exposed at point-blank range.

His tuskless cow was also interesting, at least from my perspective. We got into a herd just at sunset as the elephants were feeding in open mopane, and we closed on a lone, tuskless cow from the side. Jones had the .700; I had his .600, just for fun. With the combination of poor light and open sights, Jones's brain shot was off, and his follow-up body shot, though true, didn't take immediate effect. Figuring I now had a turn, I stepped to the left and forward to get clear and went for the going-away hip shot. Both barrels went off, and I remember being pushed backward, completely out of control. Fortunately, the elephant was down because that's the last thing I remember for several minutes. I will never know whether it was a mechanical failure, or if, in recoil from the first barrel, I inadvertently hit the second trigger. It doesn't matter much; my left shoulder has never been the same. I've handled heavy recoil differently ever since.

My last sojourn to the Lower Zambezi for several years was in 2010. It was, and is, a marvelous slice of wild Africa, a land where dangerous game roam as they always have. Because of its wildness and the localized densities of prey species, it is one of the best (and most affordable) places I know to hunt leopards. Although the ivory is rarely large, it is also one of the best places for a traditional tracking hunt for elephants, and it's a real sleeper for surprisingly good lions. Unfortunately U.S. Fish & Wildlife's 2014 decision to restrict the import of sport-hunted elephant trophies from Zimbabwe, and its 2015 decision to "uplist" the African lion, has hurt not only the operators but also the wildlife. Time marches on, but I'm very happy I had the opportunity to hunt in the Zambezi Valley when it was at the zenith of its hunting history.

Chapter Four

An Ending in Botswana

Readers of previous volumes of my African odyssey will recall that I was incredibly fortunate to enjoy several wonderful safaris in Botswana in the 1980s. Things were different then. I never hunted lions in Botswana—that was a hunt I couldn't afford—and in those days, elephant hunting was closed. Botswana was magnificent! Although it seems amazing today, in the 1980s Botswana had virtually unlimited buffaloes and teemed with plains game. Prices were competitive with Zimbabwe for shorter buffalo-and-plains-game safaris and were amazingly productive. Whether in the Okavango or Chobe region, buffalo herds would be encountered on most days just by driving or looking, with little tracking required. I took my first leopard there in 1986. In the islands and along the channels at that time it was not a problem to take a sitatunga, and red lechwes roamed in thousands. In the drier thornbush, zebras, wildebeests, and impalas roamed in big herds; kudus were plentiful, and warthogs were legion.

Nearly twenty years passed before I again hunted Botswana, and things had changed. The ban on lion hunting was hard on other wildlife. Key species such as sables were taken off license. Elephants not only multiplied, but Botswana also received immigrant elephants in the thousands, including refugee elephants from Angola and Zambia and overflow from the overpopulated Hwange Park corridor in Zimbabwe.

The tents at Johan Calitz's Kukama Camp were on elevated platforms. This soon proved a really good idea as we had fresh lion tracks through the camp every morning.

Chobe National Park and the edges of the Okavango took on the appearance of a nuclear blast zone,

Johan Calitz and I kneel next to my best elephant. He was a wonderful old bull, for sure, and hunting elephants with Johan Calitz was one of my very best experiences in Africa.

and elephants spread out across the sea of scrub mopane that is central Botswana. In that arid region, with natural water only seasonal, operators sank boreholes and pumped water, supporting elephants and other species. Elephant hunting was reopened, but a bulls-only harvest that never quite reached the CITES quota of 350 had little impact on the overall population. In 2014 it was believed that Botswana might hold 150,000 elephants. A coordinated aerial survey early in 2015 proved this number false. As of that year Botswana held 250,000 elephants that, with the wave of near-continent-wide elephant poaching, could well be a third of the entire continent's total of wild elephants.

As we know, elephant hunting is again closed in Botswana, as is all safari hunting on government land. Rumors continue, and it seems almost imperative—a management no-brainer—that some form of elephant hunting must resume; perhaps this will have happened by the time these lines see the light of day. When I hunted Botswana in 2007 and 2008 the handwriting was already on the wall, and it seemed clear that the noose was tightening on hunting.

I had met Johan Calitz at the various hunting shows, and at that time, he was the largest elephant outfitter on the continent. He also seemed a perfect gentleman, a guy I wanted to hunt with. When I decided to invest in an elephant safari, Botswana elephant hunting hadn't taken a sharp increase in price, and I thought it offered a chance for a better bull than I had taken previously. As a goal, I was looking for something in the sixty-pound class, so I struck a deal with Johan Calitz.

At the time I was hunting in the Zambezi Valley where, although Chifuti took a couple of seventy-pounders, a fifty-pounder was considered far too good to pass. Most mature bulls were in the forties, and a lot of elephant hunters settled for bulls in the high thirties. I never hunted a trophy elephant in Zimbabwe, and, perhaps, I should have. Just recently, near Gonarezhou Park in the southeast, a monster 122x119 tusker was taken, the largest known elephant taken on the continent in thirty years.

In June 2007 we hunted from Kukama Camp in his CT2 area, near the Zimbabwe border and along the elephants' movement pattern from Hwange National Park. Donna came with me, and I have to say it was one of our very best safaris. Johan's camp was marvelous, with "Botswana-style" tents erected on tall poles. This was a good thing because lions and leopards roamed the camp every night, leaving tracks directly under our tent! That was one of the most single-purpose safaris I've done. I had an elephant permit, and that was all. At the tail end Johan would come up with a big surprise, but the intent was "elephant only" . . . and what an elephant hunt it was.

Central Botswana is quite different from anything I'd ever seen. Tall trees are rare; instead, the relatively flat country is covered by scrub mopane. Stunted, I suppose, by the arid climate and sandy soil, it grows to a fairly uniform height of perhaps eight to ten feet and that's about it. Calves and sometimes mature cows are totally obscured, but the skulls and backlines of mature bulls show above this sea of brush like great gray battleships cruising hull down with a full load of fuel and ammo.

Properly butchering an elephant is pretty much an all-day task depending on how much help you have. While the work was ongoing, Johan set up quite a spectacular brunch.

They can be glassed at great distance and this makes it sound easy, but while the upper profile clearly differentiates bulls from cows and some level of maturity

This elephant had a world-class nerve, so the ivory weight wasn't what we'd thought it might be. For me it didn't matter; it was plenty heavy enough . . . but I thought Johan Calitz was going to cry.

can be seen, it's very rare to actually see the ivory when these great ships are passing. So, while it often isn't tracking in the traditional sense—finding appropriately large tracks with the worn pad indicators of older bulls—following up on sightings is usually a time-consuming matter of taking a bearing on a sighting, hoofing it until tracks are crossed, and then evaluating and following the tracks until the ivory is seen and a ruling can be made.

A shortcut is to wait at waterholes. Like most good Botswana operators, Calitz invested heavily in boreholes and diesel pumps, and from late morning onward elephants and other wildlife would come to water. We spent many pleasant hours simply watching, often spreading out lunch in the shade while watching game come to water. Calitz's rules were clear in that absolutely no shooting would be done within several kilometers of water, so if rifles were handy at all they were only present for the unlikely event of self-defense. We'd stay quietly downwind of the water, and while we glassed and followed many bulls in the thornbush to get a close look at the tusks, I lost count of the number of bulls we saw at the waterholes. Some of these we followed up just to rule them out.

I was totally impressed by the calm, deliberate, and painstaking way Calitz approached his elephants. We saw a lot of youngish bulls in the forty-pound class—bulls

The Okavango Delta from the air, one of the great natural wonders of the world.

you'd be hard-pressed to pass up on elsewhere. He would often comment, "That will be a fine bull in another fifteen or twenty years," knowing, I suppose, that he was unlikely to have so long to enjoy this paradise for elephants. Others were beautiful bulls with badly broken tusks, and there were bulls I was pretty sure we shouldn't be passing.

I think it was on the third day when we glassed a big battleship just a few hundred yards off into the mopane. He seemed to be stationary, feeding, so we got the wind right, took a line, and closed in. He was feeding in a very thick place, and in order to see the ivory we closed to within twenty yards. I started my African hunting, and my elephant hunting, during the rampant commercial poaching of the 1970s and 1980s, and this bull was among the top five best elephant bulls I had ever seen. I make no claim to being able to judge ivory, but Calitz certainly can. We agreed that his heavy, even tusks would exceed sixty pounds and probably reach sixty-five. This was my goal, and I was beyond tempted . . . *compelled* is a better word.

In his calm and confident way, Calitz suggested we might do better, and as the bull finally sensed our presence and turned to confront us, he whispered, "Let's back out lest we have to shoot him."

Without question Johan Calitz is the best elephant hunter I have ever had the honor to hunt with, and the calmest. And well he should be, for he controls some of the largest and best areas in Botswana—some, by his own admission, much better than others. At the end he was managing a quota in excess of a hundred elephant bulls, with an average tusk weight of slightly north of sixty pounds per side. Obviously he didn't guide all these hunters personally, but he insisted on strict standards among all his PHs. A minimum of fifty pounds per side was his firm rule. In order to enforce this, if a PH was uncertain or a client insisted, then the drill was to back off—which could usually be done with these incredibly calm Botswana elephants—and call Johan with a description so that he might make the ultimate decision.

Donna was really sick that day, but she rallied well enough to make a watery stalk on her red lechwe.

A couple of days later, we passed yet another obvious sixty-pounder, though smaller than the first. This time there was no discussion; Johan believed we could do better. It's always part of rolling the dice, but he could have been wrong. This time he was right.

Every night we had elephants coming into the camp waterhole after dark. Someone—I can't remember who—checked out some elephants in the moonlight, and he observed what seemed to be a particularly large bull. The bull was with a small group, so in the morning we took the tracks, following laboriously until we finally caught them in midmorning. But there was no obviously big bull among them, either in body or tusk. I figured a poor-light mistake, but Johan and his veteran trackers (including a licensed Botswanan PH named Mongoose) were certain we'd either crossed tracks or taken the wrong track from the start.

We repaired to camp, had a quick lunch, and started over, this time more carefully analyzing the tracks of the supposed extra-large bull. Honestly, I was pretty certain this was a fool's errand, and I was starting to greatly regret the sixty-pounders we'd passed. Fortunately I kept my mouth shut as we carefully plodded along in the midday heat.

I said it before, but it bears repeating: These Botswana giants, largest-bodied of all elephants, are the calmest I have ever seen. Only a fool, however, takes liberties

Johan Calitz and Donna with what was probably the last red lechwe from the Okavango—a very nice bull.

with any elephant, especially cow herds. These we avoided with religious fervency, but even the cow herds we encountered were the calmest I have ever seen.

This is unquestionably a function of Botswana's unique situation. There has never been any culling, although with an obvious and increasing overpopulation, this might someday (soon) be required. There has been very little problem animal control (PAC) shooting because, with a small rural population and limited agriculture, human-elephant conflict is uncommon. Since Botswana's reopening of elephant hunting in the mid-1990s, fewer than two thousand were ever harvested, a decreasing percentage of less than one-tenth of one percent annually. These were all bulls, and most were executed with surgical efficiency. As for the bulls, they were even calmer than the cows. In central Botswana, thanks to the endless seas of mopane, the overpopulation is not yet serious, so they tended to travel relatively short distances between watering, foraging, and resting areas.

So it was that we caught up with them before three o'clock in the afternoon, and this was a different group of bulls. As we had several times before, we started sorting through them one at a time. Yes, there was one bull clearly larger than the rest. We made several approaches, and at one point I had a clear shot at less than twenty yards. Instead of taking the shot, Johan led us straight away for a conference. The major tusk was huge, showing marvelous length, good circumference at the lip, and relatively little taper. The minor tusk was slightly thicker with less taper, but the tip was clearly broken off. He was, to my eye, a no-brainer, but Johan's retreat, an amazing concession to his client, was to ensure that, although this was clearly an old bull with heavy ivory, I was OK with mismatched tusks.

Yes, I was! Now, however, as we closed for the shot, the bull became aware of our presence, not yet spooked but shifting nervously. We had two or three bad-angle opportunities, and then, as he stood in a very thick patch, we moved in. The bull swung to face us from maybe twelve yards, head up. I took the frontal shot, then the shoulder shot as he turned, and managed to recharge the double to shoot him twice more going away. I believe Johan took one shoulder shot as well, reserving his second barrel. Collectively, this was plenty.

This was definitely the bull I sought, old and with gorgeous tusks. A lady named Debbie Peake does the official measuring and weighing for Botswana's records and export licenses. She created a matrix, sort of like a mileage chart, to estimate tusk weight: Down one side is exposed tusk from lip to tip; across the top is circumference at lip. Read down and across, and average weight is listed. This cannot account for the great unknown, the size of the nerve, but it can be adjusted up or down for exceptional thickness or unusual taper. By this chart the major tusk could have been 88 pounds, so I thought Johan Calitz was going to cry when we drew out the nerves, and they kept coming and coming! No matter—the broken tusk met my self-imposed goal of 60 pounds, and the major tusk was well into the 70s. What beautiful ivory, and what a perfect hunt!

Then came Johan's surprise. We had days remaining, and he had excess plains game quota in his Okavango area Ivory Camp, soon to be lost to Botswana's invincible photographic safari industry. We returned to Maun, quickly refitted, secured red lechwe and tsessebe licenses for Donna and impala and bird licenses for both of us, and then headed off for a quick holiday in the Okavango.

We took a short helicopter tour of the delta, surprising this young lion on a buffalo kill.

By now, though, Donna had come down with some sort of ailment. She was deathly ill, several times requiring a stop so she could stumble to the verge and throw up. The next morning I was a beast; she desperately wanted to stay in bed, but the key licenses were in her name. Somehow she managed to soldier on, taking a great lechwe, a fine tsessebe, and a good impala in what must have been a very long day.

The next morning, while she lay nearly comatose, the staff discovered an overturned chair by our tent. Investigating, they discovered a very large black mamba in the corner of the tent, and dispatched it while she lay blissfully unaware.

I took a good impala with little difficulty, and, using Johan's magnificent pair of Westley Richards 20-gauge guns, we had a marvelous "driven shoot" for francolin. On our last day Donna rallied enough to enjoy (sort of) a fantastic helicopter tour of the islands, channels, and floodplains of the Okavango, and we spotted numerous red lechwes, a couple of big buffalo herds, and a magnificent lion dining on a buffalo. Although elephant hunting would continue for a brief period, we believe hers were the last lechwe and tsessebe licenses issued as the Okavango transitioned to photo safaris only, lost as a hunting area seemingly forever. Although Donna tells it as a good story, today she is very happy that she made that last Okavango hunt.

A second elephant safari into Johan's better areas was financially out of the question, but at that time he had what he considered "marginal" areas, meaning not fewer elephants but, on average, poorer ivory. He was offering these hunts at greatly reduced rates, essentially Zimbabwe prices. This we could afford, or at least we thought we could, so as a wedding present to each other, I bought two, one for Donna and one for me. Bill Jones joined us and, with *Boddington on Elephant* still in progress, Ivan Carter came, too. Since Ivan was not properly licensed in Botswana, Mongoose was our PH of record.

My experience had been with the much smaller Zambezi Valley elephants, so all Botswana tracks looked big to me. It takes some time to change the mind-set and look for really big *tracks!*

Bill was kind enough to agree to the time-honored principle of

Donna's elephant was a beautiful bull with long, perfectly matched tusks. Her six-yard frontal encounter wasn't what we'd wanted, but she made it work.

"ladies first," and Ivan's agenda was to take three bulls in this first "marginal area," Masami, as quickly as possible, and then go on to Kukama, where Johan had a leftover quota available for Bill. We had trouble finding elephants in Masami, but on the third day we ran into a small group of bulls. One was a beauty with long, perfectly matched tusks, clearly viewed on a gentle slope from several hundred yards. It was a no-brainer, the decision easily reached.

By this time I'd done a couple of Zimbabwe elephant hunts with Ivan, and I understood his confrontational approach. Donna was using our Heym double in .450/.400 3-inch, a great little cartridge but possibly a bit marginal for the frontal brain shot on these huge-headed Botswana giants. She shot it well and certainly wasn't afraid of it, but it was her first elephant, and it's really too heavy a rifle for her to comfortably handle offhand. I took Ivan aside and asked him to take her in for a side-on brain or shoulder shot—and use sticks if the circumstance allowed.

Hell, I might as well have been talking to a wall. I stayed back to keep the footprint down and watched in horror as he took her straight in, bumped the elephant, and of course her only choice was a fast frontal brain shot at six or seven yards. Her shot was a bit left, just under the eye, but under the circumstances pretty good. Of course, the elephant turned, and Ivan got in a non-effective shoulder shot, much too high. A moment later Donna fired her second barrel, a well-placed quartering-away hip shot that, ultimately, saved the day.

Then things got even weirder. Until this point I'd seen a lot of elephants that needed additional shots, but I had never seen an elephant move out of sight from the first shot. This one did, the brush closing behind it, and Ivan took off like an Olympic sprinter. I assume the theory is to try to keep the elephant in sight, but in my view two other theories were proven: First, that a fit PH can outrun clients a quarter-century his senior and, second, that no man can outrun an elephant through house-high bush.

After a bit he came back and we took the track. After a few dozen yards we could see that Donna's second shot obviously had had its intended effect, for the bull was dragging his left hind leg, and he clearly wouldn't go very far. We caught him a few minutes later, standing in thick thorn, and she shot him well on the shoulder. Twenty more yards and he was down, anchored. It wasn't the way anyone wants a first elephant hunt to go, but it was a beautiful bull with perfect tusks.

Now it was Bill's turn, and a couple of days later he took a fine bull with his .577 double. The shot placement looked good, but the bull turned and ran, and this was the second time I saw Ivan's sprinting act. We recovered the bull just fine, and then it was my turn. The next day we got into an amazing parade of bulls coming into water, and we were pretty sure we saw a really good one with long, heavy ivory. Ivan and I crept this way and that, but there were just too many elephants. Aside from that one quick glimpse, we never saw him again, and we had no way to sort out his tracks.

Although the exposed ivory is fairly short on this bull, he had thick tusks with little taper. He exceeded expectations and was exceptionally good for the area.

Another day we found a great gray battleship cruising through the mopane, headed

Botswana's giant bulls are the calmest elephants I've ever been around. Close encounters like this, terrifying at first, are commonplace and often the only way to properly see the tusks.

out from a waterhole. This bull looked really good to both Ivan and Mongoose, but I underestimated him—bulls that have the short, heavy "Botswana" ivory are hard for me to judge. Well, they know more about elephant than I will ever learn, so I followed their advice. With the wind good, we cut across and took the tracks.

We hadn't seen the forehead secretions, but from the telltale penis secretions between the tracks, the spoor told us this bull was in musth. We tracked for only a thousand yards or so, catching him in a rare grove of tall trees. Ivan advised caution, and, of course, he was right, but in order to see the tusks, there was really no option but to go straight in. Even though we were really close, both head and shoulder were obscured by branches—but the tusks, though short, were plenty thick, and looked a whole lot better up close. One more step and the bull whirled.

Knowing the angle was too steep, I put the first Hornady solid up into his face, turning him, and as the head came around I put the second barrel just ahead of the earhole. Down, reload, another solid through the top of the massive skull, and it was over. Yeah, I suck with the first barrel, but I'm hell on wheels with the second!

Funny how things happen. I felt unnecessarily rushed to take that elephant, and since we all paid the same money, I had a right to that feeling. If I'd been as assertive as I should have been, I would have turned it down and kept looking—and I would have

The inhabitants of a small village gather to help with the butchering—and claim their share. Elephant meat is highly prized and never goes to waste.

been wrong. Mine was a huge-bodied bull with a lot of unseen ivory in the skull, and it carried the weight well. It was right at 60 pounds, better than estimated, and better than the area's average. Although Donna's was very close, mine was the best of the four elephants taken on that safari. As I've written before, on any given safari you want to do as much as you can, but it's a mistake to try to do too much in the available time.

It took a bit of time recover the meat and chop out the tusks, but in a couple of days we were headed to Kukama. It's a long and roundabout journey, but in that dry, sandy country, Botswana has good roads. As expected, at Kukama the elephants were on parade. We saw lots and lots of bulls—but we couldn't find any monsters. The best bull we saw was well over seventy pounds on his good side, possibly approaching eighty, but the minor tusk was broken off quite short. It was a tough call that I'm glad I didn't have to make.

Bill passed, wanting matched tusks, and with time growing short he took a nicely matched fifty-pounder. Once again his shot placement looked perfect, but while we got the bull down, the legendary .577 failed to penetrate. It was a mystery until he got home and chronographed the ammo—instead of the 2,050 feet per second it was supposed to produce, the actual velocity was down around 1,800 fps, just not enough to overcome the resistance encountered by that large-caliber bullet. Funny, we all shot the rifle, and it seemed to have *plenty* of recoil . . . but I guess it needed more.

When all was said and done, 2007 was a much better safari than 2008, but I'm really happy that I managed to do those two hunts in Botswana. At the time it was the best elephant hunting on the continent. When it reopens, and I remain sure it will, it will again be the best, but it won't be same, and I fear it will be even more unaffordable.

CHAPTER FIVE

ACROSS FROM OL DOINYO LENGAI

Ol Doinyo means "mountain" in the Masai tongue. Best known is Kilimanjaro, followed by Mount Meru and the Ngorongoro Crater, but many isolated mountains—and few genuine ranges—rise from the mile-high Masai Steppe. In years gone by I've hunted in sight of "Kili" and Mount Meru, and in the very shadow of Ngorongoro at M'to Wa Mbu. On this hunt above Lake Natron in northwestern Masailand, we would be almost constantly in sight of the mountain that, to the Masai, is the most famous and sacred of all: Ol Doinyo Lengai. The eerie spire of the "Mountain of God" is still an extremely active volcano.

Tom Fruechtel with a really fine gerenuk from the thornbush flats around Lake Natron.

I guess it doesn't matter where you are in Masailand. To me it remains some of the most beautiful country in Africa, and certainly some of the most pleasant. At this elevation the days can be dusty and blistering, but nights are always pleasant and cool. I've been fortunate to have taken almost all of the Masailand species: Thomson and Grant gazelle, gerenuk, lesser kudu, white-bearded wildebeest, and Coke hartebeest. In 1988 I took a very nice Masailand lion, and I suppose the way things are going, that will never happen again. Of course, Masailand is perhaps most famous for really big buffaloes, and in 1993 I took the kind of buffalo that, well, people go to Masailand to search for. My only real gap is missing the spread-horned Roberts gazelle, but it's hardly worth mounting a safari for it considering Tanzania's prices. I'll have to admit, however, that I would like to do one more safari in Masailand.

This hunt in October 2007 was not my safari. Leupold's CEO, Tom Fruechtel, was preparing to retire, and this safari was his swan song. At that time Leupold was the optics sponsor for *Petersen's HUNTING Adventures*, so I was invited to come along and, of course, get it on film. He would be hunting with Tanzania Game Trackers (TGT), one of Tanzania's most prestigious and famous operators. His three-week safari would start at Lake Natron in the north, and then travel down to the Ugalla River in western Tanzania. I couldn't do the whole hunt, but no way could I pass a chance to spend a few days in Masailand.

So Conrad Evarts, my friend and frequent videographer, and I joined Tom on the flight into Arusha. PH Andy Wilkinson met us there and we drove straight through to their Lake Natron camp. I didn't know Andy, but I'd heard good things about him for many years. A native of Zimbabwe, a few years my senior, he's an old African hand and very competent PH. This I would expect of TGT, as I'd expect a spectacular camp, which surely awaited us.

The plan was to spend the first couple of days hunting plains game, with emphasis on lesser kudu and gerenuk and such, and then go to a fly camp "up the mountain" for buffalo. Tom's primary goals were a lion and leopard, but these would wait until he went on to western Tanzania. In no way was I a full partner on this safari—it was Tom's hunt—but I'm the world's worst observer, so I brought a .375 and had a seven-day license. If time and circumstances allowed, I might take a buffalo and perhaps one or two of the common species.

This is a really nice lesser kudu bull, so I was wishing hard for Andy Wilkinson to give Tom Fruechtel the go-ahead. The bull didn't quite measure up, so we didn't shoot this one, but Tom got a fine lesser kudu before departing the area.

Let me get it over with right now and spare the suspense: On this safari I fired exactly one shot on my own behalf. On my last day, in full sight of Ol Doinyo Lengai, smoking from a recent eruption, Andy and I stalked and shot a beautiful Grant gazelle, easily the best I've ever taken. That's not a big bag to go so far for, but, as I said, it wasn't my hunt . . . but it was a good safari, and most interesting.

The Masai count their wealth in cattle. Today there are a lot of Masai in Masailand—and a lot of cattle. Regrettably, there are very few really good Masailand concessions remaining. I'm not nearly current enough to tell you which ones remain good and which are depleted, but I can say that the Lake Natron area was *spectacular*. There was lots of game, rarities like lesser kudus and gerenuks, common game like impalas and Grant gazelles. It was also beautiful country.

Andy was extremely picky, which I gather is part of TGT's credo. Down on the flat Tom made a beautiful shot on a fantastic gerenuk, and he took a really fine Kirk dik-dik. With Conrad's camera rolling, I was really hoping we could get him taking a lesser kudu on film, but while we saw a few bulls, we didn't see any that met Andy's exacting specifications. After we left, Tom had a couple more days in Masailand, and he got an exceptional lesser kudu.

The main event was the mountain hunting, and after a couple of days down on the dusty plains we took a precipitous track up the mountain. Like Ol Doinyo Lengai, our mountain rose to about 10,000 feet and was also a volcano—but fortunately not an active one for many centuries. The road stopped just short of a spare, but well-appointed, tent camp set just a few hundred yards below the western rim of the shallow crater. October is one of the hottest months in Masailand, just before the short rains, but it wasn't hot up there. It was freezing cold at night, and fog was a recurring problem during the day.

At the very outset of my African experience I hunted buffaloes as high as 10,000 feet up on Mount Kenya, and in the middle years I hunted buffaloes on other Masailand mountains with Michel Mantheakis. So the presence of buffaloes way up there wasn't a surprise. Nor, I suppose, is it to many of us since Masailand's mountain buffaloes have achieved something of celebrity status. I also wasn't surprised to learn there are some very big bushbucks up there, and they are pursued by some big leopards. There was one surprise: On the first evening, on a tall ridge across from camp, we glassed a small herd of elands. Exactly what they're doing up there, and why they go so high, I simply cannot explain—but I've heard there are elands farther up Mount Kilimanjaro than any other species, so perhaps that's a normal thing.

From camp we would hunt buffaloes strictly on foot, and anything done on foot at 10,000 feet elevation is strenuous enough. I had the impression that camp was pretty much at tree line, at least insofar as actual tall trees go, but the mountain was capped with extremely thick brush. There were scattered clearings where buffaloes came out to graze, both in the crater itself and on the slopes around the rim, but the actual brush where the buffaloes lived and bedded was far too thick to effectively track. It was, in short, some of the most difficult buffalo hunting I've

TGT's buffalo camp was far up on the mountain at nearly 10,000 feet elevation, not far below timberline. Up here the weather was really different, and very cold in the mornings and evenings.

Tom Fruechtel with his mountain buffalo, definitely not a huge bull by Tanzanian standards, but still a good, mature buffalo—and very hard won up on the mountain.

done, maybe not as difficult as hunting the forest buffalo in Central and West Africa, but as far as Cape buffaloes go, it was the most difficult I've done since, well, since I hunted along the edges of the bamboo forests on Mount Kenya. This made it very interesting, but our goal wasn't for it to be interesting. Rather, our goal was to get Tom a buffalo, and get it on camera.

In the mornings we climbed up from camp in heavy fog, not a hard climb as we had most of the elevation we needed right from camp, but the fog was a problem. Fresh tracks were always there, but by the time the fog lifted, the buffaloes had moved down into the thick stuff and we couldn't do much about it.

On the third morning, we were glassing from a rocky outcropping. Just as the fog lifted we found a little herd of buffaloes right below us, maybe a hundred yards, already in the thick stuff but right at the edge. There was a good-looking bull with them, bedded and obscured . . . but sooner or later he would move. We waited and we waited, and we waited some more. Sooner or later he would move . . . surely. Or was he down for the day?

Andy had gone a little way to the right to glass into another pocket when the bull stood up. I'm not really proud of this, and for darn sure it was neither my call nor any of my business. We had the shot, and it seemed to me it was time to take the shot. I don't recall exactly voicing that, and if I did I surely won't admit it, but I was thinking about it awfully hard. The bull was almost broadside, with a good window to the vitals open, but that window wouldn't stay open for more than another step or two.

Tom took the shot. I saw him just the other day, and we laughed about it, as we often have. Had it been my buffalo, I surely would have taken the shot, and I remain convinced it was the right thing to do. But, even with the best of intentions, things don't always turn out exactly as planned. The bullet hit a bit too far back, and the bull was instantly lost in the brush. So when Andy came rushing back, we had a bit of a mess on our hands. A consummate professional, if he was angry he kept it to himself—and whether the right thing or the wrong thing had been done, no doubt he was angry, and for that I don't blame him. *Nobody* would want to follow a wounded buffalo into that mess. *Nobody* included me!

The herd was small, just a handful, and from our vantage point we could watch their progress, just glimpses of black moving through the thorn. Although we were below the crater rim, the pocket below us was a little bowl. Fortunately the buffaloes didn't bomb straight down into the worst of it; they stayed more or less level, stopping about halfway around the bowl. Using what cover we could find, we worked our way around until we were above them again. By that point, they were just dim forms in the brush. I doubt we could have worked out which animal was ours, but the buffaloes told us when another bull came in and horned one of his buddies.

The victim didn't respond, so we concluded this was the injured animal, and he was hurt worse than we had thought. Tom was a bit to the left and I don't remember whether Andy was with him or with me, but, like Tom, I had a scoped .375. We were a bit far for Andy's open-sighted .404. The tableau broke for an instant, and the bull we thought to be the correct one took a couple of steps forward, clearly limping, and just for an instant he came clear enough. This time I was totally culpable: I took matters into my own hands and took the shot I had. I knew it was a bit too far back, but I knew for sure this was the correct buffalo, and I figured if we had to go down there into that nightmare, a second bullet *anywhere* was better than just one.

I'm flanked by Tom Fruechtel and my buddy and frequent cameraman Conrad Evarts (right) with a very good Grant gazelle. This is easily my best . . . but because it was the only animal I took on the trip, it was probably the costliest Grant gazelle ever taken in the history of African hunting!

At my shot the group broke and ran, a bit down but mostly laterally around the bowl. They stopped again, the stricken bull out of sight, but we could see a second bull horning *something*, and then several buffaloes moved out, no sign of one lagging behind. We waited for a long time—*nobody* really wanted to go down there, but available evidence was that one buffalo was lying in some bushes out of sight. Whether it was dead or alive, we had no idea.

Eventually we had to find out, so we outlined a route, fanned out three abreast, and headed down. Once off the rim, visibility shrank to feet, and it was a scary and slow descent. Fortunately, the buffalo was right there in a little depression, and even more fortunately, he was stone dead.

We needed to go back to camp to get some help, so Andy marked the spot and we took the gentlest slope up. As we topped out, a group of elands—perhaps our camp herd, perhaps another group—appeared out of nowhere. A really good-looking bull stopped on the far side of a meadow, hardly a hundred yards, and Tom pasted him once and then again. Now we really needed some help!

The presence of eland up at 10,000 feet really surprised me, but I've heard that elands are found farther up on Kilimanjaro than almost any other species, so clearly there's something they like at higher elevations.

The next morning we climbed up into the crater hoping to find a buffalo for me. We saw him, a wide, good-looking bull with a small herd, working his way up through scattered openings toward the far rim. I would like to have had him, but dense fog came in, and when it lifted the herd was gone, probably over the top into nasty brush on the far side. We tried again that evening, but no buffaloes came out, and then we were out of time. Well, we were on a schedule, and that's the way it was.

We came down off the mountain the next morning and headed back to the main camp where, the following morning, Conrad and I would have transportation back to Arusha. On the way we ran into a nice group of Grant gazelles, and Andy agreed to a stalk. I'm quite sure my .375 would have been adequate, but the country was really open—and I didn't want to blow it. So I borrowed Tom's .30-06 with a larger scope, and Andy led me on a very nice stalk through scattered thornbush. Technically, I suppose you could call it a one-shot safari . . . almost.

CHAPTER SIX

MAYO N'DUEL

By now it's no secret that I'm an African junkie. It isn't hard to make excuses to keep going back, and, indeed, I still have plenty of them, including the places I haven't been and the animals I haven't hunted. So there's still a bucket list. Among the almost endless variety of antelopes, the spiral-horned group holds special interest. An old friend of mine, Dr. Ed Chatwell, long gone now, was equally fixated by Africa. I remember being in his den and seeing a mounted addax and scimitar-horned oryx that he took in Chad, and being awed by these creatures that I would never get to hunt, at least in their native range.

At that time, the late 1970s, Chatwell was among a fairly small group of hunters who had taken all nine of the principal spiral-horn antelope: bongo, bushbuck, common eland, giant eland, common nyala, mountain nyala, greater kudu, lesser kudu, and sitatunga. In those days I could scarcely imagine accomplishing such a feat, but he told me he had a further goal: to take two of each, and from separate countries, except mountain nyalas, which only occur in Ethiopia. There's nothing wrong with establishing hunting goals based on dreams, and I guess this stuck with me.

To my knowledge Dr. Chatwell never accomplished this lofty African quest, but by early 2008, albeit somewhat by accident, I was actually quite close. Counting races and subspecies I didn't have *all* the spiral horns, and I suppose I never will. I'm still missing both the Abyssinian bushbuck and Abyssinian greater kudu, and I'm missing both an island and a forest sitatunga. But I had multiple races of bushbucks and common elands from several different countries, likewise greater kudus. I had lesser kudus from Kenya and Tanzania, and bongos from C.A.R. and Cameroon. I had two mountain nyalas, obviously both from Ethiopia, which I took in 1993 and 2000, and I had sitatungas from Botswana, Tanzania, and Zambia. I had taken three nyalas, all from South Africa, but I was booked for a hunt in coastal Mozambique in October 2008, and a primary goal was a native-range nyala. Surely that would happen!

I had just one Lord Derby giant eland, a monstrous old bull with worn tips and huge bases, taken on my second attempt in C.A.R. in 1994. I'd hunted in northern Cameroon's giant eland country in 2004, but the license there is sort of odd. The animals are divided into classes, ranked, if you will, and you can only take two Class A animals. I didn't have two other important Class A beasts, the western roan and savanna buffalo, so I hunted all three until I took a fine roan, then a buffalo, and was tagged out. Hunting in the Mayo Oldiri block and adjacent Mayo N'Duel of Cameroon, we tracked elands several times and saw quite a few, but I just didn't get a shot. I had no regrets, and indeed, just those few years back, I'd never even thought about this silly "double-spiral-horn" quest.

However, when a chance came to hunt again with Mayo Oldiri in early March, I thought about it quite a lot. To me Lord Derby giant eland is one of Africa's most imposing and magnificent creatures, and in my experience one of the most physically demanding to hunt. Hey, sitatungas are very specialized, and both bongos and mountain nyalas are difficult, but with bongos, despite the heat and humidity, you're walking in shade. In Ethiopia much of the climbing is done on horseback; it's more a matter of glassing and being extremely patient rather than a back-breaking physical challenge. Of these four prized spiral horns, the hunt for the Derby eland is probably the most successful in today's Africa, but it's a tracking hunt done in extreme heat and in the open Terminalia forest where there is no shade.

The herd was on the far side of a big, open burn with scant cover. Using the "butt-scooting" method, we covered several hundred slow, agonizing yards.

Mayo means *river* in the language of northern Cameroon. My outfit would be the Mayo Oldiri group, which also utilizes the adjacent Mayo N'Duel block where I would hunt. Once again my guide would be Guav

PH Guav Johnson and I flank my fantastic Derby eland bull, at this time the largest Derby eland known to have been taken in Cameroon. I had one chance, a shot with a .375 Ruger from about 250 yards.

Johnson, a great Zimbabwe hunter who, between Zimbabwe and Cameroon, probably puts in more hunting days per year than any professional hunter I know. As I keep telling him, he's paying the price. Though still young, he's rapier thin, and has suffered just about every tropical ailment known to man. I keep telling him he needs to slow down . . . yet the only way I would do this safari was if Guav Johnson guided me. And I hope he has still another safari in him because I have more work to do in Cameroon.

Hunting with me, or at least that was the plan, would be my old friend Kirk Kelso. This part of the plan went awry. For reasons known only to the outfitter we were separated on arrival, with Kirk going to an altogether different area. This was disappointing, but not a train smash. He shot his Derby eland before I shot mine, and he filled out his license on A and B animals before I did.

Getting to northern Cameroon is a long trip. We overnighted in Douala, then took an internal flight to Garoua, and then drove several hours to Mayo Oldiri. At this stage Kelso was whisked away, a bit cross and no doubt thinking his buddy, Craig, had shafted him and he was getting second-class treatment. To tell you the truth, that's exactly what I feared, although I had nothing to do with it and could do nothing about it. Fortunately, we were both wrong. Mayo Oldiri is a quality outfit, and Kelso probably went to its very best Derby eland area.

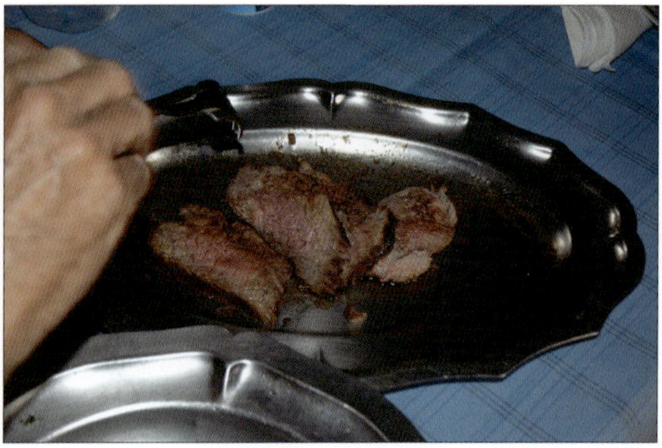

Most African hunters are in agreement that the eland offers some of the very finest wild meat! When done properly, there's simply nothing like filet of eland.

From the Mayo Oldiri headquarters Guav took me some three hours north to the Mayo N'Duel camp. It's a much older camp of adobe huts, but I was happy because, at least four years earlier, it was pretty clear there were more Derby elands and more buffaloes in the Mayo N'Duel block, although generally more game overall in Mayo Oldiri. This time our priorities were clear: We would hunt giant elands until successful, and then we'd take things as they came, provided only that "things" included buffaloes.

On the one hand it was a very easy giant eland hunt, but on the other, it became one of the longest and tensest hunts of my life. We struck fresh tracks of a big herd on the afternoon of the first day and followed with maybe two hours of daylight. That's a chancy deal at that time of day, but we had to try. The elands hadn't gone far and we might well have gotten into the herd except they made a hook and got around the wind. We were in a really thick patch when the herd exploded just ahead of us, branches cracking and joints clacking as only elands do. One of the trackers knew there was a big burn ahead, so we ran quickly to the right and up a little kopje, hoping to catch sight of the herd in the open.

By the time we gained enough height to glass, they were right in the middle, about eight hundred yards away and, thus, totally unreachable—but now spread out and walking. It was a big herd, seventy or more, and there were at least four mature bulls in the group, distinct by larger body size and dark neck collars. But here was our blessing and potential undoing: Right in the middle of the herd was a monster, huge in the body with incredibly long, straight, and wide horns. He dwarfed the other bulls in the herd.

You see, here's reality: Nobody passes a mature giant eland bull. In a herd like that, on level ground, we would almost never see all the bulls, and certainly not in one viewing. Had we gotten into that herd before this unusual sighting, we would have taken the first mature bull to offer a shot. Yes, I already had a giant eland, and I had time to be picky. As I said, however, though a marvelous trophy because of age and horn circumference, my Derby eland had short, thick, worn-down horns. I loved him and still do, but *all* the mature bulls in this herd had longer horns, so I would have taken any of them. Now that we had seen this monster, we knew we'd stay with them until we got him . . . or until we lost them completely.

There was enough light for one try, so we watched until they crossed the burn, then scrambled down and dashed across the burn, picking up the tracks on the far side. With dark coming on I thought they would stop soon, but they did not. When

With the eland in the salt, we turned to buffalo hunting. A few days later we tracked a small herd and took this excellent bull just at sunset. This is a Central African savanna buffalo, and with it, I filled my license that allowed only two "Class A" animals.

it became too dark to follow, we gave it up and headed back to the truck, but we were back on the tracks twelve hours later, just as dawn was breaking.

The herd hadn't gone far during the night. We had them in sight before 7 A.M., while it was still cool, and one of the lesser bulls stood in a clear spot under a tree. Normally the hunt would have ended there, but we knew a monster was in that herd, so we kept maneuvering. Inevitably they spooked, so we took the tracks again. By the time we bumped them a second time, it was already hot, and the heat continued to build through a very long day. I don't know how many times we got on them, or how many chances we had at every other bull in the herd, but we kept at it, looking for the big boy.

For several miserable midday hours I worried that the big bull might have gotten nervous and left the herd, as older animals will sometimes do. Then, finally, as they clacked off for the umpteenth time, we got a glimpse of him. He was in a press of cows, and there was no chance for a shot, but we now knew that he was definitely in the herd. That time they went a long way. We gave them a half-hour before starting again, and an hour later we stopped in some shade and took a water break. It was very hot and we'd logged some miles, but I don't want to make it sound more difficult or heroic than it was. We were walking slowly, holding the tracks. We would keep at them until nearly dark, and if necessary we'd start again the next morning where we left them. We all knew this bull was worth it.

A few hot kilometers later we finally got a break. We started out of a tree line with a big, open burn beyond. The herd had stopped at the far side of the burn, probably six hundred yards away. We couldn't see the big bull, but he was

With the eland taken early in the hunt, there was no pressure and things slowed down dramatically. We took it easy and enjoyed "tea time" along the Mayo N'Duel.

In both northern C.A.R. and northern Cameroon, the kob is the most numerous antelope, essentially replacing the impala of Southern and East Africa.

surely there. The eland herd had been moving into the wind, and although breezes get fickle in the heat of the day, the wind was still good.

Leaving the trackers at the tree line, Guav and I and our cameraman moved forward. At first there were some scattered trees and unburned clumps we could use by walking doubled over. Part of the herd was in some trees on the far side, but they were spread out, so it wasn't too long before we had to get lower. The ground was burning hot from the ferocious sun and we still had a lot of ground to cover. The best expedient was what we call "butt-scooting"—feet planted ahead of you, butt on the ground, rifle horizontally over your lap, hands behind you for balance. Reach forward with your feet, scoot your rear forward a foot or so, do it again. It's slow, but less exhausting than crawling, and a whole lot easier on your knees and elbows.

This went on for quite a while as Guav led us from tree to tree, clump to clump, antheap to antheap. We stopped numerous times to glass . . . we were sweating and breathing too hard to talk, but I don't think Guav had a visual on the big bull until we were nearly in range. For sure I didn't, and it was just as well because I was plenty nervous enough.

Then we found him towering over some cows in the deep shade under a tree. At that point we were 275 yards out. Guav took us at an angle around some obstructions, and I suppose we'd gained about twenty-five yards when Guav stopped and slowly opened the sticks, spreading the legs wide so I could shoot from a steady sitting position.

At this moment the bull was blocked, but none of the elands were bedded and the cows were drifting back and forth, so we were in a good position to wait until he

This is a really old harnessed bushbuck, probably the most colorful of all the bushbucks. They're plentiful in Mayo Oldiri's blocks, but they are widely scattered and encountered only sporadically.

was clearly visible. I worked on the position a bit, making sure I was dead steady, and I verified that the distance was right at 250 yards. A couple of cows moved off, and then the bull stepped out. I really didn't look at his horns again; the body size was distinctive, as was the regal black collar. He moved away from the tree and stood broadside, wide open. Giving myself as much leeway as possible, I held on the rear of the shoulder about six inches above the horizontal centerline—and felt steady when the trigger broke.

At the shot the herd exploded, but as I worked the bolt I saw the bull swap ends and run to the left. I lost him completely behind the trees, and then there was a mass exodus of elands, raising a huge cloud of dust as they exited the plain and stampeded up a low ridge beyond. We stood and dusted off a layer of ash, and then moved forward. My assumption was the bull had gone with the herd, at least for some distance, but he hadn't at all . . . he was stretched out just on the other side of those trees, pretty much where I'd lost sight of him.

What can I say but "*wow!*" His huge body with a prime winter cape and neck ruff made him one of the most magnificent animals I'd ever seen. His horns exceeded 52 inches, a fantastic Derby eland. Neighboring C.A.R. has always produced the largest horns, and I suppose always will, but this bull was bigger than any giant eland previously recorded from Cameroon.

At that point the safari was a huge success, and anything else that might happen was a pure bonus. The next few days were spent primarily hunting buffaloes. Mayo N'Duel is usually very good for buffaloes; on my previous trip there we got into buffalo herds almost every day. For whatever reason, at this moment they were a bit scarce, but we saw several small groups and passed a couple of bulls. These buffaloes are Central African savanna buffaloes, smaller than buffaloes to the east and typically with separated horns and no distinct boss. My impression is that mature bulls tend to be darker, but there is usually a good mix of tan, red, brown, and black buffaloes in the herds.

A few days later, just at sunset, we glassed a small herd coming up out of the riverine brush and got on their tracks. We caught them in an open glade, and the bull appeared to have exceptionally long, sharp horns. With dark coming on fast, I shot him three times as quickly as I could, and, fortunately, he went down and stayed there.

Well, that was it for my two Class A animals, and there was nothing else in the area that I didn't already have. So we hunted sort of randomly, seeing what we could find. I took an exceptional Nigerian bohor reedbuck and an ancient harnessed bushbuck, and one morning I simply couldn't refuse a really good warthog. We still had days left when I finished my license with a nice western kob, and then we packed up to join Kirk back at Mayo Oldiri.

He had taken his giant eland on the first day, his buffalo on the second, and then had finished his license—like me, with days to spare—with several more fine animals. He was fishing in deep pools in the river when I caught up with him. Mayo Oldiri not only has good areas but this safari group also works hard to control poaching. Even given the good areas, Central African safaris aren't usually quite that easy. Of some nine hunts that I took in that part of Africa, this was easily the very best.

Chapter Seven

A New Beginning in Mozambique

Africa is a land of change. Political changes can happen overnight, while changes to wildlife populations are a bit slower. When areas are left uncared-for, poachers and squatters can move in unhindered and turn a game-rich area into a wasteland in just a season or two. These things I have long known because I've seen them happen. In 1977, at the beginning of my African odyssey, I was among the last to hunt in Kenya. The closure of hunting there was totally unexpected . . . and, for Kenya's wildlife, the results were catastrophic. With legal safaris out of the way, the poaching gangs moved in. Today, thirty years later, Kenya has some of the finest national parks on the continent but, outside of those protected enclaves, Kenya is wall-to-wall people and villages, with no hope for the wildlife that once existed.

Since then I've seen two short-term closures in Zambia, both political moves for "area reallocation." Safaris moved out and poachers, woodcutters, and squatters moved in. Fortunately hunting resumed, but when it did some areas were already ruined, and few were as good as they had been. As I write these lines in 2016, all government concessions in Botswana have been closed for nearly two years. At this moment I believe—and hope—that this closure is temporary, but if Botswana reopens it will not be as good as it was.

The Botswana Defense Force is one of the continent's best militaries. With a "shoot-on-sight" policy they are doing a good job preventing ivory poaching, but I'm told there is more meat poaching than ever before. Perhaps worse, the overpopulation of elephants is extremely hard on all other species, and that problem continues to escalate. In Africa it is easy to be gloomy about the future for both hunting and wildlife given that these are just three of many negative examples.

In recent years, however, I have learned that wildlife is more resilient than we often believe. Given a bit of care, remnant populations can rebound. It takes much more time

We used Canadian Argos to gain access to the swamps, which was a whole separate experience all by itself.

to rebuild an area than it does to destroy it, but with good stewardship—including effective antipoaching efforts—it is possible.

I'm often asked about my favorite areas in Africa. The answer depends a whole lot on the game as well as hunting conditions, which, subjectively, I want to be both interesting and exciting. For me, as a broad brush I can easily say that what I love most about Africa is the variety: On any given day when you leave camp, you have no idea what you might see. I love wild Africa, and while I love the rich diversity of antelopes and other nondangerous species, I love most of all areas where some or all of the dangerous game might be encountered.

In this context my favorite areas have changed over time. In the 1980s, Botswana's Okavango teemed with plains game and buffaloes, and in that same period, Zambia was amazing. Later in the decade, and into the 1990s, Tanzania was fantastic, but hunting there became too expensive for most of us, and in all three countries, for different reasons, I have seen the number of good areas diminish. In the early 2000s, Zimbabwe's Zambezi Valley was my favorite, for it was wild country where buffaloes and elephants roamed, and almost nightly I could hear lions roaring, leopards coughing, and hyenas laughing.

Right now I can easily say that coastal Mozambique, in and around the delta of the mighty Zambezi, has become my favorite area. This is actually quite amazing to me. I first hunted in Mozambique in 1989, just as her long civil war was winding down. In the wake of that struggle, Mozambique was in tatters and her game in scattered remnants. I believed, and I wrote, that the wildlife could never recover.

Fortunately I was very wrong. Fast-forward to 2006. Together with Donna and my friend Joe Bishop I enjoyed a great safari at Mahimba in coastal Mozambique, north of the Zambezi. That was a good area then, and remains a good area today. We found plenty of buffaloes, and the only downside was (and is) that species diversity is limited: There are lots of waterbucks, reedbucks, warthogs, and bushpigs; there are scattered sables and bushbucks . . . and little else.

I suppose others might classify me differently, but as a hunter I'm not really a "collector" except in the context of collecting experiences. But, given Africa's almost endless diversity, in any new area—meaning new to me—I have always tried to hunt those animals that I have not previously hunted. As a country, Mozambique has almost no indigenous rarities—species not found elsewhere.

She does hold two animals that, in 2006, I had never hunted: Livingstone suni and Natal red duiker. Both are fairly rare north of the Zambezi, but extremely common in the woodlands surrounding the Marromeu Reserve to the south. It was these two animals that introduced me to the Zambezi Delta. At that time (and again today) J. P. Kleinhans had the Mahimba concession, and on the way out he arranged for me to stop in Coutada 10, south of the river, to do a short hunt for these two animals. Portuguese is the *lingua franca* of Mozambique, and in that language *coutada* simply means *hunting area*, government land in large numbered blocks tendered to outfitters as concessions.

One thing I learned: Coastal Mozambique isn't really "open-sight country." We ran out of cover at a bit over a hundred yards, and the herd was bedded. With the bull spotted and plenty of time to "practice" the shot, I made it work, but it was a long poke with iron sights.

Gert Saaiman had Coutada 10, and I easily took both a fine

Donna, Willem van Dyk Jr., and I with my first Marromeu buffalo, taken with a Turnbull 1886 Winchester in .475 Turnbull. This is a really good buffalo from this area, and still one of my best.

suni and a good red duiker there. I was only in Coutada 10 a couple of days, certainly not long enough to really see the area, but a quick tour through his skinning shed told me all I needed to know: lots of buffaloes, good sables and nyalas, and a wide variety of other fine trophies. I had made a surprising discovery. A few months later, at the SCI convention, Joe and I booked a safari for 2008.

However irrational, I usually try to find a good excuse to hunt in a certain area. Since I already had the suni and red duiker, coastal Mozambique held no "new" species for me, but buffaloes always draw me, and Donna wanted a sable. I had taken nyalas in South Africa, but in Mozambique's native range, free range nyalas were intriguing. Then, as I wrote in the preceding chapter, this crazy idea of a second assembly of Africa's nine spiral-horn antelope, each in two countries, began to take shape. Our Coutada 10 hunt was set for October of 2008. Seven months earlier, in February, I took my second Derby eland in Cameroon. From that moment on, a nyala became my primary goal for the Mozambique hunt.

Gert Saaiman met us in Johannesburg and whisked us up to Beira for customs clearance and then on to camp in his Beechcraft twin. He had a little surprise for me that he held to the last: Our professional hunter would be Willem van Dyk Junior, son of my PH on my first safari in Kenya. Willem Senior, long retired in South Africa, would join us for part of the safari. I had hunted with him several times in the 1980s, but I hadn't seen him for twenty years. That alone made it a memorable hunt, but it was more than that. Young Willem proved an exceptionally capable PH, very much a chip off the old block, and, as I'd expected, Coutada 10 proved to be a marvelous hunting area.

This was my first experience in hunting Mozambique's "swamp buffaloes." Biologically they're the same old Cape buffaloes, but hunting them is quite different from the tracking hunts I was used to. So different that I wish I'd known more about this when I wrote *Buffalo!*—but, as always, you don't know what you don't know.

The Marromeu Reserve is a vast floodplain cut by papyrus-lined channels. The reserve proper is not hunted, but Coutadas 10, 11, and 14 border the reserve and run onward into the surrounding *miombo* woodland. There are buffaloes in the woodlands, more every year as the numbers continue to grow, but the great majority of the buffaloes roam in big herds out on the swamps and floodplains. In part this is

Willem van Dyk Jr. and Joe Bishop (right) with a good Natal red duiker. These red duikers are extremely common in this area but, unlike the suni, aren't confined to specific habitats. Give it a few days, and you're almost certain to run into one.

A sable antelope was at the top of Donna's wish list. This is country where you'll see sable almost every day, so it's a matter of time. We caught this beautiful bull just at sundown, feeding in a big pan with his herd.

undoubtedly because there's plenty of water, good grass, and cover in the form of dense sawgrass out there, but also undoubtedly because lions don't like to get their feet wet. Even when there were lots of lions in the *miombo* woodlands, few ventured into the swamps.

We accessed the swamp in Canadian-made Argo amphibious vehicles, designed for negotiating swampy muskeg. The buffalo country is surrounded by miles of wide-open grasslands, covered in water during the rains and starting to dry out in July and August; the only trees are on slightly raised islands. Buffaloes rarely venture out into the grasslands, but that's home territory to numerous species.

On the way to the swamps you see lots and lots of reedbucks, big herds of waterbucks, and numerous warthogs. Daylight sightings of bushpigs are common out there, and there are also sables, Lichtenstein hartebeests, Selous zebras, and elands. The swamps begin beyond the last island and run for many more miles. That's where the buffaloes roam, but, oddly, there are few other species out in the swamps. Once in a while you'll encounter warthogs and the odd waterbuck bull—usually at exactly the wrong time—but the swamps are buffalo country, and they congregate in big herds.

If there's a norm, it's probably a couple hundred buffaloes, but I've seen many groups much larger, and once, years later, I saw a massive herd of at least two thousand animals. Obviously such herds can be tracked, but in the swamps buffaloes are located mostly by glassing. You can't see over the tall papyrus, and taller sawgrass can swallow even the biggest herd, so you aren't looking for buffaloes. Instead you're glassing for birds. White cattle egrets follow the buffaloes to pick insects, so they are constantly swooping and circling above the herds. So that's what you're looking for, and you can see them through the mirage and haze from a couple of miles away.

We plowed through the deep channels with the Argo and then through stands of six-foot sawgrass. There are no vantage points for glassing, so the drill was to stop frequently and stand up on the Argo. There are lots of buffaloes out there, but it's a very big place! We left the last island just after daybreak, and it was late morning and hot when we finally saw egrets on the horizon. We left the Argo, and now began the real buffalo hunt.

As I would learn, sometimes it's hard and sometimes easy, but this time it was all new. We had to circle a bit to get the wind right. On the ground the swamp all looks the same, but the trackers have spent their lives out there and this is their home. Somehow they'd marked the spot, but by the time we got there, the buffaloes had moved on, so we took up the tracks.

By October the waters have mostly receded, but we still had to wade through several channels. Donna was with me, but she's a whole lot lighter than I am. I quickly learned that Donna could step across the papyrus whereas half the time I'd sink into the muck. It's very hot out there and there's no shade, but you have to stay covered up. The sawgrass will cut, and there are leeches in the channel, so long sleeve-shirts and long trousers tied at the cuffs are essential. Later I'd figure out that gloves and kneepads help a lot.

The buffaloes had passed through some tall sawgrass and onto a wide-open short-grass savanna, and when we caught up, they were just starting to lie down. This was good and bad: They were totally unaware and we had them dead to rights . . . but we were completely out of cover. The herd was a couple hundred strong, with the closest buffaloes within a hundred yards, not too bad—but some were fifty yards farther on and in a tightly packed mass.

There was a really good-looking bull lying broadside on the left-hand side of the herd, so we shifted a bit and set up at the last bit of cover. I was carrying a Doug Turnbull-customized 1886 Winchester in .475 Turnbull. There's plenty of power in that cartridge and the rifle is wonderfully accurate, but I was just at my limit for the open sights. Eventually the bull would probably get up, if only to shift a bit, so while we waited I had time to practice. The front bead covered an awful lot of buffalo, but if I had a decent shot presentation, I was pretty sure I could pull it off.

Sunis are extremely common in thick forest habitat that is known as "suni forest." A common way to hunt them is to walk along the forest roads very slowly with a shotgun.

It seemed we waited for a long time, but I don't think it was much more than an hour later when the bull got to his feet and drifted to the right. For a time he was blocked by other buffaloes, but then he came clear and offered a good quartering-to presentation. With the rifle on the sticks, I buried the bead in the buckhorn rear and shifted the sight picture up, down, and sideways until I was really certain I had it right.

The big bullet hit the bull hard, and, instantly, the herd was in motion and he was lost in the mass of black bodies. But he was already slowing and quickly fell to the rear, offering another shot as the herd passed us diagonally. He made a couple hundred yards and then went down to stay. He was a beautiful buffalo, and he offered me a good lesson. I love hunting buffaloes with open-sighted big bores, but when working the big herds in Mozambique's swamps, it isn't always possible to get as close as you might like. From that point on I've done most of my buffalo hunting there with scoped rifles.

On this hunt a sable was at the top of Donna's short "wish list." Like everything else, the sable was extremely scarce when Mozambique's long civil war ended, but they've recovered nicely and today the sable is probably the area's most plentiful large antelope. Most days you'll see sables without really looking for them, and if you look for them they aren't hard to find. I figured this out after a couple of days, with the extended thought that finding a good bull was just a matter of time. This is correct, and it's even better today, eight years later, because the sable has continued to flourish. That said, sable bulls in this region are rarely huge, so it takes a lot of looking to find

Willem van Dyk (center) with Joe Bishop and me and two good sunis. I hunted with van Dyk in Kenya in 1977 and in South Africa a few times in the 1980s, but at the time of this hunt I hadn't seen him for twenty years.

one approaching the magic 40-inch mark. We had a couple of stalks that went awry, and somewhere along the way Donna missed a last-light shot at a nice bull.

Even so, I still believed that, in this area, a good sable was just a matter of time. In the *miombo* forest it's common to find slight depressions that hold water. Called "pans," these depressions tend to be very open around the edges, often with stands of tall papyrus in the center where water remains throughout the dry season. Good grass grows in these pans and, although important to almost all species in the area, is irresistible to warthogs and seems especially attractive to sables and nyalas.

This lends itself to a somewhat unusual hunting technique that, at least in my experience, is unique to coastal Mozambique: observing the pans. When you're near a pan, you'll almost always stop the vehicle a few hundred yards out and stalk in, hoping to catch animals there. In that critical last hour of light you might rush around madly, trying to check several pans. Another option is to simply choose a pan and sit. Depending on the moon and weather, this might be done morning, afternoon, or even midday, or, if you have the patience—which I really don't—pick a good pan and sit all day. You will definitely see game, but whether you'll see the game you seek depends a bit on luck.

So we had the folding chairs out and were watching a big pan to our front, and our two trackers were a few hundred yards away watching another pan. One of them came running to say that a herd of sables had entered their pan. We hot-footed it over, and in thick grass on the far side, maybe six hundred yards away, a big herd was feeding along—with a beautiful coal-black sable bull in their midst. It was nearly sundown, so Willem took Donna on a quick frontal approach, using the papyrus bed for cover.

Joe Bishop was with us that evening, so Joe and I hung back, watching the show through binoculars. We saw the bullet hit squarely on the shoulder before we heard the shot, but the bull ran well with his herd for a hundred yards before he staggered and fell. He was a beautiful sable, old and heavy-horned, right at the magical 40 inches and with a glossy black coat. Wow!

Neither Joe nor Donna had hunted a suni. The Livingstone suni occurs sporadically in Natal and Zululand, but they're the very Devil to hunt there—the saying in South Africa is "I'm going looney looking for a suni." In coastal Mozambique they are also found in very specialized habitat, tall-tree forests called "suni forest"—but there they are so plentiful that I'm pretty sure Stevie Wonder could take one.

Much more time would pass before I'd have a better understanding of the nuances of the Marromeu region, but in 2006 and again in 2008 it was clear that neighboring Coutada 11 held the majority of the suni forest. Although they are obviously competitors, several outfitters pool their resources to some degree. Coutada 10 has far and away the most waterbucks; 11 and 12 the best nyalas; 14 the most buffaloes, and so forth. So, with permission, one day we made the long drive across to Coutada 11, and both Donna and Joe took good sunis with little incident.

This day was noteworthy because, along the road, we met Coutada 11's outfitter, Mark Haldane of Zambeze Delta Safaris. Although I'd heard of him, I'd never met him, but we chatted a bit and he seemed a good guy. As we parted he said something like, "Well, you're seeing Coutada 10, but next time you need to hunt with us." At the moment that meant nothing, but in months to come I would remember those words, and they would change the future of my African hunting.

On that hunt, our wish lists weren't long. I can't remember what Joe took, but he was looking for some "non-Namibian" species for his house in Namibia—an oribi, bushpig, suni, red duiker, this and that. Joe also got a blue duiker, found along with the sunis but much harder to come by. Donna had the sable she had long wanted, and a great suni as a bonus. I'd experienced hunting swamp buffaloes, and one evening Willem and I got a big bushpig—but I was still struggling for the nyala.

Later I would understand that there are lots of nyalas, but they're almost invisible. They stay lost in the forest until the small waterholes dry up, and then they start to hit the big pans. We were there in October, very much the right time, but we were badly hampered by a bright moon. We spent several afternoons watching big pans, but we saw very few nyalas. And then, almost like magic, it happened.

The pan was six or seven hundred yards across. On a particularly sweltering afternoon we'd been sitting and sweating in folding chairs for a couple of hours when, a half-hour before dark, a small group of red female nyalas fed out on the far side . . . followed by a dark, monstrous bull. Willem and I started at a trot, hugging the cover on the edge. We quickly slowed to a doubled-over walk, and then we crawled the last few dozen yards to get into position. So far, so good—the bull was feeding peacefully, and Willem got the sticks spread out low for a steady rest from the sitting position. The distance was about three hundred yards, a fair poke for a .30-06, but I'd used this Ruger and its 3–9X Trijicon scope for several seasons and I knew it well. Or thought I did.

The bull was broadside when I took the shot, and it felt good. Amazingly, I hit him again as he ran for cover, and then he was gone into the dense forest on the edge of the pan. Still, so far so good. I was sure we'd find him quickly. But the blood spoor didn't look good, and it quickly got dark. At dawn we checked the rifle . . . the scope had shifted right and low, just three inches at a hundred yards, but it would have been nine inches off at three hundred. I knew we were in trouble, but, of course, we spent the day looking. The sparse blood was quickly gone, and there was no further trace.

Africa rules apply: The trophy fee would be paid. Because nyalas don't show up in numbers until later in the season, this is a quota that, unlike more visible animals like hartebeests, sables, and waterbucks, is almost never filled. So, sick at heart, I continued to hunt nyalas our last few days, but we never saw another good bull. I had failed to complete the totally silly but somehow compelling concept of the "two-country, double-spiral-horn" challenge.

Willem van Dyk Junior is a great professional hunter, just like his dad, but with a wife and young family he elected not to return to Mozambique after the 2008 season. I still wanted a nyala from Mozambique, but I'd learned that, although Coutada 10 was and is a great area, 11 and 12 are better for this species. So I remembered that chance meeting with Mark Haldane along the road in a dense suni forest, and at the SCI convention early the next year we made a plan to try again for a nyala in Coutada 11 with his Zambeze Delta Safaris. Today this has become an annual event in a most amazing part of wild Africa . . . but, of course, I didn't know that then. I only knew that I still wanted a nyala from Mozambique.

CHAPTER EIGHT

FISHER'S CORNER

Zambia has been exceedingly good to me. Once called Northern Rhodesia, Zambia is blessed with a significant number of indigenous rarities, animals not found elsewhere. I hunted there several times in the 1980s and 1990s, and Zambia was generous, giving me my best lion, my best sable, two of my very best buffaloes, and most of her specialized species. Although it's a great hunting country, I didn't have a real reason to return. Well, I never took a Crawshay defassa waterbuck, but, after all, with the great diversity of African antelope, *nobody* lives long enough to hunt them all.

Then I met Pete Fisher. His great-grandfather was a missionary to Zambia in Dr. Livingstone's time. His grandfather was born there, and joined up for the little fracas we call World War I. Badly wounded in the Battle of the Somme, he went home to Africa to recuperate, and established a cattle ranch in extreme northwestern Zambia. If you look at the map, there's an odd little boot-heel of a projection up there, Angola to the west and Congo to the north and east. The area is perhaps best-known as the source of the Zambezi River, with the headwaters just a small spring not far from Pete Fisher's modern-day headquarters.

When the borders between Northern Rhodesia and then-Belgian Congo were surveyed, the Fisher clan adamantly refused to come under Belgian rule, so the odd projection of Zambia called "Fisher's Corner" was created, and remains. Pete Fisher, the fourth generation, still raises cattle, but, together with his

For much of the year Nchila is the Fisher family home as well as safari headquarters.

I knew one horn was broken on this bush duiker before I squeezed the trigger, but this is a really nice old ram with very thick horns. Even with one horn broken I was really glad to have him.

American wife, Lynn, and their children, he also raises sables on their private Nchila Wildlife Reserve. With genes strongly influenced by Angolan sable, he has the largest private sable herd in Africa that also produces some of the longest horns.

I didn't really need another sable, and although his country is big and natural, I didn't really want to hunt one in an "estate" situation. But my then-partner at Safari Classics, Dave Fulson, very much wanted a big sable, and there was more. Fisher also had Crawshay waterbucks, and since he was right on the Angolan border his bush duikers were Angolan bush duikers. He also had natural and native sitatungas. Remembering that his area is a projection of Zambia into Congo, he believed his sitatungas were not Zambezi sitatungas, but the more northern forest sitatungas.

African authority Peter Flack and I agree on this: Fisher's sitatungas are different and geographically separated from the sitatungas farther to the east in Zambia, although to this day the DNA samples don't exist to prove that difference. At any rate, we had the makings of a very interesting hunt in the farthest corner of Zambia. At that time we were knee-deep in the *Tracks across Africa* TV series, so the plan was for Dave and me to spend ten days with Pete Fisher, and then fly back through Johannesburg, on up to Beira, and do a safari with Mark Haldane's Zambeze Delta Safaris.

More than a decade had passed since I'd flown into Lusaka, but not much had changed. Gun clearance was no problem, and after a short wait we took a fairly long charter up to Nchila at Fisher's Corner. The camp was beautiful, overlooking a grassy plain where, several times, we watched herds of sables passing by. The sables were the Fishers' pride and glory, a totally amazing spectacle. I have never seen so many beautiful sables, but our goal was to find an older bull, past breeding age. We looked at a lot of beautiful sables—and a lot of other game—before Fulson took a beautiful bull.

Initially a waterbuck was top of my wish list. Waterbucks are not nearly as common or visible as sables, so we spent quite a bit of time looking. Dark was coming fast when I got a shot at a nice bull, and although the shot felt good, he dashed off into thick cover. I was worried, but we quickly stumbled onto him in the dark. He was a fine bull.

We took the Angolan bush duiker by calling, always a really interesting hunt. The duiker came in fast, as they do, and stopped about twenty-five yards away from us. I could see that one horn was broken off, but the intact horn was extremely long, and only a third of the broken horn was missing. Quick decision: Keep looking? With a rarity like this, how many chances can there be? Take the shot!

Somewhere along the way we had a little problem. This was a Ruger No. 1 safari: I had a .300 H&H for plains game, and a .450/.400 3-inch that we would use for buffaloes in Mozambique. Dave was trying to shoot something—I think a lechwe—with the .300, and his bullets were striking about six feet low. We repaired to the range and checked the rifle, and the Trijicon scope was hopelessly out. We re-zeroed, and it came back in just fine . . . but after we had it all ready to go I thought I'd better check one more time. Good God, it was more than a foot off again. Fortunately Pete Fisher had a new-in-the-box Leupold 3–9X, so I bought it from him . . . but since Leupold wasn't a sponsor of the TV show, we put black tape on the signature Gold Ring. That's just one of many "accommodations" made in television production!

A herd of pukus feeding on an open dambo. *Pukus are extremely plentiful in this area, more than I've ever seen.*

Just past the midpoint in the safari, all of our primary goals had been accomplished and we had some time. I like to hunt sitatungas, but I'd taken two Zambezi sitatungas in Zambia and one in Botswana. I understood the argument that Fisher's sitatungas were forest, not Zambezi. They probably are, but I also understood that this wasn't proven and perhaps never would be. The sitatunga is an expensive animal, so this was a whimsical and perhaps unwise decision. On the other hand, it matches the credo I've long followed: I was there and the costs were already incurred. Once there, cartridges, film, and even trophy fees are fairly minor expenses! With several days left and no major animals remaining, I told Pete we should hunt sitatungas.

Unlike almost all other sitatunga country I've seen, there was no papyrus in this area. Instead the sitatungas lived in small riverine forests, so their habitat is also more similar to that of forest sitatungas than the areas where I've hunted Zambezi sitatungas in both Botswana and Zambia. For that matter, it's also dissimilar to East African sitatunga country I've seen in both Tanzania and Uganda. The population is not large, but occasionally sitatungas will be seen along the edges, and Fisher believes he can comfortably take three or four bulls in most years. Although the country looks different, these sitatungas are homebodies, just like all the swamp fairies, so hunting is done from machans sited on the edges of known haunts.

We were hunting a specific bull known to frequent a particular stretch of river. We actually caught a quick glimpse of him one evening while we were looking for waterbucks, before I'd made a firm decision to hunt sitatungas. These are generally not long-horned sitatungas but tend toward thick bases without extreme length, like forest sitatungas. It was just a quick flash, but this seemed a good-looking bull, fully mature with horns in the mid-twenties.

The Crawshay waterbuck is the smallest race of waterbuck, and can be hunted only in western Zambia. It was almost dark when I got a shot with the .300 H&H, and we had to follow the animal a few dozen yards into the thick forest before we stumbled over him.

The machan was sited across the river and a few hundred yards upstream from where we'd seen him, covering a wide bend in the river with good grass. Built on

Geographically separated from other sitatungas in Zambia and surrounded by Congo and Angola, these are forest sitatungas according to Fisher, and I agree, but so far it's been impossible to establish this through DNA testing.

stout poles, it was a sturdy platform with thatched walls, a comfortable place to sit and watch the world go by. The first afternoon we saw a couple of mouselike sitatunga females drifting through the area, so we were in a good place, although I was still a bit skeptical as to why *that* bull might choose to cruise by *that* place. Well, even though it wasn't a country of floating islands and impenetrable papyrus, the riverine was too thick to still-hunt, so hunting from stands seemed the best approach.

I can't keep you in suspense: This was the easiest sitatunga I ever shot, and I didn't even get my feet wet. On the second afternoon the bull came out from the right, headed across our front wide-open and in the clear, in full sunlight. He was walking very slowly and cautiously, not much more than a hundred yards away, and when he hesitated I shot him on the shoulder with a 180-grain Hornady.

He ran for the narrow river, plowing brush as he went, and we found him on the far side, having gone down in mid-stride. I wish I could claim him as a forest sitatunga because that's an animal I don't have and perhaps never will. Also, that's what I think he properly is, dark in color with shorter, thicker horns. But I neither make the boundaries nor, without all the proper evidence, do I have the opportunity to change them. So he is what he is, a nice sitatunga bull. Even that makes him unique, a good representative of a highly specialized spiral-horn antelope that, in my estimation, ranks just slightly below the three great prizes: bongo, giant eland, and mountain nyala.

By walking along forest roads slowly with a .22, Dave Fulson finally got this beautiful blue duiker on the very last evening.

With its huge northern border with Democratic Republic of Congo (DRC) it's hard to characterize exactly to what region of Africa Zambia belongs. My old friend Peter Capstick liked to call it part of Central Africa. However, Zambia clearly lies south of the great forest zone, so I tend to think of it as the northernmost country in southern Africa. It does, however, have a unique mix of species: three varieties of lechwes, sitatungas, and indigenous species such as pukus and Cookson wildebeests. There are also pockets of yellow-backed duikers in some of the northern blocks, and quite a few blue duikers.

Fisher didn't have yellow-backed duikers as far as he knew, but he had a lot of blue duikers. Fulson had never taken one, so we spent the last couple of evenings walking along forest trails looking for blue duikers. These tiny little antelopes were far more plentiful than I'd expected. Although we recognize just one variety of blue duiker, my assumption is there must be differences between the populations in Central Africa and Cameroon and the blue duikers of the Eastern Cape and coastal Mozambique. My further assumption is that those in Zambia must be the same as the Central African blue duikers, but whatever or whichever, I saw more of them at Nchila in Fisher's Corner than I've ever seen anywhere else. Getting a shot is easier said than done, but just at dark on the very last day Fulson came through and took a very nice blue duiker, completing a marvelous hunt in a very out-of-the-way corner of Africa.

CHAPTER NINE

FIRST HUNT IN COUTADA 11

The Beira airport is hot and tropical, and the firearms clearance, though better now than then, is tedious. Sooner or later they get it done, and then you're cruising north over palm-studded wetlands, the Indian Ocean glimmering off the right wing. The destination is Mungari airstrip, headquarters for Zambeze Delta Safaris. There you will find Coutada 11 and farther inland Coutada 12.

It was early October, and with the waterholes drying quickly, the pans were becoming ever more active. We would go to the swamp to hunt buffaloes, of course, but the primary goal was a nyala. The timing should have been perfect, and Mark Haldane was full of confidence. Well, he should have been; he knows his country and he has lots of nyalas. Me, well, after the beating I'd taken the year before, I had a sense that this was a more difficult animal than it really is. A couple of years later, I would see thirty-five nyala *bulls* in one day—in the same places at much the same time! But let's not get ahead of our story.

Dave Fulson took a very good suni, which was one of the animals he really wanted on the trip.

On the nyala scene Mark was perhaps a bit overconfident, while I was anything but confident. So it was that, on about the second evening, well before dusk, Fulson had the camera rolling over my shoulder, I was on sticks, and we had a lovely nyala bull walking left

An aerial tour of the Marromeu reveals huge herds of buffaloes, some of the largest herds I've ever seen. On the ground it's a whole lot different, but even from this altitude the circling white birds are obvious.

to right through some dry grass, not sixty yards away. Oh, yes, I would have shot him. He wasn't the 30-inch monster we dream of, but he was within an inch or so with good shape and plenty of mass.

Mark hesitated, and even if I think I know better, I know well enough that the wisest course is to listen to one's PH. He whispered that we could probably do better, so I backed off the trigger. Eventually we would get a better nyala, but it wasn't going to happen on that trip. Years later, after months in the field together, Haldane and I still laugh about passing that nyala on the second day we ever hunted together.

Oh, we saw plenty of nyalas. We even saw plenty of mature, shootable nyalas—but all were in the middle range, twenty-six or twenty-seven inches. We waited at selected pans, and on some evenings we did the mad rush, checking three or four pans in the last golden hour of light. Plenty of nyalas and plenty of bulls, but the big boys didn't want to come out to play.

Late in the hunt, with time growing short, we consciously settled. We came into a big pan just before sundown. There were some red females on the far side, and we picked up the dark color of two bulls, then the white of their dorsal crests. One was a good bull, dark, heavy, and absolutely shootable, but his horns had too little flare and not enough in and out to have extreme length.

We knew this, but we were running out of days. The nyala was the main goal on this hunt. We'd put in a lot of time, and of course the TV camera was running and we hadn't taken a great deal of other game. At this stage the decision wasn't hard, and we couldn't agonize over it. Much ground must be covered, and light was starting to fade.

Mark led us back into the woods to get out of sight, and we hopped from one game trail to another, hustling as best we could. We'd marked a big termite mound down at that end of the pan. Once we got close it would give us cover, so when we had it in sight—with the nyalas on the far side—we left the tree line and made a direct approach. Some of the termite mounds in this area are huge, fifteen feet tall, often with stout trees on the crest. They can offer good vantage points for both glassing and shooting, but in this case the ground beyond was flat and open. So we tucked in behind the mound, got our breath, and then slipped out to the right where Mark put up the sticks.

The females were about two hundred away on the edge of the tree line, as they had been, but neither bull was visible. Then we saw a ghostly line of white just to their right, in the dark trees. It was the dorsal crest of a nyala, white hairs erect—perhaps it had been fighting or was doing the display ritual. The smaller bull was gone and this was the one we wanted. I was shooting the Ruger single-shot in .300 H&H, the 3–9X Leupold turned up all the way. The sticks were steady, but I still had a horizontal wobble, almost unavoidable at that distance.

Controlling it as best I could, I got the shot off. It felt good, but the bull turned and ran deeper in the trees and we lost sight of him. The next few moments were agonizing. This time I knew the rifle was on, but I feared I might have hit him a bit far back. With light going fast now, we crossed the bottom of the pan and entered the trees, me feeling a healthy dose of *déjà vu* from the year before and fearing the worst. Fortunately, the bull was down just inside the trees, well hit.

We were still walking toward him when Mark stopped and pointed. A huge red duiker stood not thirty yards away, thick horns obvious even in deep shadow. "Craig, that's a giant duiker; you'd better shoot him as well."

With the deepest channel crossed, we stop to get papyrus out of the treads and have some coffee. The real buffalo hunt is about to begin.

Here it's open enough to see the black mass of buffaloes, but often all you can see over papyrus and sawgrass are the white cattle egrets circling the herd.

He started to put up the sticks but I waved him off—we were too close, and that takes a lot of movement. I took the shot offhand, flattening the duiker, and we made sure of him before walking up on our main prize, the nyala.

Everyone has their favorites. Kudus are amazing and sables are stunning. All elands are awesome, but the Derby eland in winter color is matchless, and the burnt-orange of the bongo is almost unimaginable, especially up close. For me, however, I vote for the nyala as Africa's most beautiful antelope: long, silky coat; orange and white on legs and undersides; bright white nose chevron; white side-stripes; and white accents on the flank . . . and of course, those thick lyre-shaped horns. In years gone by I'd taken three in South Africa and thought each one was the most beautiful antelope. I had long wanted one in Mozambique and now, on the next to the last day, we had one, and he was every bit as beautiful as the others.

Scientists have not identified any divergent races or subspecies of nyalas as they have with most other species of antelopes. This is probably because their native range is fairly small: central and southern Mozambique into Zululand and Natal, across Malawi, and along a few rivers in southeastern Zimbabwe. That's it. The small, bright-red, harness-striped females are so different they don't even seem the same species as the larger, darker males. I have the impression, and it's just an impression, that the nyala bulls of coastal Mozambique aren't quite as dark as nyalas I've seen in South Africa. You do see bulls that appear nearly black, but the ones I've taken and seen taken, now quite a few, seem to be more brownish or dark gray.

In any case, I had my nyala from Mozambique and, thus, at least doubles of all nine major spiral horns with, excepting the Ethiopia-only mountain nyalas, specimens of each from two different countries. It was a silly goal, but I'd been thinking about it for a long time, so this nyala was a major event. To my knowledge, though I could be wrong, Peter Flack is the only other hunter who has taken two of each, although I don't know if he also included that silliness of two different countries wherever possible.

On this hunt we concentrated on nyalas, but there is so much game in the coastal *coutadas* that it's pretty difficult to hunt a single species in a vacuum. We went to the suni forests and Dave got a fine suni, and early one morning he took a nice red duiker. Bushbuck is another favorite. The bushbucks in coastal Mozambique are the red Chobe bushbucks, and the area produces giants—but it's a funny deal in that, unlike most places, bushbuck habitat isn't obvious. There are plenty of them, but they are here and there, everywhere and nowhere, so this is a very difficult animal to hunt.

Fulson hadn't taken a Chobe bushbuck, so we were always looking, but of all the species found in this area, bushbucks and blue duikers are probably the hardest to come by. On the last evening, after we finally had the nyala, Dave took a nice bushbuck—but, regrettably, not one of the really big ones the area can produce. Come to think of it, now after eight or nine hunts in this area, I haven't yet taken a really big bushbuck—or a blue duiker.

Needless to say, we also went to the swamps to hunt buffalo. Actually, on this hunt we had fresh tracks out in the forest several times and got into several herds. This is pure tracking, but because the forest is dry and noisy, it's very difficult. Although the buffaloes are exactly the same, around the camps we speak of "swamp buffaloes" and "forest buffaloes" because hunting them is so different. The herds tend to be smaller in the forest, but it's difficult to sort through the herds. We saw bulls, but we never saw a mature bull. So, at some point in the hunt, it was time to go to the swamp. This was still "BBV"—before the outfitter started using the large tracked vehicles called Hägglunds BVs—when all the hunting was done from Argos, which are slower and have a more limited payload.

We're lucky here with a bit of papyrus for cover, but even so, crawling is part of the game with these swamp buffaloes. Later we'd add kneepads and gloves to our hunting essentials for these animals.

We stayed in a fly camp on the last island the night before so as to get an early start. With relative ease we found where a big herd had spent the night, but they were moving and had covered a lot of ground, so, as usual, it was a blistering hot midday before we closed on them. By this time they had bedded on an open flat, which is common—but we were lucky because they were fairly close to a strand of papyrus with some sawgrass on the edge. A bit of wading and a bit more crawling, and we were very close to this big herd. The nearest buffaloes were barely forty yards, but there were at least four hundred individuals in the herd. That meant that we couldn't see them all and probably never would, and Murphy's Law being what it is, the buffalo we wanted would probably be at the far end.

As usual we never saw all the bulls, but on the right-hand fringe, almost in the clear, a very old bull was bedded. He was very mature but flat-horned and, honestly, kind of ugly. We watched and sweated for a couple of hours. Although a herd might stay bedded all day, individuals will get up and shift around a bit. So if you have cover and the wind stays constant, with patience you'll see at least a significant portion of the herd. We saw other bulls, but mostly youngsters and no giants. There was no hurry, but we didn't yet have our nyala and that was the main order of business. When that old, flat-horned bull stood, I was pretty sure we'd get a shot, so we got ready and I kept an eye on him while Mark continued to scan the herd.

Mark Haldane and I with a really old, ugly swamp buffalo that I took with a single 400-grain Hornady from the Ruger single shot in .450/.400-3".

A snappy double on the next-to-last day landed these! We were walking toward our nyala when Mark spotted a huge red duiker, much too big to pass. This is a nice nyala, not as big as we'd hoped but hard won. There would be more chances for a bigger one in years to come.

Undoubtedly there were better bulls somewhere in the mess, but nothing else showed, and there's never anything wrong with taking an old buffalo. Eventually he stood, and instead of walking into the herd, he walked into the clear. *Perfect!* Unfortunately for the buffalo, just too perfect.

I was shooting a scoped Ruger No. 1 in .450/.400 3-inch with 400-grain Hornady DGX bullets. The buffalo had been bedded at 125 yards, but when he stopped he'd ambled a few yards closer. I shot him very carefully on the shoulder, and the herd exploded. Of course, I had to reload the single-shot, but the bull was covered up so quickly there would have been no second shot with a double rifle, let alone with a bolt action. They moved off quickly, and as they vanished, our buffalo was in their wake, down and dead.

I learned a lot on this safari. I learned more about the Marromeu complex, much more about nyalas, and more about swamp buffaloes. I also learned that Mark Haldane not only had a great area, but also ran a great camp. And perhaps most important of all, he made it *fun*. He had a wonderful team, an interesting mixture of eager young PHs and extremely experienced hands, these last including his brother, Glen, and Mike Curry and Craigh Hamman. It would be a couple of years before I'd hunt with him again, but I knew I'd be back, and since then I've been back again and again.

Chapter Ten

Secrets of the Eastern Cape

South African hunting was in its fledgling stages when I started hunting in Africa. There were very few outfitters—Norman Deane of Zululand Safaris; Deane's onetime apprentice, Gary Kelly, in Natal; Bowker & Scott down in the Cape . . . and not many more. Opportunities were limited, but clearly they grew. As did the game ranching industry! The Professional Hunters Association of South Africa estimates wildlife in South Africa has increased thirtyfold since about 1970. Today there are good areas and good operators in virtually all regions, and South Africa hosts something like 50 percent of all hunting safaris annually on the African continent.

Although the country offers the entire Big Five in limited numbers, South Africa is perhaps best known as a destination for the first-time hunter in search of a plains-game safari. In this market it competes directly with Namibia. Which is better can be argued endlessly. Daily rates in South Africa tend to be a bit less, while trophy fees are often a bit lower in Namibia. Both are good, take your pick . . . but one thing that cannot be argued is that South Africa has a more extensive game list, and a lot more indigenous rarities. Heck, I'm not done with either country, but for the veteran African hunter there are probably more excuses—*er, reasons*—to return to South Africa.

This especially applies to South Africa's Eastern Cape. This region probably has the longest game list of any similar-size area on the continent. This is because several varied habitats are found in proximity. In the course of a day you can go from dense, almost tropical coastal thornbush through a narrow belt of coastal plain, then to brushy hills, and up to tall mountains. Beyond the mountains, and studded by more mountains, lies the windswept Karoo, an arid semidesert region.

Naturally these areas hold a tremendous variety of wildlife, but thanks to game ranching, the list has expanded considerably over the years. In this area "game ranching" is not necessarily synonymous with "high-fenced." Some properties are, but many are not. Either way, the average farm (the preferred term in South Africa) tends to be large.

South Africa's Eastern Cape is one of few areas where permits can be obtained for some of the strange night animals such as aardvark and aardwolf. This is the aardvark or "earth pig," which are hunted in fields containing termite mounds.

For beginners the Eastern Cape offers a great hunting experience; for experts, well, it takes a number of visits there to work through the extensive game list.

At the beginning of this volume I wrote about a hunt up in the Cape Mountains for a Vaal rhebok and mountain reedbuck for Donna and a lechwe and fallow deer for me. In years gone by, the Eastern Cape yielded a bontebok, white blesbok, blue duiker, oribi, Cape grysbok, and much more . . . even, on Russell Lovemore's farm, a bat-eared fox.

This last is a good example of one of several secrets of the Eastern Cape: The wildlife authorities there will issue permits for several animals that, although widespread and often plentiful, are rarely on license. One is the aardwolf (earth wolf), which is a small, nocturnal, and beautiful relative of the hyena. Another is the aardvark (earth pig), not exactly beautiful but kind of cool. It took Russell Lovemore a lot of effort to get licenses issued for these two animals, and, in fact, they came in separate years—but in the Eastern Cape, such things are possible.

The aardwolf is considered one of the world's most selective feeders. Although sheep farmers have hated them for generations, they eat termites almost exclusively, and are said to have hearing so sensitive that they can detect termites digging. The aardvark also preys on termites. The mounds in that region tend to be small, sort of like wide, stunted fireplugs. If you see a termite mound with a round hole drilled just above ground level—and you will see many like this if you look—you can tell that an aardvark has come to call.

The Eastern Cape is also extremely easy to reach: It's a quick flight from Johannesburg to Port Elizabeth, and the outfitters I know there are generally within a couple of hours from the Port Elizabeth airport. So for a specialized hunt for a couple of rarities, it's pretty easy to "drop in" for a few days before, after, or during another hunt in southern Africa. With my wishes on the game list limited, this has often been my *modus operandi* in the Eastern Cape, and the area has never disappointed me.

Over the years I've seen quite a few aardwolves cross the road in the dark, and once one came to a call while we were hunting jackals—so maybe they aren't as selective as believed. I've even seen several in the daylight. Although they are even more nocturnal, I've seen several aardvarks moving just at dusk. But to find either species on purpose, well, both times I made sure to allow plenty of time.

In neither case was the time needed. Both times we were fortunate to catch calm, cold, clear evenings when the animals were moving. Though in different years, both hunts were essentially the same, with us starting in the rapidly cooling dusk and prowling the edges of termite mounds. Both times we hunted through the evening, nearly freezing to death, and when we were just about to give up, *voila*, there they were!

The aardwolf is about the size of a jackal, but slimmer in build. I used a .223 borrowed from Larry McGillewie, and it worked perfectly with little pelt damage. The aardvark, on the other hand, is a stout, stocky animal, and I wasn't concerned about such niceties. I used the rifle I had, a .375 Ruger, and its impact against such a solid animal was one of the loudest *thumps* I've ever heard. I have both animals mounted life-size on either side of my entryway in Kansas, two unique and interesting African animals.

Larry McGillewie and I are standing in prime aoudad country, which is on the northern fringe of the Great Karoo. Aoudads are not especially widespread in South Africa, but in the areas where they've been introduced, they've done very well.

I'm sure some hunters would have the restraint to travel all the way to the Eastern Cape for just

I was hunting with Larry McGillewie when I took this nice South African aoudad. In body and horn size, these aoudads are more similar to the native North African aoudad; they usually don't get as big as the aoudad in the American Southwest.

one animal. I lack that degree of restraint, but the Eastern Cape holds plenty of other animals that I, personally, find interesting, so there's no waste of time for me to hunt there. It's a fantastic area for bushbucks, always one of my favorites. The Cape bushbucks are rarely extremely long in the horn, they're nearly black, and they're always beautiful. Over the years, hunting with Larry McGillewie and his partner, Russell Lovemore, I've taken several beautiful bushbucks.

One time we were actually hunting hog deer, a nonnative that, although not plentiful, has been in the Eastern Cape for a long time, long enough to occasionally turn up in odd places. We were chasing a rumor of a big buck seen at the edge of a hayfield. The hog deer didn't show, but as the morning wore on and it seemed unlikely he would appear, a beautiful bushbuck did, in broad daylight, no reason for him to be there at all. We changed directions and made a quick stalk, and I got a fine, dark bushbuck ram.

We did get a hog deer that trip. Russell Lovemore and Larry McGillewie were sort of tag-teaming me on that hunt. When a couple of other rumors didn't pan out, Larry McGillewie and I went down to Ervin Tam's place. Technically I suppose these are fenced but, just like jackals, steenboks, duikers, and pigs, I'm not sure it's possible to fence such a small animal either in or out. But Ervin does have a genuine breeding herd of hog deer that hang out in a wandering, brushy streambed.

Asian hog deer have been introduced into several areas in the Eastern Cape. Larry McGillewie and I got this one on Ervin Tam's property. His herd is fairly small, but he can take two or three nice bucks every year.

Still-hunting on foot, as one might hunt bushbucks, Larry and I slowly worked our way along the edges of the cover. We jumped several female hog deer and one small buck, along with impalas, springboks, and nyalas. Near the end of the heavy cover, seemingly a dry run, a nice buck broke cover and dashed across the open streambed. It took a couple seconds to get on him, and in another moment he'd be gone—but I got the rifle on him, and with the .375 Ruger I wasn't worried about the angle. I got the shot off just as he disappeared, and when we crossed the riverbed, we found a very fine buck. This unusual African trophy is only found in the Eastern Cape.

There are several other unusual nonnatives in the Eastern Cape. I looked into water buffaloes, but the only ones known were in small paddocks, not really a hunt and definitely not for me. There continue to be rumors of free-range Himalayan tahr. At one time there were definitely a few in isolated hills. They might still be there, but my contacts believe predators cleaned them out. Whether this is true or not, there are quite a few aoudads in scattered populations.

Hunting again with Larry McGillewie, we drove endlessly through the wee hours to a rough bit of country, deep canyons and steep, rocky ridges that looked a lot like aoudad country, and it was. A local tracker took us to a deep canyon, and we hunted on foot from there. We glassed up a big herd with several good rams, got the wind right, and planned what turned out to be a perfect stalk. Resting over a rock, I took the shot at less than a hundred yards, pounding what appeared to be a big ram.

It was a big ram, but judging an aoudad is always a matter of perspective. Aoudads are a favorite animal of mine, and I've hunted them a lot in Texas as well as in Chad and southern Spain, so I know something about judging them in the field and the importance of perspective. The aoudads in Chad are much smaller-bodied than those in Texas, so you lose inches of horn to body size. This proved true in Spain, and equally in South Africa: My ram was a good, mature specimen, but not as big as I'd thought because the body size is smaller than the aoudads in Texas.

In any case we got a nice aoudad, and it was a good hunt. On the trek back to the truck we saw another herd that we'd missed. There must have been a hundred aoudads, with more scattered across a rugged hillside—a magnificent sight. This is another little known but most enjoyable Eastern Cape hunt.

Another secret of the Eastern Cape is the excellent pig hunting, especially interesting if you're a pig hunter like me. Years ago, when I first hunted in this region, warthogs were almost unknown. None of the landowners know exactly what happened—whether they were introduced or somehow moved in—but today warthogs are common, and the Eastern Cape produces pigs with very good tusks. So warthogs are another favorite pursuit in the Eastern Cape.

Hunting along the boundary of the Addo Park, one can glass incredible tuskers, but so far the big ones have always been on the wrong side of the fence. Russell and I shot a good one once, on a neighbor's farm just across the road from his place, but I'm sure I'll keep looking because big warthogs are always an interest of mine.

So are bushpigs, and the Eastern Cape is one of the two great places to hunt this elusive, nocturnal swine. (The other is coastal Mozambique.) Back in the 1980s I got my first bushpig in the Eastern Cape, hunting with dogs. For many years that was my only bushpig. Hunting them with dogs is a young man's sport, and I'm way past my ability to run a marathon down the long cut lines. The other option in the Eastern Cape is baiting, something of a fine art in the area.

That was kind of a funny deal. I was hunting with Russell Lovemore, but Eardley Rudman of Blaauwkrantz had done a lot of work with baiting and trail cameras. Some work remained to be done, and at that time he hadn't quite earned the title of Hogfather. (See chapter twenty-five.) But he was keen, and he wanted to show us what he was up to. So, one afternoon, Russell and I hustled over to Blaauwkrantz. Eardley showed us some sets and trail cameras, and he picked a bait to sit over. Sure enough, some pigs came in, but it was so dark it was impossible to size or judge them. I shot one, sort of a barbecue pig.

The Eastern Cape is one of the very best places to hunt bushpig, and the most common techniques are baiting at night or hunting with hounds. This excellent boar was taken over bait at Russell Lovemore's place.

Now, in the Eastern Cape all the outfitters are competitors, but most of them are also friends. You don't see the back-stabbing viciousness that occurs among neighboring outfitters in some areas. So Russell was good enough to take me over to Eardley's, but I suspect he was secretly delighted when the "sure thing" didn't quite work out. Except that issued a challenge—could he produce a good bushpig?

Two nights later he did. We were on his family farm, now regrettably sold. We went to a bait site he'd kept going for years, next to dense Addo bush and overlooked by a tower blind. The setup is perfect, and it produces a few bushpigs every year. Everyone has his or her tricks for baiting. Russell had a red light above the bait, a constant source that the pigs either get used to, or they don't.

These pigs didn't mind. Three came in to the bait, grunting and snuffling, and then a fourth pig, obviously bigger, joined them. The distance was perhaps thirty yards, but it was really dim. Through a binocular I could clearly see the largest pig, but through the scope it wasn't quite so easy. But I was sure I was on the correct pig, and reasonably sure I could see my reticle. Pigs on bait are always grunting and shifting; when the one I was watching shifted and opened up a broadside shot, I fired the .375 Ruger.

Of course, all hell broke loose. I was blinded by the muzzle flash, and the pigs exploded in all directions. We thought the group went left while the stricken pig went right into thick thornbushes. Maybe we heard him crash, maybe we didn't . . . but now everything was very quiet. We waited a little while, then we climbed down, got our headlamps going, and started digging into the horrible Addo bush. Our pig was right there, a beautiful boar with good, well-matched tusks. I guess you have to be a pig hunter to appreciate a bushpig, but to my thinking they're one of the best secrets of the Eastern Cape.

CHAPTER ELEVEN

BY FOOT IN COUTADA 14

The heat was palpable. It was late October and the sun glared from a cloudless sky. The buffaloes were there, a thick black line dancing through mirage and heat wave. They were on the move, as were we . . . but we weren't getting closer, and we were into the heat of the day. Whether we could reach them was questionable, but we had to give it one more try.

I was hunting in Tony Wicker's Coutada 14. I'd hunted in Coutadas 10 and 11, the other two blocks that border the Marromeu Reserve, and I had hunted in Coutada 12, adjacent to and inland from 11. Hunting in Coutada 14 sort of created a "Marromeu grand slam" for me. Tony's 14 is the northernmost region and closest to the Zambezi. As I would eventually come to understand, though all these blocks are close together, they differ quite a bit.

Coutada 10 has the most waterbucks by far while 11 has the most suni forest, and, thus, the majority of suni and red duiker. Lacking an actual Marromeu frontage, 12 has the fewest buffaloes, but probably the most nyalas. They're all huge areas, but 14 is the smallest, with perhaps the greatest concentration of buffaloes and with the least plains game. None of these distinctions matter a great deal because the operators trade back and forth. Even so, it's interesting to note the difference within such a tight area.

Tony Wicker, longtime operator of Coutada 14, had generously donated a buffalo safari for auction. Texan David Porter had purchased the hunt, and was accompanied by his old buddy Walter Foss. So there we were at Tony's scenic camp that overlooked a pool frequented by hippos and crocodiles. This developed into a great buffalo hunt, but it was a bit different in a couple of ways. For one thing, Tony Wicker is a bit of a traditionalist; he doesn't use swamp vehicles to hunt swamp buffaloes.

It helps that his area has a lot of buffaloes, and their primary habitat is a bit closer to the tree line than in the other *coutadas*. Also, although you're going to get your feet wet, the way his area is situated there aren't any major rivers to cross. There's something else that I simply cannot explain: In both Coutadas 10 and 11 bachelor bulls—*dagga boys*—seem rare, or at least are rarely seen. However, there are mature bulls in the big herds, so the answer to that is pretty obvious: hunt the herds. In 14, for whatever reason, there are usually quite a few bachelor bulls, alone and in small groups, in isolated patches of papyrus and sawgrass around the edges.

So his buffaloes are more accessible by foot, and he solves the meat recovery issue by sending a whole bunch of porters out with the buffalo hunters. Typically a hunt starts by glassing from the last tall trees at the edge of the swamp. Sometimes you see the actual buffaloes, but as with all the swamp hunting, what you're really looking for are the white cattle egrets swirling over the herd.

Once you find the egrets, from there it depends a bit on luck, and in more ways than one. If a herd can be glassed, it's probably accessible by foot—providing it's not moving away—but it will take at least a couple hours of hard slogging to get in striking range. If no herds can be glassed, it's a bit foolish to simply take off walking, so lack of visible buffaloes from the vantage points is the cue to start digging around for a bachelor group or to spend the morning hunting something else.

There's another aspect to luck. This is hot country. August and September are usually tolerable, but the rains end late in coastal Mozambique, so the earlier one hunts the cooler the weather, but more wading is required. By October into early November the swamps are about as dry as they're going to get, so walking is easier, but the midday hours are beastly hot, and once you leave the tree line, there is no shade. However, it isn't like much of southern Africa where clear skies are the norm in winter and early spring. Because of proximity to the Indian Ocean it is always blessedly cool at night, and even in the hottest months, cloudy days aren't uncommon.

In this kind of buffalo hunting, you're certain to get your feet wet!

Debbie Visser's system for finding buffalo is to have one of the trackers carry a stout pole. She's light enough that her trackers can hoist her up, and that's enough elevation to glass at considerable distance for circling birds.

So if you're lucky, you can march off into the swamps under cloud cover. If you're not so lucky the sun will beat on you like a hammer. That particular day was one of the latter. Oddly, although I become a sniveling wimp when it gets cold, I'm not unduly bothered by intense heat. But sometimes you're better off not knowing. Some idiot brought a thermometer, and as we were watching that buffalo herd drift off through the heat waves, we were told that it was 130 degrees Fahrenheit where we were standing. Yes, Virginia, that's hot.

The books say it doesn't get much hotter than that, but that's actually not true. In 2002, on a blistering day along the Iraq-Kuwait border, my German battalion commander came to me somewhat sheepishly and said, "Sir, I'm not sure if you really want to know this, but it's 72 degrees where we're standing—that's 162 in your Fahrenheit." I knew it was hot, but I'm not sure I wanted to know it was *that* hot! On that day we shut down until, near sunset, it was a blessedly cool 120-something.

On this day, with the heat sucking moisture out of our bodies faster than we could take it in, we had buffaloes in sight, and we were already several miles out from the nearest shade. There was little choice but to proceed.

There was one more thing unique about this hunt. Our professional hunter was Debbie Visser, petite, blonde, and at that time a twenty-something-year-old. I don't want this to sound sexist—I've hunted elsewhere with female guides, and many times with female hunting companions—but to be hunting dangerous game under difficult conditions with this slip of a young lady was a new experience for all of us.

Trust me, there was no competence issue. At this time Visser had guided in Coutada 14 for nearly a decade. She's a good hand and knows buffalo, and although she never had to use it on our safari I had no doubt she knew exactly how to handle the worn Cogswell & Harrison .404 Jeffery she carried. There was also no toughness issue. She was fully acclimated to the heat, and was at least twenty years younger than any of us.

She was also carrying, well, let's just say *fewer* pounds than the rest of us—by a bunch. In the swamps I'd already learned from hunting with Donna that this makes a huge difference: A 120-pound person can skip lightly across places where 180-pounders get wallowed—or swallowed. Put it all together, and Debbie Visser could walk us to death. But of course, in our macho world, we would die horribly before we would admit it. She had one more weight-based advantage: One of the trackers carried a stout pole, so to gain some height she would stand on the pole, and they'd hoist her up so she could glass over the sawgrass.

We continued, and a tough hour later we caught the herd in a wide-open savanna with one last strand of sawgrass allowing a good approach. Walter Foss, who had not taken a buffalo, was the designated hitter. Debbie took him in and put up the sticks; he made a good shot on a nice bull, hit him again on the move, and he went down in the open with no incident.

By now it was pushing one o'clock and nobody wanted to look at the thermometer any more. The herd moved off slowly, across the savanna and into sawgrass, but deeper into the swamp. In other words, they were going the wrong way. There were other bulls in the herd. With these swamp buffaloes you often have the opportunity to make a double play. Except, honestly, we were pretty well finished, and we already had a long walk out of there.

Tony Wicker's camp in Coutada 14. This is a really pretty spot for a camp, with crocodiles and sometimes hippos in the lagoon.

Visser, of course, was raring to go, and we couldn't very well refuse.

Debbie Visser and David Porter smile over their truly spectacular warthog. Debbie had seen this boar several times, and others had shot at it before. This time it made a mistake and showed itself to the wrong hunter!

So we made a couple more tries, but the herd was wary and on the move, and we finally had to do the sensible and un-macho thing and call it day. Except that wasn't the end of the day; we still had to get out of there, and our dozen-odd helpers were burdened with meat. Dusk was falling when we stumbled back to dry ground and the truck.

Most of the places where I've done a lot of buffalo hunting we've focused on bachelor groups. This is certainly true in Zimbabwe, perhaps a bit less so in Botswana, Tanzania, and Zambia. But, typically, if you can find bachelor groups that's what you go after since there is a greater likelihood of mature bulls and fewer eyes, ears, and noses to defeat. Most of the hunting I've done in coastal Mozambique, both before and after this hunt, has been different. There are mature bulls in the herds, and the big herds are much easier to find, so usually we hunt the herds, and over the course of a full decade of hunting in the area, I can recall few sightings of bachelor groups.

This made Coutada 14 unique, at least to my experience in the area. We'd done our death march in the swamp (and we'd do it again), but, closer in, there were bachelor groups . . . not necessarily easier to hunt, but offering easier access. So if we aren't able to glass (seemingly) accessible herds, one or another tracker would usually know where we might look for *dagga* bulls.

As part of the auction package David had also won a Rigby double rifle, and, of course, he wanted to use it. Honestly, way out in the swamps it is *not* double rifle country, or at least not open-sight country, and with the big herds it's difficult to get quite close enough. So looking for bachelor groups seemed like an exceedingly good idea.

We found a group hanging around some sawgrass and papyrus that surrounded a little pond. It looked easy, but this turned out to be a wet spot miles from the true swamp, and getting around the group was a nightmarish slog, going through mud above our knees and in a couple of places water up to our chests. Well, at least for David, Walter, and me. Even Debbie couldn't keep her feet dry, but she never sunk in as deep as we did. Aided by a strong breeze, we caught the bulls in some sawgrass and crawled in really close. Debbie identified the best bull, and David made a brilliant shot with his .470. Bull down!

David wanted a second buffalo, and since I was there I wanted one as well. Walter was more interested in hunting some plains game, so we separated on some days. Walter took a nice sable and a couple other animals, and both Walter and David took nice sunis—really a must-do in this region. One afternoon David took a spectacular warthog that Debbie had seen several times. But the primary focus remained buffaloes. We went back to the swamp on another blistering day and closed on a nice herd, but, unusually, there just weren't any mature bulls. Then, finally, we caught another group of five bachelor bulls.

It was an unusual situation. We'd picked up their tracks—very fresh—on dry ground and followed, but they'd gone into a stand of tall sawgrass. Fairly certain they weren't far ahead, Debbie took us on a mostly foot-dry circle, using some termite mounds to peer into the nasty stuff. Yes, they were there, maybe seventy yards in, just their horns and backlines visible. Debbie set David up on sticks on a slight mound—considering the distance and circumstances he wisely used his scoped Dakota .375—and we waited

David Porter's first buffalo was in a small group, and he dropped it with a brilliant shot from his double rifle. Although not especially wide, the bosses are excellent. It is a very nice bull.

David Porter, Debbie Visser, and I pose with our "double" on buffalo, two bulls from a bachelor herd in really scary sawgrass.

them out. Finally, what appeared to be the best bull stepped onto his own raised spot, showed his shoulder, and David pasted him.

The shot looked good, but all we could see was bobbing horns, and then the buffaloes stopped and milled, only heads and horns visible. It appeared there were now four . . . was David's bull down, or was there one we couldn't see? At this point I did a very risky thing. I took David's place on the sticks, handing off my Krieghoff double .500 and using his .375. There was an old bull with terrible horns in the group, but all I could see above the sawgrass was head, horns, and ears. I studied the shot for a long time, also evaluating how steady I was. Finally the bull turned quartering away, offering a bit of broad neck just up from the base of the ear. I took the shot and the bull vanished while bobbing heads and horns scattered.

It was a foolish thing to do because now we had a totally unknown situation. Did we have two buffaloes down? One buffalo down? *Two* wounded buffaloes in deadly sawgrass? There was only one way to find out, and, of course, we had to do this the macho way. So I gratefully took back my big double and David took his, and we circled while Debbie and Walter stayed on the high ground to direct us.

Inside the sawgrass the buffalo had created a little clearing where they'd bedded, probably numerous times. There was one black form—David's. He fired while I covered—no movement. One dead buffalo. Now we re-oriented ourselves and went through a hallway to another flattened alcove. Another still, dark form. This time David covered while I fired. Two dead buffaloes, both down on the spot.

As I said, it was a great buffalo hunt.

Chapter Twelve

Kigosi and Kilombero

Western Tanzania's Moyowosi block is one of the country's most famous areas, made so by the movie *In the Blood*, and also by Mark Sullivan's early videos. Not so well known, though nearly identical, is the Kigosi block just to the east, with the Moyowosi River as the boundary. In November 2010 I had a chance to hunt not just in the Kigosi but also in two other excellent areas in Tanzania: the Kilombero Valley east of the Selous Reserve and the Rungwa region in west-central Tanzania, all great hunting areas and all places that I had never seen.

The circumstances of the hunts were quite different. First, in Kigosi, I'd join Remington's Linda Powell and Carlos Martinez, Swarovski's Dean Capuano, and John Zent of NRA publications. Immediately following I would meet my old friend Michel Mantheakis for a few days in the Kilombero. On the third hunt, we'd go up to the Rungwa to host Ron Bird on a hunt that Michel had donated to SCI.

My goals were quite different on the three hunts. Kigosi is usually good for buffalo and cats, and has a wide variety of plains game. Although I expected to hunt buffaloes, for once I didn't care about the dangerous game. On previous Tanzania hunts I'd failed to get an East African roan, and I'd never been far enough west to get a topi where they occurred, so these were at the top of my list. In Kilombero, well, like always in buffalo country, I

Jaco and his team had the bull marked well, and we walked right to him. We then put him on a tarp to carry him out of the swamp.

John Zent needed a buffalo for lion bait really badly and there just weren't any buffaloes around. Late one afternoon we got onto a herd, and Carlos Martinez took the best one, not a big buffalo but we were now in business for lion baiting.

was hoping to hunt buffaloes—but the real goal was a single-minded quest for a Roosevelt sable. In Rungwa I would just be an observer, like Andy McDonald who was filming the hunt for *Tracks across Africa*. I'll leave Rungwa for the next chapter and stick with the first two legs of what would be a near-epic six weeks in Tanzania.

In Kigosi we'd be hunting with Jaco Oosthuizen of Game Trackers Africa. It was a large group, five of us trying to cram in as much as possible. Based on the available quota, we divvied things up, which worked out very well for me. Although each of us could take a couple of buffaloes, we were allowed only one lion and one leopard for the group. John Zent had never taken a lion, so he put dibs on *simba*. Linda Powell had never taken a leopard, so she staked her claim to *chui*. That gave me both running room and trading material. I spoke up for the one roan, but although the sable antelope is plentiful in Kigosi and quality can be fantastic, I couldn't take one because of the follow-on hunt in Kilombero. So I grabbed one of the two available sitatungas and Zent grabbed the other one. More common game such as topis, reedbucks, and waterbucks weren't a quota problem, so we all had plenty of options, and, more or less, opportunity for the animals we wanted most.

In any group, success is going to vary. Technically it's a level playing field, but hunting luck isn't even-handed. One hunter does very well; another does poorly. It worked out pretty darn well for me, but not so well for everyone else. Although John and his PH baited well and conscientiously, they never got a mature male lion on bait. Hunting mostly with Jaco and me, Linda also worked hard, and we had a couple of leopards feeding. She and Jaco sat in a blind for several evenings, but no leopards came to the bait while they were there.

Oddly, the buffalo hunting was also terrible while we were there. It had been a very wet year, and the story was that the famed Moyowosi herds were on unreachable islands along the Moyowosi River that divides Kigosi from the more famous Moyowosi block. During the course of the hunt we had near-constant run-ins with poachers, both fish poachers and game poachers. Heavy poaching may have had something to do with the absence of buffaloes. On the other hand, the plains game was plentiful and, in general, very calm. So who knows? Timing is everything, and for buffaloes and cats we weren't there at the right time.

At the time of this hunt the Remington group had just taken over Dakota Arms, and Carlos Martinez was (and is again now) Remington's product manager for Dakota. So he was the gun guy, and we had a rare opportunity to use some really awesome Dakota rifles. I had a left-hand .375 bolt action that I used for the trip; in Kigosi I also used an amazingly accurate Model 10 single-shot in 7mm Remington Magnum, both topped with Swarovski scopes. (Yes, you guessed it, Dean Capuano was the optics guy.) Ammo was, of course, Remington, loaded with Swift Sciroccos in the light rifles and A-Frames and Super Solids in the heavies.

It looks like a perfect bait situation for John Zent's lion, but although we baited hard for a lion for John and a leopard for Linda, we had absolutely no luck getting cats to come to it.

As I said, we all had expectations of taking a buffalo or two apiece, but it just didn't happen. Early in the safari Carlos got his first buffalo; later in the hunt Dean also took his first buffalo. Somewhere in the middle John Zent took a very nice bull,

I had never been far enough west in Tanzania to encounter topi, so together with the roan, a topi was at the top of my list. We saw quite a few, and I took this excellent bull with the Dakota .375.

well over forty inches in spread with a lovely curl, a fine buffalo for anywhere. And that was it for buffaloes.

Jaco, Linda, and I got into a couple of herds, but we couldn't find any mature bulls. I never had an opportunity at a buffalo at all, but one afternoon, when Linda was with us, we bumped into a very nice bull wandering alone in the open. We got ahead of him and Jaco got her on the sticks, but while the bull had nice shape and curl, he was still soft-bossed. So we let him go, and that was the only chance she had at a buffalo.

Plains game worked out quite a bit better. My sitatunga was almost an afterthought. I'd hunted sitatunga on the Ugalla River well to the south some years earlier. Although I got an East African sitatunga on that hunt, there weren't many around, so I expected much the same. I was wrong.

The hunt started in the dark of the moon, the best time to hunt sitatungas. Jaco suggested that if I wanted a sitatunga, we'd best get to work. In the northern part of the area, where the Kigosi flows into the Moyowosi, there are floodplains and papyrus beds—ideal sitatunga habitat. Our game scout told us he knew of a good bull hanging out not far from a village. Of course, I've heard this before, but with animals like sitatungas, all leads are followed.

On the second afternoon we pulled into a small village, and one of the local fishermen took us west a few hundred yards and showed us a tall and wonderfully convenient termite mound on the edge of the swamp that continued on into the far horizon. Yes,

This buffalo bull wandered in front of us in broad daylight, and he was the only chance either Linda or I had at a buffalo. She was all set up with her .416, but he was just a bit too young and we let him go.

I've seen this before, too, but we set up as if this was really going to work. I broke down my shooting sticks and set them up for a sitting position, plumping up my pack so I could use it for elbow support. Jaco put his sticks high, in case I needed more elevation to see down into the grass. And we waited, accompanied by swarms of mosquitoes.

Amazingly, after an hour or so a female sitatunga came out, just a couple hundred yards from us in the swamp. Shockingly, she was soon followed by a really nice bull. For the longest time we could only see the top of his head now and again—he'd vanish completely, feeding, and reappear briefly a few yards away. It could have gone either way; my pessimistic side was quite certain we'd never get a shot. But it might happen any moment, so I stayed on the rifle endlessly with my 5–15X scope turned all the way up in the hope of an opening. There were no actual clearings in that sea of grass, but in some places it was slightly less thick than in others. After a long time and with the sun starting to set, the bull took a couple of steps and his shoulder became clear.

The bullet seemed to hit hard, and I thought he was going down when he vanished into the long grass. I wasn't certain I had anchored him until we splashed out and found him. A week later, John Zent also got a very fine sitatunga. Clearly, I'd underrated Tanzania's potential for this wonderful swamp-dweller.

We had three professional hunters for the five of us, so we mixed and matched a bit. Linda was looking for a big sable, and by my estimation the sable is the most plentiful large animal in that area. We saw herds every day, but, of course, Linda wasn't with us when we saw big bulls. She eventually got a good one while out with another group. I had exactly the same situation with roan. Compared to sable, there aren't many roans in the area, but we saw a few almost every day. The problem was we couldn't find a decent bull, while, almost every day, someone else reported seeing a huge roan. I wasn't worried, but we were a week into the project before we finally found a small herd tended by a good bull.

It was late in the evening, and there was not enough time, but we tried an approach and ran out of daylight. The next morning we located the herd again, but the bull wasn't there. That sent me into a panic, but Jaco was convinced he had either wandered off a bit or was lying down where we couldn't see him. After a while, the bull sauntered in from left field and joined the ladies.

It turned into a long day. I lost count of how many approaches we tried. The herd was in fairly open country. We could see them easily from a half-mile away, but we just couldn't get in close to them. Finally, in midafternoon, they wandered into an opening

This beautiful East African roan was worth the wait. The shot was fairly long for a .375, but we got as close as we possibly could. I then took several deep breaths and made the shot.

In Kilombero the rivers were running in full spate from the recent rains. We knew there were big buffaloes on a big island, but we got hopelessly mired trying to get to them.

and started to lie down. We couldn't get close, but we thought there was enough low brush to get us in range. Marking a prominent termite mound, we tried one more time.

That termite mound gave us a last bit of cover. Jaco slipped to the right and put up the sticks, and I slid in behind him with the .375. The bull was about 260 yards away when he got up. Of course, he walked directly away, so he was quite a bit farther when he finally turned and offered a shot. I held high and heard a solid *thunk* when the bullet hit. Then he ran and I couldn't hit him again. He went down a hundred yards later and stayed down. I finally had an East African roan.

The rest of the game came fairly easily. There were lots of bohor reedbuck, and I took a dandy. There weren't *lots* of topis, but there were enough and I eventually got a very nice topi. Likewise I got a nice defassa waterbuck at the tail end of the hunt. Everyone else had similar results on the common game, and John Zent took a magnificent greater kudu, a rare animal in western Tanzania.

Toward the end we had three incidents worth recounting. Dean Capuano was with me on the back of the truck as we were driving along the edge created between a floodplain and a tree line. The plain was on the left, and there was a grass fire burning a couple hundred yards away. Somebody hollered, *"Mamba!"*

Yep, there was a very big mamba coming at speed, obviously fleeing the fire and heading for the tree line . . . with our truck directly in its path. Jaco speeded up—good thing, too, because the snake struck the canvas that was stretched over the rear of the truck. I can't remember exactly what our trackers were saying, but by then Dean and I were on the roof of the cab, squealing like little girls.

We celebrated Linda's birthday (never mind which one) in camp. As you can see, the chef made her a really nice cake!

I think it was the last evening, as we headed toward camp at dusk when a jackal took off beside the track and ran across a burned plain. This far north and west these are side-striped jackals, not the common black-backed. I'd been looking for one the whole trip, and this was my first and only opportunity. I grabbed the Model 10 while Jaco started squeaking—but when the jackal finally stopped, it was a long, long way out on the burned plain and looked really tiny through the scope. I held as steady as I could, but nobody was more surprised than I when the jackal dropped, flattened.

On the way out we chartered to Mwanza on the shores of Lake Victoria to catch a commercial flight to Dar es Salaam. It was a warm afternoon and we had a bit of time, so we went to a hotel and enjoyed a couple of beers while looking out across Lake Victoria, a sight we all recount every time we see each other.

From Dar I took a plane to Kilombero, where Michel Mantheakis scooped me up. I had first hunted with Michel in Masailand back in 1988, and we've hunted together several times since. I think of him as a little brother, and as a professional hunter, he's a guy in whom I have the utmost faith. We were there for just a few days, strictly for a Roosevelt sable. Well, not strictly. Here there were plenty of buffaloes. We let ourselves get sidetracked by several herds, but we never found a really good bull, so no shots were fired, and on the last day we got spectacularly stuck trying to cross a river that a herd of buffaloes had apparently crossed quite easily. That said, we were mostly there for a sable.

The Roosevelt sable is a smaller sable, typically with reddish tints in the black hide even when the animal is fully mature. At one time they were thought to be confined to the Shimba Hills in coastal Kenya, but in more recent years DNA testing has proven they extend into and around the Selous Reserve in southern Tanzania.

Michel Mantheakis and I took this really good Roosevelt sable in the Kilombero Valley south of the Selous Reserve. The Roosevelt sable tends to have a reddish tint to the coat, and is definitely smaller in both body and horn than the common sable.

Personally, I'm pretty sure they also extend southward through coastal Mozambique at least to the Zambezi. In 2006 I took a sable at Mahimba, just north of the Zambezi, and I'm convinced these sables are Roosevelts. But that remains to be proven, so I was in the Kilombero looking for an "official" Roosevelt sable.

It wasn't so easy. Sables are not especially common and they are very widespread. I've spent entire hunts in the Selous and never saw one, but on the other hand, I'd never looked specifically for sables in this region. It still wasn't easy. We saw a few but no good bulls, and then on the fourth morning we drove around a little hill and bumped smack into a herd with a very good bull. They ran while we scrambled, but they held up on the crest of a ridge just long enough for Michel to get the sticks up. I was excited, nervous, rushed—and I missed!

We tracked them all morning, now losing the tracks, now finding them again. They led us along a burned hillside, then over the top. They hadn't run far, but they'd been walking steadily. Now they spread out to feed, and tracking got a whole lot slower. It was the heat of the day, and we were tracking slowly along the flat top of the ridge when a tracker stopped and pointed.

Ahead of us, in some rocks, a sable bull was staring at us. He had us—the only chance was an offhand shot. It isn't clear whether I hit or missed with the first shot, but he angled past us at full speed, headed for the rim. Come to think of it, it isn't clear whether I hit him with the second shot or the third, but somewhere in there I hit him a couple of times. We found him about eighty yards down the far slope. He was a really good Roosevelt sable with thick bases covered in secondary growth. He was hard earned and almost lost, and I think he's my favorite sable antelope.

CHAPTER THIRTEEN

RUNGWA

My safari to Rungwa in central Tanzania in November 2010 was unusual in multiple ways. For one, it wasn't "my" safari. It was Ron Bird's, auctioned at SCI with me as window dressing. Exactly why I agreed to that is open for discussion. Three weeks is a long time to spend with a stranger, and for me, an interminable time to spend as an observer. On the other hand, I'd never been to the Rungwa region of Tanzania. There was nothing there I craved, but it was an area I wanted to see. Also, Michel Mantheakis is an old friend, as I said, and we all sometimes do crazy things for friends.

It was a bittersweet experience because the safari was to be conducted in Michel's Rungwa concession, an area he had managed and developed for years. Unfortunately, due to the fickle nature of Tanzanian hunting, as the safari was conducted he was losing the area. He would go on to acquire and develop other great areas, but as famous as Tanzania is as a destination, Tanzanian hunting is really about the area . . . and good areas are increasingly rare. I had just spent two weeks in Kigosi, a famous area. Among our party we had seen few buffaloes, and despite serious effort no male lions or leopards had taken our baits. Results in the Rungwa would be far different.

This colorful bushbuck was on a termite mound outside my tent when I arrived at Michel Mantheakis's Rungwa camp. He stood like a statue for more than an hour, and I never saw him again until the morning we departed, three weeks later . . . when he was on the same termite mound.

Another unusual aspect to this safari was that ours was primarily a single-minded quest for a good lion. In case you have any doubts, let me quell them: This is not a spectator sport! I can easily say that I enjoyed the buffalo tracking—we did a lot of it, because we needed bait—but being along on a lion hunt as an observer is like watching paint dry. Fortunately, Ron was a great guy, good company, and a good hunter. I'd be happy to share another camp with him.

Cat hunting over bait is a painstaking ritual of looking for tracks, dragging bait, hanging bait, checking bait, building blinds, sitting . . . and repeating all the before mentioned. We did, however, have a lot of excitement along the way, and it started early in the hunt. The first order of business was to get some bait, preferably something large. There are no "extras" in Tanzania; bait animals come off the license. When available, it's common to take a hippo early in a lion safari, but this was an area of rocky hills with springs and small streams—not hippo habitat. Fortunately, buffaloes were plentiful. Over the course of the safari Ron would take all three buffaloes he had on license: one good bull, one monster bull, and an old, broken-horned bull when we needed bait really badly.

At the outset the buffaloes weren't cooperating. We found tracks easily enough and got into a couple of herds with no problem, but we couldn't find a mature bull. So we were still looking for buffalo tracks late in the morning on the third day. By now we really needed to get the baiting process started. We'd come up out of a grassy streambed and were ascending a gentle ridge when we spotted a young elephant bull just to the right of the track.

Rungwa isn't thought of as a good elephant area, but just the evening before we had gotten into a huge cow herd, at least seventy strong, and elephant sightings would continue to be regular events. This young bull was feeding placidly by the side of the road, so we started taking pic-

Michel takes Ron Bird in for his elephant. Rungwa has a lot of elephants but isn't known for good ivory, so to run into a group of bulls like this was a great gift.

Sixty pounds per side, long and very heavy ivory, make a great elephant in Tanzania today. Or, for that matter, anywhere in modern Africa. And now we had plenty of lion bait available!

tures of him. I think Michel had just commented that it was odd he was alone when we heard a branch break off to our left. More elephants had arrived. Our young bull crossed the road and wandered in that direction, so we followed him.

As Michel had already guessed, it was a group of bulls, seven or eight. They were spread out feeding very calmly, and the wind was good. This is a situation where Michel excels as a PH; he is very calm and very patient. We checked them all out, then backed off to assess. Several of the bulls were legal. In Tanzania there is a minimum for weight of ivory and an alternative minimum for length of tusk. A couple of these bulls were legal by length, meaning they had long ivory that was thin and light.

One seemed to have it all—mass, length, weight—but he was in the middle of the group. So we waited, and when the elephants moved a bit, Michel took Ron in. He got the shot from about twenty yards, and his bull was down in another twenty yards. The tusks were evenly matched and would weigh in at sixty pounds each, a spectacular Rungwa bull—and now we had all the lion bait we could possibly need, at least for a while.

Michel had hunted in this area for years, so he had a number of favorite bait sites already picked out, and we found others. Of course we looked for tracks, and of course we dragged bait. We put out trail cameras, too, and a couple of days later we started to see lions. Some baits were hit by prides, others by lone males, and one bait was hit by two big males. Ron wanted a good, big lion, but the "six-year rule" was in effect: To be legal, a lion must be six years old, and ethics demanded that it also be a nonpride male. Most of the males we saw on the trail cameras were easily dismissed as obviously too young.

There was one beautiful young male, probably just three years old, but already carrying a good mane. He was aggressive in defense of his meat, and we saw him several times, close enough to see that he had already broken a canine. We also saw two brothers hunting together, both big lions, but with manes just coming in, probably four years old. One morning, checking a bait, we saw a lion that was questionable. He had an excellent blond mane, and was borderline in age. The distinction between five and six years old is subtle, and it's a tough call to make. Michel called him five, and we left him in peace.

It was about the tenth day when we picked up a new lion on a trail camera. It had a dark mane and a long face that showed some scars. This one made the age grade for sure! We already had a blind; Michel believes in building a blind when he hangs a bait because then the disturbance is minimal if the bait is hit. So, with a blind in place, Ron and Michel sat the next morning. The lion came in, and he was plenty old enough, but his mane was scruffy. They passed. I was horrified.

This was a very nice lion, yet his age was borderline. It was not impossible that he met the six-year rule, but since he was probably five years old, we passed.

Two days later we were driving through a burned area with some buffalo meat. It was a hot midday, and a lion appeared out of nowhere and darn near climbed into the back of the truck. He was old and emaciated, with broken teeth, and would have been a wonderful lion to take. But his mane was skimpy, and as near as I could tell no thought was given to shooting him.

At this point, just past the safari's halfway point, we'd encountered a dozen male lions. Nine were clearly too young. One, the best-looking so far, had been questionable on age, and I think the correct decision had been made to pass. And then we'd seen two fully mature lions, neither of which had the quality of mane that Ron had in mind.

Between trail camera photos and actual sightings, I lost count of the number of leopards we saw—probably eight or nine. This picture is comical enough, but I missed the shot a few seconds later when the leopard lost its grip and fell.

To continue our tally, we had a sixty-pound elephant, an incredible and unexpected bonus. So far we hadn't done much on plains game, but we'd been busy. At this point I think Ron had taken one nice buffalo, and we had two on license in reserve as we needed bait. Oh, did I mention the leopards? We had trail-cam photos of several leopards on our lion baits.

Once, when checking a bait, we found a leopard sleeping in our pre-built blind. Out it dashed as we approached. Another leopard, a nice tom, had hit a lion bait while we were in the blind. Remember, lion baits aren't planned for leopards—this cat jumped onto the bait, and actually fell off once while trying to figure out how to feed upside down!

Ron had a nice leopard from a previous safari, so he wasn't interested. That's fine—it was his call . . . but the opportunity was clearly there. An optimist might think that things were going very well, and in due time we would find the lion Ron was looking for. A pessimist, on the other hand, might think that things were going *too well*, and this cornucopia would come to a halt.

The Rungwa is pretty good for sable and roan—which we never saw—but a good kudu bull is a rare prize. This is a really fine East African greater kudu, taken one afternoon in a chance encounter.

For some days it appeared the pessimist was winning. After that hungry old lion tried to climb into the truck, we went a week without seeing new lions *anywhere.* By now our elephant baits were long gone. Ron had taken a second buffalo and a really good Lichtenstein hartebeest. One afternoon when we were headed back from checking a distant bait, somebody saw movement off to the left. We dismounted, made a quick stalk, and Ron shot an excellent East African greater kudu. That's a rare trophy in the Rungwa region. Although we saw some youngsters, we never saw a mature sable bull, and we never saw a single roan, even though both species are more plentiful in that area than kudu.

Lions had dried up. If I were Michel, I'd have been slashing my wrists, but I'm not Michel. He remained confident and positive and he is, after all, the best cat hunter I've ever known. And a good thing that is because luck came to us with mixed messages. On the eighteenth day we picked up a trail-cam photo of a new lion, our thirteenth lion, far up in the corner of the concession and hours from camp. The angle of the photos wasn't adequate for aging, but he looked good. So, of course, we sat and waited for him and . . . nothing happened.

Along the road we found tracks of a big lion headed toward another bait a few miles away. *Hmmm.* While sitting on the one bait, we put a trail camera on the other. Bingo. There was our lion, but he was coming in the dark, and night shooting is illegal in Tanzania.

We switched to that bait, as the lion had, but again nothing happened. With time growing short, Ron had taken his third buffalo, a monster this time, so we had fresh meat, but Michel wanted more. We got lucky and found a herd of zebras, and Ron took a fine stallion. By now we were in spike camp mode, sleeping on the ground, betting everything on this lion that we had never seen.

Serious cat hunters have all kind of tricks. Whenever you hang bait, it's common to put leafy cover on top of it so the vultures won't find it, and thus it will last longer. Now we put a "vulture bait" in the open, near the lion bait, so the vultures *would* find it. The theory is that the lion will be infuriated by the vultures finding his meat and will lie nearby to protect it. We also moved the bait, taking it down from its perfect tree and dragging it to another tree, as if some interloper had discovered it.

These were all great ideas, but through a long twentieth day only two vultures cruised by in a cloudless sky, and they must have been myopic. They never gave our vulture bait a glance. In the cold dark on the morning of the twenty-first day, the last day, I dropped Ron, Michel, and cameraman Andy McDonald at the blind, and then swung noisily out so that any sensible lion within earshot would know the humans had departed and the coast was clear.

We captured the lion on a trail camera, and now we had a handful of mane hair . . . but we were down to the last couple of days.

I drove to a flat spot on a ridge some distance away, and I lay on

It was the morning of the twenty-first and last day when Ron Bird shot a fantastic lion, perfectly—but he was also perfectly guided by Michel Mantheakis.

the ground in the morning chill, watching the stars, sorry I wasn't in the blind but happy that I wasn't undergoing that kind of pressure. I tried to sleep, but as the horizon lightened I was drawn inexorably to my watch. Shooting light was coming, and in a matter of minutes we would know whether all the tactics and all the gambles would pay off—or if it all would come to naught. It was still very gray when I heard the shot.

It was a beautiful lion, worth all the gambles. Michel knew this lion; he had seen him on bait three years earlier when he judged him to be solidly six years old. So now he was at least nine, possibly ten, still in perfect condition and with a mane that most other wild lions would envy. He had come to the bait shortly after the truck left, and had stayed until the light grew bright enough for a shot. Perhaps oddly, I wasn't jealous in the least . . . this was Ron's lion, hard-hunted and, on the very last day, shot well. I remained at peace with having taken my own last lion, but I was extremely happy to have been a small part of an epic hunt for this magnificent cat.

Chapter Fourteen

Ghana

The story is that the royal antelope got its name because, in West African tradition, its tender flesh was reserved for royalty, the tribal kings. Whether this is true or not, the tiny royal antelope is the smallest creature in the world with hoofs and horns. This tiny antelope only occurs west of the Dahomey Gap, that odd break in West Africa's forests. East of the Gap its place is taken by the slightly larger Bates pygmy antelope. West of the Gap the royal antelope is discontinuous, but until recently most royal antelopes taken by sport hunters came from Liberia. This is a bit confusing because *no* royal antelope have been taken since Liberia reopened five years ago. Historical records prove they occur there, but obviously they are neither common nor widespread; their primary habitat is farther east.

Specifically, they live in the forests of Ghana. Although the country holds a variety of game, Ghana had never been open to outsiders until American expatriate Steve Kobrine made inroads and set up shop. Although a legendary African animal, the royal antelope is not exactly a kudu; Kobrine didn't have people beating down his doors to hunt them, but there were enough long-gone African fanatics to make a business out of it. I was not among the first to try my luck at hunting in Ghana, but obviously I was among those who had a desire to go to there.

A safari in Ghana does offer some variety. There are black duikers, Maxwell duikers, palm civets, and more. Bongos and other forest species do occur, at least historically, and in the north there are buffaloes, kobs, waterbucks, and other savanna species. But the real reason to hunt in Ghana is the royal antelope.

I hunted in inland forests about a hundred miles northwest of the capital of Accra. As weird African hunts go, it was pleasant. Kobrine housed his hunters in sort of a motel, with decent food and air conditioning that more or less worked. As far as the hunting, it was good, but very dependent on luck.

The royal antelope is the smallest animal in the world with hoofs and horns. Its actual range extends up and down the coastal forest, but Ghana has offered far and away the best opportunity to hunt this amazing little antelope.

The hunt for royal antelopes is done almost entirely at night by walking along forest trails with spotlights. Some will say this is not ethical, and my only answer is there is no other known technique for taking this small animal. Unlike forest duikers, royal antelopes are not known to come to a call, and because they are almost entirely nocturnal, options for hunting them are extremely limited. I was very lucky: I got my royal antelope on the first night.

There's more to that "luck" aspect. We had walked through most of the night, taking a few breaks along the way. It was hot and I was soaked in sweat, also exhausted from both jet lag and tropical heat. We continued in the wee hours and still saw nothing. Vaguely I think I saw eyes to the right, but they were gone instantly. Instead, I saw the red dot of my guide's laser pointer, which told me I was to shoot.

As I raised the single-shot 12-gauge, I actually saw the animal for the first time. I fired as it turned away, and my guide rushed forward to claim our prize. The tiny size of this antelope is simply amazing—both hoofs will fit on a thumbnail with plenty space remaining. I suppose both horns would fit as well if the angle could be found.

Here's where luck came into play: My royal antelope actually had horns. It was a male. I was blessed, and also very lucky. Unlike so many species, the royal antelope doesn't freeze for a light, but typically turns away, as mine did. Even if a royal antelope would stand, or by some miracle be caught out in daylight, the horns are so tiny that I'm not sure they could readily be seen. In other words, this is an animal that is almost impossible to properly sex and judge. So it comes down to luck.

Realistically, any royal antelope is a great trophy. Some hunters have taken females and are perfectly happy. The license allows for multiple royal antelopes, so in the beginning the outfitter allowed hunters to try again in the hopes of getting a male. Although it's easy for me to say since I got a male, this probably isn't a good idea. There aren't a lot of royal antelope, and it's just as easy to wind up with two or three females and still not get a male. I was there in the second or third season. Success seemed to be diminishing a bit, so Steve Kobrine was leaning toward a "one-to-a-customer" rule for royal antelopes.

In any case, it's not a sure thing. I got spectacularly lucky, but other hunters walked the forest trails every night through their entire hunt and never had a chance. You have to be a long-gone Africa freak to mount a safari specifically for one of the pygmy antelopes, but to some degree it's an acquired taste. Initially most of us are drawn by high-profile animals like the kudu. Then comes dangerous game, and in time perhaps one is driven toward the great antelopes like bongos and giant elands. Along the way one is almost certain to pick up a few of

Most of the small forest animals are nocturnal, but the black duiker is diurnal. We set up to call, and a black duiker actually came in . . . but he came in behind me and I couldn't swing around in time.

Outfitter Steve Kobrine and I sit behind a Maxwell duiker, probably the most common animal in the Ghana forest.

the pygmy antelopes. The bush duikers and open-country animals like steenboks and oribis will probably be taken incidentally, in chance encounters. Animals like the Vaal rhebok, suni, and blue duiker require specific hunting in the proper habitat, but will probably not be the primary focus of a specialized hunt. Finally, you get to difficult animals that are only found in out-of-the-way places, like the royal antelope and the great prizes in Liberia's forests.

Years ago I would have said that I would never mount a safari specifically for the little guys . . . and, obviously, I would have been wrong! They grow on you. In the course of this book I'll have been to Liberia twice in search of zebra duikers and water chevrotains, and the royal antelope is the primary reason to hunt in Ghana. I got lucky, and although the royal antelope is a tiny little animal, it rates high on my list of my best and most prized African animals.

With time available, we spent the next few days hunting other game, primarily Maxwell duikers and black duikers. The Maxwell duiker is slightly larger than but similar to the blue duiker, which it replaces west of the Dahomey Gap (similarly, east of the gap the royal antelope is replaced by the slightly larger Bates pygmy antelope). The black duiker is larger, sort of a medium-size duiker, very dark and extremely attractive.

I got a Maxwell duiker with little difficulty, and I almost got a black duiker. Unlike many of the small forest antelopes, the black duiker is diurnal, and like most of them it is fairly territorial. We found tracks that had to be a black duiker, so we set up to call. Actually, we found more than one set of tracks, and made several calls. At one stand the duiker actually came in . . . but we'd guessed the approach wrong, and it came in on the wrong side of the tree. The local hunter I was with saw it clearly, but it was gone by the time I could swing around.

Ghana was an interesting place. The people were friendly, and the old fort from slave-trade days was horrifically fascinating. I admire Steve Kobrine a lot for scouting out this situation and getting it open, for among Africa's many good outfitters, few can successfully claim to have opened up a new country. In 2015 the Ebola outbreak across West Africa effectively shut down all tourism, and at this writing it's unclear if Steve will go back. Although it was not an expensive hunt, it is clearly a very specialized destination.

I'm glad I went when I did. There are always uncertainties in African hunting, especially in her out-of-the-way destinations. I'll be honest: I'm not crazy about being first into a new destination. Even for the best outfitters and PHs, it takes time to learn the country and game, and although pioneering an area is both an honor and an adventure, I have long fig-

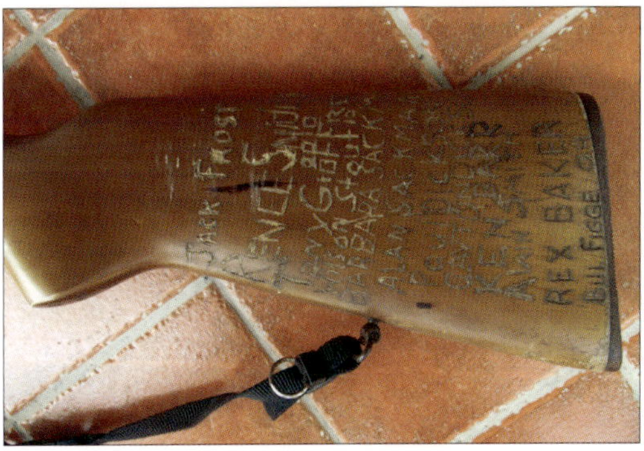

It's impossible to bring firearms into Ghana, so Kobrine supplied shotguns. This is the royal antelope gun, a single shot with fiber optic sights; every hunter who has taken a royal antelope with it has carved his or her name into the stock. My name is on the other side.

A serious row of old blackpowder cannons still guard the harbor.

ured being first was better suited to hunters more well-heeled than I. On the other hand, some chances are fleeting. My timing was perfect in Ghana, also in Chad in years gone by . . . but I missed the last window when Gabon was open, likewise the Republic of the Sudan. You can't win them all, and right now it's unclear if hunting in Ghana will be available again.

Ghana is a fragile destination, and the royal antelope is a fragile resource. Locals can hunt legally, and do, which is one thing for genuine subsistence and another for the bush meat trade. Kobrine carved out a big chunk of forest and was protecting it by placing value on the wildlife. But along the roads, carcasses of duikers, cane rats, and royal antelopes were offered for sale. On the last evening we went to a local restaurant, and Kobrine insisted I try the cane rat with maize meal. I did. The flavor was a bit strong, but the gravy was excellent.

CHAPTER FIFTEEN

THE PEARL OF AFRICA

"The Pearl of Africa" is what a young Winston Churchill dubbed Uganda, and he was exactly right. It is a beautiful country, verdant green and tropical . . . and it's a very small country, sandwiched between Kenya and the Democratic Republic of Congo, with Sudan to the north and Rwanda and Tanzania to the south. We think of it as East Africa, but it is a landlocked country that rides a fence between East and Central Africa. On the east side one finds typical East African species: lesser kudus, fringe-eared oryxes, big Cape buffaloes. But on the west, in the Nile drainage, one finds Nile buffaloes and Nile bushbucks, and Uganda's national animal, the Uganda kob. To the southwest the elevation rises quickly to one of the last strongholds of the mountain gorilla.

Hunting never officially ceased in Uganda, but it ground inexorably to a halt under Idi Amin's reign of terror. Ruark hunted in Uganda in the early 1960s, taking one of Walter Dalrymple Maitland "Karamojo" Bell's .275 Rigbys with him. Later in the decade Robert E. Petersen and Tom Siatos of Petersen Publishing made their first safari to Uganda. When I was shopping for my first safari in the mid-1970s, I considered Uganda. Even though the country allowed five buffaloes on license, the "Last King of Scotland" was in power, and hunting there just wasn't a good idea. So the new millennium was more than a decade old before I finally got to Uganda.

Uganda's game had nearly been wiped out during Amin's excesses, civil war, and her brief war with Kenya—but, with protection, it had started to rebuild. With not just protection but because of the value placed on wildlife, the rebuilding process continues. Even so, it's fair to say that Uganda's wildlife today is found in pockets. It is no longer the "general bag" destination it once was. Many key animals are not currently on license, so it's a specialized safari destination. Even so, the pockets are very good, with the game occurring in excellent quality.

The Nile bushbuck was the first animal I took in Uganda, and it was one of the animals I wanted most. This is a very small bushbuck with an extremely red coat, much like a harnessed bushbuck but with fewer white markings.

I flew straight from the royal antelope hunt in Ghana to the Entebbe airport, site of the famous Israeli hostage rescue. Ghana is a country where firearms cannot be imported, so I had used outfitter Steve Kobrine's shotguns, which was just fine. Bringing firearms into Uganda is not an issue, but since I was coming straight from Ghana, my hunting partner, Bill Jones, had graciously agreed we could share his. He got in the evening before me and had cleared his .416 Rigby and his Bill Wiseman .300 Winchester Magnum with no issues.

Although Uganda is small, it offers at least three separate safaris, some of which can be combined depending on time. You can head northeast, up toward the famous Karamojo region, and find big Cape buffaloes, monstrous East African impalas, and some specialties such as Guenther dik-diks and Chanler mountain reedbucks. You can stay in the south and hunt Ssese Island sitatungas on islands in Lake Victoria. Or, as we planned to do, you can go north and west, and find altogether different species.

First we would go north to the Kafu River, a few hours from Kampala. There Bill wanted to hunt sitatungas, and we hoped to find Nile bushbucks. From there we'd continue north and west to hunt Nile buffaloes and kobs in the Aswa-Lolim area. Time permitting, we might even get up to the northwest corner to Rhino Camp, where Kermit and Theodore Roosevelt hunted in 1909.

It seemed an ambitious plan, but in fact was not. We were hunting with Christian Weth of Uganda Wildlife Safaris, with veteran PH Tony Moore also in camp and sort of tag-teaming us, depending on what we were hunting. The species available on license were limited, but what was available was there in plenty.

I figured Bill's sitatunga would be one of the tougher nuts to crack. On the mainland these are considered East African sitatungas, which is kind of silly since the Ssese Island sitatungas obviously got there by swimming from the mainland, or stowing away on floating papyrus. No matter, I don't make the rules. I elected not to hunt sitatungas because I'd taken a good one in Tanzania the previous year. I didn't really need another, and my experience with this difficult animal is such that I figured getting just one for Bill would be a tough enough proposition.

In this I was totally wrong. The Kafu River area has miles of papyrus, all of it sitatunga habitat, and much of it never, ever hunted. When Uganda was open in the old days, it was a destination for heavy-tusked elephants, well-maned lions, and big leopards, and remember those five buffaloes that were once on license. The antelope species were taken along the way, but rarely specifically hunted. As I would learn, the mainland of Uganda must offer the best sitatunga hunting on the African continent.

It was a hot midafternoon when we reached Christian's tent camp near the Kafu River. We stowed our gear, checked the rifles, and then Bill and Tony went sitatunga hunting, using machans that Tony had built and looking for sitatungas he had scouted.

Bill Jones (left) took an exceptional East African sitatunga in just a few days. I am absolutely convinced that Uganda's mainland offers the best sitatunga hunting in Africa today, with miles and miles of untouched papyrus habitat.

They saw sitatungas on every outing, which is not like most sitatunga hunting, and they passed some smaller bulls, which

Christian Weth and I are seated behind a very nice East African bohor reedbuck, probably the most plentiful antelope in the Kafu River area.

is also not like most sitatunga hunting. On the evening of the third day Bill took a huge bull with no difficulty. Meantime, Christian and I dug around for other antelopes. This was an area of private land with small farms, and clearly the people were not poaching but were looking after the game. From the tracks I saw, sitatungas walk around the edges of the villages like goats. Several big ones have been taken, and I predict a new world record!

The area didn't have great species diversity: sitatungas, Nile bushbucks, East African bohor reedbucks, oribis, and bush duikers . . . but these last five also walked around like goats! The Nile bushbuck was my primary goal. It's one of the smallest races of bushbucks, very red in color with unimposing horns, but, hey, it's a spiral-horned antelope that I didn't have, and I needed a reason to be there, right? Bushbucks are always wary and often difficult. Understanding that Uganda's game is very much on the recovery trail, I didn't expect it to be easy, but it was. I have never seen bushbuck so calm, nor have I seen so many at midday.

Even so, the big ones don't get big by being dumb. We saw a monster, just a brief flash of very long, sharp horns, and then gone into some thick bush. Needless to say, we fixated on that one and tried to find him, but we never saw him again. I suppose we could have kept looking, but one afternoon we spotted an exceptional old ram with very thick horns, and I stalked and shot him with Bill's .416.

I took a very good reedbuck, too good to pass—and it was a really interesting stalk with Bill's .416. I had plenty of gun, but not plenty of scope for the smaller antelopes, so I needed to get close. I also shot a very nice bush duiker—they are, of course, East African bush duikers, but their coloration is different from what I'd seen in Kenya and Tanzania. I have heard a rumor that they might be separated out as a subspecies.

By now Bill had his sitatunga, and he played a bit of catch-up because we wanted to get up to the buffalo area. In one afternoon he took an oribi, a reedbuck, a bushbuck, and a duiker—very good trophies all, which says much about the area and its game.

The drive north was beautiful, and it was another hot afternoon when we reached the Aswa-Lolim area, a collective of farms situated along the northern boundary of Murchison Falls National Park, east of the Albert Nile. This is a much more difficult area. There are some resident kobs and, depending on the rains,

The Murchison Falls National Park was full of amazing animals. Our kob was very good, well into the top ten. This one, photographed in the park, is a whole lot bigger, almost certainly of world-record quality.

buffaloes, Uganda defassa waterbucks, and Jackson hartebeests come and go. It was dry when we were there, with most of the water inside the park—but there was good feed on our side. So, except for the kobs, it was essentially a park boundary hunt, as we hoped to catch buffaloes outside the park in the morning, or coming out to feed in the late afternoon.

Now, inside the park there were wonderful Nile buffaloes, incredible kobs, quite a few hartebeests and waterbucks, and a good number of elephants. We took midday drives through the park and licked our chops because on our side of the line it was tough sledding. But we had time, and it worked. One morning we glassed a herd of kobs on a distant ridge, made our way there, and I shot a nice one. A couple evenings later Bill shot a monster. Fortunately, there are two kobs on the license because a day later we saw one just as good as his, and I couldn't resist. On another morning, patrolling for buffaloes, we caught a herd of Jackson hartebeests north of the boundary, and I got a nice one.

In Uganda the defassa waterbuck can grow exceptionally large, and we saw some good ones deep in the park, along the Victoria Nile. The conditions were such that we never caught any waterbucks outside the park. It might have happened, but did not. That was no problem since we were really there for buffaloes . . . and that wasn't looking so good, either. Every day we glassed groups of bulls just inside the park, but they didn't want to come out to play.

One day we took a break and drove up to Rhino Camp, crossing the bridge over the Albert Nile and heading northwest toward the Congo border. That's where the Roosevelt party shot nine northern white rhinos. Even in 1909 the northern white rhinos were growing scarce, so this was one of the most controversial excesses of Roosevelt's epic ten-month safari. Christian had the area where Roosevelt hunted as a concession, but it needed care and development and there was very little game. We knew that, but it was worth taking the drive to say we'd been there.

This hunt was in 2011, very early in Uganda's new hunting program. With protection and hunting revenues, things have continued to improve. There are more outfitters now to protect and develop more areas, and Christian Weth's Uganda Wildlife Safaris has expanded into more of the country. I had hoped to get back in 2016, before the period of this book concluded, so I could write about the improvement. We couldn't work out the dates, so I look forward to seeing Uganda

I took this excellent Uganda kob in the Aswa-Lolim area. This animal is the national animal of Uganda, and while they were not numerous outside the park, there were enough and quality was really good.

again in 2017. We did well in 2011, but by all accounts the situation is considerably better today.

Back then the Nile buffalo situation was iffy. As are, realistically, all park-boundary hunts, whether elk along the Yellowstone, elephants along the Kruger boundary, or wherever. Sometimes they come out, and sometimes they don't. We were patient, and we were lucky. One morning we caught a group just outside the boundary, made a quick stalk, and got a shot.

Then, with time growing short, villagers reported a lone bull in some hills several miles north of the park. Christian's scouts found the tracks, and it was a blistering midmorning when we took the spoor. We didn't follow all that far—old buffalo bulls are lazy, and never go too far. But it was hot, and I was uncharacteristically breathless as we ascended a major ridge. *Too much caffeine, not enough water?* I wondered.

The top was a plateau with scattered groves of trees, catching a nice breeze. Now the tracks meandered, and we found where the buffalo had bedded briefly and then continued on, probably looking for better shade. We followed, my discomfort now forgotten, and then one of the trackers saw the mound of a bedded buffalo, not quite as black as the black shadow he lay in.

I had the .416; Bill had the .300. We had agreed he would fire just after me so as to take no chances. We moved in slowly, a step at a time. I doubt we were thirty yards away when the buffalo stood. As he stood, he offered his shoulder. I fired, heard Bill fire next to me, and then I fired again, and the bull was down.

We went forward, checked him, and I was giving our government game guard a high-five when the world started spinning and I went down. I was only out for a few seconds, but I was sweating profusely and having trouble breathing. With no reason to think otherwise, we assumed I was suffering from heat exhaustion, so they got me into some shade and started splashing water on me. It helped, and after a half-hour or so I got up, went over to the buffalo, and we did some filming for the TV show and took some pictures.

Christian was able to get a vehicle fairly close, so we got me and our buffalo loaded up, and we went back to camp. I lay down and rested, but I couldn't sleep because breathing was difficult and starting to hurt. It was a long night, and in the morning we broke camp and drove to Kampala, where we went straight to the International Hospital.

Amazingly, they missed what was wrong with me. And, with no history and no harbingers, I missed it, too. I was given a baggie of antibiotics for a pulmonary infection, and I assumed that would do the trick. So far I'd done everything wrong. I had not used the medical evacuation card and satellite phone that had been with me when I shot the buffalo because I immediately sought help by going to the hospital in Kampala. These decisions seemed justified. Getting on the airplane with my bag of antibiotics, unsupervised and unstabilized, however, was a dumb mistake. Like many of the decisions we take in life, however, hindsight affords clearer insights.

On the plane, every breath now became a painful struggle. Somehow I cleared U.S. Customs in Los Angeles, got a baggage cart, and pushed it down the sidewalk to my connecting terminal. I knew I didn't have the strength to get the duffel and gun case on and off the shuttle bus. When I got off the plane in San Luis Obispo, Donna took one look and told me I had had a heart attack. *Surely not*, I thought.

French Hospital, one of the best cardiac centers in the country, was just down the street. Of course, stubborn to what was now too near the end, after having flown with whatever it was for nearly forty hours, I insisted on going home and taking a

The Nile viewed from the ridges of the Aswa-Lolim hunting area north of Murchison Falls National Park.

shower. Then, feeling a bit better, we went to the square to meet some friends who happened to be in town. The reprieve was brief.

I was again in distress, so after a quick hello to our friends, I told Donna I was (finally) ready to go to the hospital. It took our local ER about ninety seconds to diagnose a heart attack, and the next thing I knew I was in an ambulance, headed back over the Cuesta Grade to French Hospital . . . except this ride cost us about $4,000—in addition to the costs incurred for a week in intensive care.

I did what they told me to do, and I got better fast. Six months later I was back in Africa, and a few weeks after that I was sheep hunting in Russia. So, although the sentiment is appreciated, please don't ask me how I'm doing. I'm fine. There was no known cause, and no permanent damage. In fact, while I was recovering my heart grew a new vessel around the blockage. It happens sometimes, so I skated by with no surgery, and no stents.

I made the decisions I did in Uganda based on the fact that I'd had a recent physical, I was in good shape, and I had no known risk factors and no family history of heart disease. My symptoms weren't classic, but, in fact, there are no 100 percent classic symptoms, so I didn't pay attention and, with no history or known risk, I also didn't pay attention to the clear warnings I had received: two periods of weird dizziness a few weeks earlier. They passed, and I blew them off. In Uganda I had a medical evacuation card (and a satellite phone), but I didn't make a call to at least get a consultation with an *American* doctor, and I should never have gotten on an

Although this bull is nothing like some we saw in the park, it is still a very fine Nile buffalo. Although I didn't know it, I'd had a heart attack about a half-hour before this picture was taken. So excuse me if I look a little pale. . . .

airplane with that stuff going on. Today I'm 100 percent fine, but after they got me into ICU, the doctors told Donna that I wouldn't have made it through the night without medical help.

This is a private matter, and I'm a private guy, but it's a story worth telling because it can happen to anyone, and it was a very close call. I offer this simply as a cautionary tale of what might and could happen to any of us, anytime.

Chapter Sixteen

The Kasserine Pass

Joe Coogan and I stood in the high valley of the Kasserine Pass, looking westward toward Algeria. I never fought in any real armored engagements, but it brought to mind so many of my own "tank battles" in the Mojave Desert, both at our own Marine Corps base at Twentynine Palms and the Army's Fort Irwin. I could envision Rommel's outposts and his clever reverse-slope defense, and see how the green American troops were led into a cauldron created by the Desert Fox. We all remember the early scene from *Patton* as he surveyed the carnage. In fact, our famous and mercurial fighting general wasn't actually there until later, but it was here, in Tunisia, that Patton turned the tables on the well-trained, well-led, vaunted, and feared—though undermanned and underequipped—Afrika Korps.

Later, south of the pass, we went into a national park straddling the top of the rugged Atlas Mountains. Near the top lay the ruins of a significant Roman outpost—no ornate temples here, but pillars and lintels were still standing. Most were pocked by bullets. Since it seems unlikely that the long-forgotten Centurions stationed here directed machine-gun fire, I could imagine an encounter by a more recent patrol, Germans or Italians, holding the high ground, and Americans or Brits seeking to take it.

This is the monument at the top of the Kasserine Pass where green American troops met Rommel for the first time. Rommel with his deep reverse-slope defense badly mauled the Allied forces here.

In an outcropping above the winding track to the top we saw a group of native-

Erik von Eckhardt stands a determined charge from a wounded boar. He has hunted the Barbary wild boar for more than forty years and believes they are more aggressive than their European cousins.

range, free-range Barbary sheep, and on the plain below a few Atlas gazelles, proof that North Africa isn't quite as devoid of wildlife as we often hear. In fact, the aoudad still occupies a broad range in North Africa from Morocco discontinuously to Egypt and the Red Sea Hills. The big game is long gone from the region. North African elephants were extirpated in Roman times through overhunting for the Roman circus. The last known Barbary lion was killed a century ago, and, surprisingly, Africa's only bear, the Atlas brown/grizzly, survived until late in the nineteenth century.

More recent losses are the big dama gazelles and the two great desert antelopes, the addax and scimitar-horned oryx, plentiful through the 1970s but quickly eradicated by desert warfare. In 2001 I was fortunate to hunt in northern Chad's Ennedi Mountains, near the Libyan border. We found a surprising number of aoudads in the crumbling sandstone heights, and plenty of the small dorcas gazelles in the *wadi*s below.

I suspect the situation is much the same across the great breadth of North Africa, along both the northern and southern limits of the great Sahara. Both Morocco and Tunisia could open hunting for aoudads and gazelles, and I'm told there are still quite a few Barbary red deer toward the Mediterranean coast. That's stuff for future dreaming. Until very recently the Republic of the Sudan remained open for Nubian ibexes, aoudads, gazelles, and the tiny Salt dik-diks. I could have gone, and one of my greatest regrets in African hunting is that I didn't get there in time . . . but the hunting potential remains. Chad is open again, but only in the south, and at this writing there is no hunting for aoudads or dorcas gazelles. At this moment, late 2016, the continent's only North African hunting is found in Morocco and Tunisia.

I haven't been to Morocco, but I'm told the conditions are similar to Tunisia. The primary game is the Barbary wild boar although Morocco also hosts good bird shooting. It's similar, too, in that both countries are "shotgun only." Tunisia lies between Algeria to the west and Libya to the east, with Morocco far to the west. Algeria and Libya are messes, but both Morocco and Tunisia have been relatively stable and safe. A stumbling block to opening hunting for other big game in both countries is the shotgun rule . . . both governments are uncomfortable with foreigners running around with rifles.

Theoretically one could *maybe* hunt aoudads with a modern, American rifled-barrel shotgun and a scope. I ran into this once before in Greece, which also has a shotguns-only rule, but the letter of the law establishes that there are to be no rifled barrels and no scopes. I hunted Cretan or kri-kri ibexes there and got a really good one, using a Remington 870 with a rifled choke tube. It worked, but it was brushy country. I'm not sure I'd want to try it with aoudads where shooting distances are likely to be longer.

The Barbary wild boar is a different story, especially the way hunting techniques have evolved in North Africa: Boars are hunted on drives, European-style. This is appropriate as the Barbary wild boar is an adaptation of the European wild boar, which has been separated by the Mediterranean for eons. They're rangier, with thinner hair and maybe a bit smaller in body, but with the same tusks. They live in the hills above vast almond groves, vineyards, and grain fields, and while the locals hate them for their crop depredations and fear

The legend is that these pigs use their eyes. I didn't believe it until I saw more than one boar almost magically slip between the guns. I took heed and used camouflage and cover when I took a stand.

Coming down a long ridge after a drive. Tunisia is truly a beautiful country, with grainfields, vineyards, and some five million olive trees in the valleys. After her conquest by Rome, Tunisia became known as the "breadbasket of the Roman Empire."

them for their legendary aggressiveness, they're hard-pressed to do much about them because the population is Muslim, so, of course, they don't eat pigs and prefer not to touch them. Consequently, there are plenty of pigs, and hunters lacking the local Muslim sensibilities are extremely welcome.

This is a hunt very few Americans know anything about, but it's actually a dandy. Europeans love their driven boar hunting, and many go to Tunisia because the hunts there are not only a whole lot cheaper than the ones in Europe but they're also very successful. One of Africa's great characters, Baron Erik von Eckhardt, has been running driven boar hunts in Tunisia for more than forty years. Widely experienced elsewhere in Africa, Eckhardt's parents retired to Tunisia and as a young man he was appointed chief game warden. That gig went out the door with a government change, but after a few years he came back to outfit boar hunting, and has been there ever since.

Nobody in the Western world knows more about Barbary wild boars than the good Baron. Organizing drives is difficult because the country is hilly and open, and the effective range of the guns allowed is at best about sixty yards (smoothbores with open sights, which most European hunters use) and, optimistically, possibly two hundred yards with scopes and rifled barrels. Complicating the equation is Erik's belief that, unlike most wild pigs, the Barbary wild boar, in its more open terrain, has adapted to use its eyes in equal preference and acuity to its nose and ears.

Needless to say, until confronted with evidence, I didn't believe this. Nor did I believe Erik's assertion that, when wounded or pressed, the Barbary wild boar is more likely than most pigs (and most species considered "dangerous") to launch an attack. This last I didn't witness—but I did observe the great care with which approaches were made on downed hogs, and I've seen the videos of Erik standing his ground on several serious charges, not necessarily more determined charges than I've seen with other pigs, but apparently more frequent.

At that time my old friend Joe Coogan was a marketing director for Benelli, and we were there to make an episode for his *Benelli on Assignment* TV series. We were armed with Benelli Black Eagle shotguns, scoped with rifled barrels, and loaded with good Federal 300-grain sabot slugs. It's a short flight from Paris to Tunis, another reason why Tunisia is a popular destination for Europeans—not only for hunting, but also vacationing along the Mediterranean coast. Gun clearance was simple, but the schedule was a bit weird in that we arrived in the wee hours, and then drove several hours to Erik's headquarters, a sprawling tourist hotel in Sbeitla.

The rooms were fine and food was good, but the best part was that hotel sat a stone's throw from some of the most extensive Roman ruins I've ever seen. Tunisia is the site of ancient Carthage, Rome's trading rival and eventual enemy in the three Punic Wars. It was from Carthage that Hannibal departed with his army and his war elephants, eventually taking them down through the Brenner Pass into Italy where he sacked Rome. The Romans got the upper hand in the Third Punic War, and in 146 B.C. Scipio's legions finally breached the city walls. Carthage was utterly destroyed, dismantled stone by stone. After that, fertile Tunisia became the breadbasket of the Roman Empire, and Sbeitla was its capital and major city; the Roman name for their Tunisian province was "Africa," from which the entire continent takes its name today. Eventually we'd have time to wander through the temples and Roman baths, but first we had some boar hunting to do.

Joe and I joined a group of six Swedish hunters, all of whom had hunted here before—some many times. That made us the "newbies," and because of our film crew, we were prominently difficult newbies. Even so it was a congenial camp, but also a bit different from most of Erik's hunts. Although a big boar might be taken at any time, either alone or with a sounder, the usual intent is to shoot a lot of pigs. The older boars are wise to the game, so when any pig is taken from a sounder the big

I took this really good Barbary wild boar at a dead run with a single sabot slug from a Benelli. On this hunt Joe Coogan and I were focusing on big boars only and not everyone even got a shot, so I was very fortunate.

boys tend to leave the group, either turning back to slip past the beaters or to the side to break through the line. The country is big, and with eight or even a dozen guns, a lot of pigs will slip past just out of range. On this particular hunt the concept was "trophy boars only," not by law but by mutual agreement.

With this restriction, it wasn't easy. In fact, it was downright difficult. On one drive, cameraman Mark Womack and I were hunkered in seemingly good cover, looking up a wooded ridge. I spotted a big, lone pig—I assumed a boar—coming down the ridge straight toward me, maybe a hundred and fifty yards away. While he was behind a bush, I stood to get ready . . . and never saw him again. One of the local farmers acting as a beater saw a big boar heading back over the ridge, so I assume he turned back. On another drive I had a big pig in brush not fifty yards away, and despite good cover he shifted to my left, passing exactly between me and the next "gun." But why? This happened enough to all of us that, eventually, I came to accept Erik's theory that these semidesert pigs have adapted to use their vision to avoid hunters.

Most of our drives were in the vicinity of the Kasserine Pass, where a lot of Tunisia's estimated five million olive trees grow. Some drives were on the edge of groves, but since it was all daylight hunting, most were in brushy hills and draws where pigs were likely to be bedded. The hunters were placed to cover as many logical escape routes as possible, and the beaters would spread out perhaps a mile away and make their way noisily toward the line.

On a normal Tunisian hunt everybody shoots pigs, usually several. The local farmers are euphoric, and at the end of the hunt there will be a few good boars in the mix. This experimental "trophy hunt" was different. We got some good boars, but not everyone even got a shot. Joe Coogan—"Coogs," as I call him—wasn't one of the lucky ones, but I was.

My stand was on a little finger dropping down into a steep-sided draw, the ground rising again into a steep ridge. It looked like a good place, and I had high hopes as I heard the beaters shouting and banging sticks up to my right and across the ridge. But nothing happened, no distant shots, and after a half-hour the beaters were fairly close. And then I heard the sound of animals moving up on the ridge—lots of animals and moving downhill fast. It was a big sounder, at least thirty pigs, sidehilling as fast as their short legs would carry them.

They broke cover on the far side of the draw, visible for just a couple of seconds and then gone. Most were probably sows because there were quite a few piglets, but near the end, running third from last, was a much bigger pig. There was no way to be certain, and for sure I didn't have time to look for tusks. But it wasn't until later that I realized I was taking a chance—at the moment I was sure, sure enough to swing with him, get ahead of him, and get the shot off just before he passed out of sight.

Instead of crossing the draw, the pig swung away around the toe of the ridge, and suddenly I was no longer so sure what I'd shot at, or even if I'd hit it. A couple of minutes later a young boy appeared out of nowhere. Totally unseen, he'd been standing on a little knoll behind us, and he pointed excitedly, telling us he'd seen a pig roll down the ridge, just out of our sight.

In approved fashion we waited until the beaters reached us, then crossed the draw and climbed up as the lad directed us. Yes, there was a pig lying there under tall pines, dead, a beautiful boar with awesome tusks.

It was an interesting and thoroughly delightful hunt, very inexpensive and yet one I remember as one of the best. In addition to the endless olive groves, it's also

Von Eckhardt's "camp" was a very comfortable hotel in Sbeitla. In Roman times Sbeitla was the capital of the province; these ruins were right next to the hotel. Fantastic!

a famous wine-growing region despite Tunisia being very much a Muslim country. Closer to the coast, the vineyards stretch forever along with the olive groves and, in camp, the local wine was just fine (as the Legionnaires stationed at this far outpost of the Empire no doubt discovered more than two thousand years ago).

We saw a lot of pigs, but they were sharp. If you made the slightest mistake or movement before they came into shotgun range, it was *game over*! Once I must have been doing it right because a jackal—in North Africa a golden jackal—passed close enough to my feet that I could have easily kicked it. But under our rules it was "pigs only," so I stayed perfectly still and let the jackal go on its way.

No pigs followed the jackal on that drive, but toward the end a small sounder came toward me. Having made a lucky guess once, I tempted fate and shot the biggest pig in the group, not thirty yards away and obviously without piglets. It was a good-size pig and looked great on the TV camera—but it turned out to be a big sow. So I took my well-deserved tongue lashing from Erik but, honestly, I didn't feel too bad about it . . . and neither did anyone else.

CHAPTER SEVENTEEN

THE LIBERIAN FOREST

The West African country of Liberia has been on-again, off-again as a hunting destination. Even at that, it has been the most reliable and consistent country for hunting in the region. There has never been sport hunting in Sierra Leone to the west or Ivory Coast to the east. To the northwest Guinea has offered a bit of do-it-yourself *chasse libre* (free hunting) for a few adventurous (and French-speaking) Europeans, but there's never been any outfitters. As described earlier, Ghana, a bit farther east, was only opened recently and at this writing has a questionable future.

Of them all Liberia probably offers the greatest variety of game, but it's highly specialized hunting, primarily for a selection of small forest animals. Several are not huntable anywhere else, so Liberia has always been attractive to long-gone African nuts . . . but there have never been enough of us to support more than a very small

Camp was near a big village, which was not good, but a motorboat gave us mobility. Being able to go several miles up and down the river allowed us to access game country.

Ralf Schneider is shown here with a very nice bay duiker. This was probably the most plentiful animal in the area, and it is an extremely attractive midsize duiker.

industry. Back in the 1980s Harry Gilmore was the lone outfitter in Liberia and, thus, in the entire region.

I knew several experienced hunters who hunted there back then, and most were extremely successful, but in those days a duiker safari was not of the least interest to me. As I've written, hunting the little guys is an acquired taste, and I wasn't there yet. Gilmore was older; after he closed up shop there was a break, and then Tom Banks tried to get hunting going again. Results were mixed, mostly because of catastrophic logistics and poor management. Banks went under, taking a number of safari deposits with him, and then came a horrific civil war that kept Liberia out of the running for more than a decade.

Weatherby Award winner Rex Baker was among a few hunters to enjoy a really successful safari during Tom Banks's brief tenure, but Banks himself left Baker high and dry. Fortunately, Baker's hunt was salvaged by one of Banks's employees, Morris Dougba. During the war Morris sought political asylum in the United States, became a U.S. citizen, and moved with his family to Pennsylvania.

Fast-forward to 2010, when Liberia had stabilized. Morris was starting an import/export business in Monrovia and had interest in reopening hunting in Liberia, so he reached out to Rex Baker. Rex contacted all his fellow board members on the Conklin Foundation, me included, and several of us put up a little bit of seed money to get Morris started. I think most of us figured it was a long shot and we'd never see the money again—or get to hunt in Liberia—but it wasn't a lot of money, and if Morris could make it happen, we'd have our pick of dates for his first season.

While this was percolating, American expat Steve Kobrine, who opened hunting in Ghana, managed to get Liberia reopened, but in a parallel development, so did Morris Dougba. To give proper credit, Kobrine was first. I discussed hunting with him in Liberia when we were in Ghana—he had hunted there himself with a diplomatic permit but hadn't yet started operating. No date was set and no money changed hands.

When Morris actually got going, I figured I had a prior commitment to him, as did the rest of us who had put up deposits. Also, something that was important to me if to nobody else—Morris's rates were a lot more reasonable! Unfortunately, Kobrine was extremely upset to have competition in Liberia. I honestly don't know if the other Conklin directors were treated similarly—I haven't asked—but at the after-party for the 2014 Weatherby presentation, Kobrine publicly and loudly attacked me. I regret this very much because he's an experienced African hand who has opened up some interesting and offbeat destinations, but, understandably, we haven't spoken since.

So I first hunted in Liberia with Morris Dougba in March 2013, paired up with German-Canadian Ralf Schneider. We were Morris's third group in his first "experimental" season. Prepped as well as possible by Rex Baker, we expected an exploratory hunt with rough conditions. That proved true and untrue. Morris is a good organizer, with ability to find good areas and the contacts in government to make it all work, but he is not a hunter himself. In that context, I was proud of him. His base camp was maybe not quite to South African game-lodge standards, but in the middle of nowhere it was a

We worked with the guys on skinning for taxidermy. They didn't really know how to prepare the animals, but they were eager to learn, and we had plenty of salt.

This is the palm civet, a small arboreal cat but obviously a totally different animal from the civet cats encountered elsewhere in Africa.

neat cluster of mud-wattle rondavels, comfortable, well-supplied, and ably staffed. His camp manager, Tony Henry, proved a good hand, and would become the linchpin in keeping things going.

That first year the camp was in the northwest, not far from the three-way border with Sierra Leone and Guinea. The problem was that it was near a large village. Every village has its hunters—in Liberia it's probably not appropriate to call them poachers—so there was virtually no game in easy proximity to camp. That's where the rough stuff came in; we had to stay in spike camps, taking a boat up or down the river as far as possible, and then walking from there. The weather was miserably humid and blistering hot, yet every couple of days we were cooled and soaked by thunderstorms. That said, we had enough bottled water and adequate food. The drill was to spike out for a couple of days, return to base camp for a much-needed shower and a night in a bed, and then spike out in a different direction.

I was fortunate to share the hunt with Ralf Schneider, not just a veteran African hand, but a serious do-it-yourselfer. He's hunted on his own in Cameroon, Guinea, and

God knows where else . . . his know-how was invaluable, and his *chasse libre* emergency kit was filled with all kinds of useful goodies, from Top Ramen to good brandy.

Remember, this was an exploratory hunt. African warfare is hard on wildlife, so it wasn't the same Liberia that had existed a decade earlier. Also, and perhaps of greater importance, there was little expertise and no corporate memory. Some experienced hunters had left Liberia, never to return, and many were killed in the conflict. Therefore, nobody left standing knew exactly where the beautiful zebra duiker, the one forest duiker that most draws hunters to Liberia, might be found. I would class the water chevrotain as the second-most-desirable animal, not an antelope but actually a small antlerless deer with fangs. They are widespread in Liberia, typically found along rivers—as the name suggests. The problem was: which rivers?

That first season was a good news/bad news story. It took some doing to get to good game country, and it required sleeping in hammocks. But since the forest duikers are mostly nocturnal, there isn't much sleeping at night, and, try as you might, it's too hot to sleep much during the day. Forest hunting is difficult and often uncomfortable, and it isn't for everyone.

The good news is: Once we got far enough from the villages, there was lots of game. The little Maxwell duikers and the pretty bay duikers were plentiful. Water chevrotains were fairly common along the river; about half of the hunters in that first season took them. There were also a few black duikers around, and some of the first hunters took them as well.

Hey, forest hunting is hard, and when night hunting is on the menu, the hours are terrible. However, I'm not a guy who likes to make things sound worse or more difficult than they are. Like all forest hunting, walking is slow and mostly in shade, and the Liberian forest is amazingly clean. There are very few biting ants, almost no mosquitoes, and relatively few thorny plants. In many ways it's a much more pleasant forest than those I've experienced in Cameroon and the C.A.R.

The bad news is: The great prize, the zebra duiker, seemed totally absent in this area. It's a funny thing: One patch of African forest looks pretty much the same as another to you and me, but it doesn't look the same to the forest dwellers, so there were plenty of duikers, but not the zebra duiker we hoped to find. There were very few bongos in this area, meaning the occasional old track, and we saw quite a few

Here we are on a forest trail en route to our last and most distant fly camp . . . still hoping to find where the zebra duikers live!

buffalo tracks, though nothing fresh enough to follow, but zebra duikers were absent, and there were only rumors of the large yellow-backed and Jentink duikers.

Sometimes there were clues to where these duikers might be found by understanding the Liberian designations for these animals. Although there are tribal languages in Liberia, to this day the common language is English.* This is important to know because forest hunting there is done directly with local hunters, so you are absent a trained PH to translate, run interference, and hold your hand.

After generations spent in North America, the original settlers named all the animals "deer" in their patois. Some names are purely descriptive: The black duiker is the "black deer;" the big-eared Ogilby is the "wide-eared deer." However, the water chevrotain is the "water deer" and is always found along flowing watercourses, and

*Freed American slaves returned to West Africa as early as 1818, and the country was established in 1847 when former president James Monroe, a prominent supporter of colonization, procured money for the settlement. The capital, Monrovia, is named in his honor. English is and has always been the official language of Liberia.

the zebra duiker is the "mountain deer." The country where we hunted was hilly, but apparently not hilly enough for this animal.

So Ralf Schneider and I hunted hard, and our local guides gave it their best efforts, but in any situation some hunters are going to do better than others, and in an initial season that saw mixed results, somebody had to get the neck of the chicken. That would be Ralf and me! We both took good bay and Maxwell duikers, but that's about it. I also got a palm civet, a long-tailed arboreal animal dramatically different from the regular civet.

One afternoon my team and I jumped what was probably a black duiker and heard it crash away, and one night I got a very quick glimpse of a water chevrotain. I'm sure that's what it was because it's the only animal in the forest with eyes that reflect red, but it ran instantly and we heard it splash into the stream.

Our lack of success wasn't for lack of effort. We hunted day and night, and I found it both interesting and intimidating. I'm terrified of snakes, and the Liberian forest is home to one of the most fearsome of all, the Gaboon viper, a snake with two-inch fangs. For hunters cursed with active imaginations, stumbling down forest trails in the dark is a scary deal. Fortunately, I never saw a single snake, although Rex Baker's son, Rex Jr., nearly stepped on a Gaboon viper on the safari previous to ours. *Ugh!*

Liberia is another country where it's impossible to bring in firearms. Locals hunt with shotguns, usually well-used single-shots; rifles are generally illegal. Morris had three good 12-gauge pump guns: a Mossberg, an SKB, and a very clean Winchester Model 25 (a cheaper version of the famous Model 12). After much discussion with the game department, he had also brought a Model 70 .458 into camp for buffalo.

The shotgun shells were made in Mali, filled with coarse shot that looked like our No. 4 birdshot but may have been a size larger. These plastic-cased cartridges had "low-base" brass rims, but were actually very strong. I didn't find the mix of game I'd hoped for, but I shot multiples of both bay and Maxwell duikers, and every animal I shot at was stone-dead on the spot.

During both day and night we would walk along the forest trails slowly, at night with headlamps, always looking. Most of the animals we saw by calling, the local hunters making that odd mewling nasal sound that a variety of forest animals respond

A very good Maxwell duiker, an ancient male with thick, worn horns. West of the Dahomey Gap the Maxwell duiker essentially replaces the blue duiker, similar in color but the Maxwell variety is larger.

to. We'd hunker on the forest floor, often in total darkness, listening between calls. Sometimes I could hear the slight scuffling in the leaves, but the forest hunters would always hear them. The problem with this hunting is that it is very random. Sometimes you can positively identify the animal, but sometimes not . . . and even if the species is known, it is difficult to determine the sex or size of the horns, especially at night. So, to a degree, you take what the forest offers you, although you try to be picky.

In the latter part of the hunt I turned down several Maxwell and bay duikers, still hoping for a great prize. This was much to the chagrin of our local guides. They were strictly meat hunters, and if Ralf and I weren't there, they would be out hunting for themselves, with total disregard for species or quantity. This, of course, is why little wildlife remains in proximity to any village. But it's still a big forest, and the small antelopes, though short-lived, are prolific, reaching maturity and breeding at a much younger age than the larger antelopes. The forest is their grocery, and they don't have to move much to sustain themselves.

As with bongo hunting in previous years, it seemed to me that the forest came alive just after a rain when the leaves were quiet and the animals tended to feel good. One night in the first spike camp it poured buckets for several hours, accompanied by some of the most violent thunder and lightning I've ever seen. When it stopped, we headed out in the middle of the night, returning at dawn with a bay duiker, a Maxwell duiker, and the palm civet. At that point I genuinely thought we'd hit the jackpot, not knowing that these were, essentially, the only species in the area. Later in the hunt, again just after a rain, we came back with a bay duiker and very big Maxwell duiker, and we'd turned down several other animals of both species. By then I knew the truth: These were the animals this forest was offering us.

I had never taken a bay duiker. I'd barely heard of a palm civet and didn't know they were so different from civets I'd hunted elsewhere. So it would be an exaggeration to say that the hunt was unsuccessful. If success is measured in animals taken, we'd done well; in species diversity, which is one of Africa's great attractions, not so well. Ralf and I had

It was very hot during the days, but since we were hunting most of the nights we had to try to nap a bit during daylight hours.

I took this good bay duiker by calling at night. Although we hunted both day and night, almost all the animals we encountered were seen at night

hoped for the great prize, the zebra duiker, so we kept at it until the last day (and night), and at the finish we were exhausted. The forest does that to you, but it's a beautiful forest, much of it still largely untouched. The hunting is highly specialized and very challenging. Some will like it and others will hate it, but I knew I'd try again.

I told Morris and Tony that they had done well in re-establishing hunting in Liberia, but now they needed to scour the country to find the right place to hunt the zebra duiker. I'm sure most of their other exploratory hunters told them the same thing. You know how it is; some people listen and others don't. After that first season, Tony Henry spent *five months* scouring Liberia, going village to village, looking for zebra duikers and unspoiled forest.

He found a spot maybe five hours' drive from Monrovia in northcentral Liberia, and it was a good spot. I couldn't go the following year, and 2015 was lost to the terrible Ebola pandemic. As these lines are written it's March 2016, and I'm back in the Liberian forest, writing under generator power, with a black duiker Tony and I killed hanging about fifty yards away. Sometimes faith is rewarded and sometimes it isn't, but this new area is proving vastly different. I'll save the stories of this hunt for later in the book.

Chapter Eighteen

Natal, Cape, and Karoo

Donna likes to say that she is "collateral damage," implying that I force her to do this silly hunting stuff. There's probably a bit of truth in that, but just the other day (when I was God knows where) she sneaked off and went turkey hunting by herself, and she's always got a "girls'-only" hunt in the works somewhere. So I don't feel too bad about co-opting her into my crazy world, and it's a lot of fun going along with her—and my daughters—on hunts that, realistically, I can't really justify the *need* to do again. So instead of "collateral damage," my preferred term is "surrogate shooter." Mind you, it's all fun, but there are always stories to be written, so whether a camera is rolling or not, there is a business angle, which makes a lot of what we do affordable.

Caroline, Brittany, and Donna with Caroline's first African animal, a really excellent southern bushbuck. I'm pretty sure Caroline had no idea how good this ram is, and she made a perfect shot.

That's neither good nor bad; it just is. For me, deadline pressure is nothing. I'm not only used to it; it's what I do. The TV camera is something else again. I didn't get into what we call "outdoor television" because I wanted to see myself on the boob tube. Rather, it was a conscious acceptance that this is now a multimedia world, and to stay employed it's important to stay current. I hate social media, but it has to be done. At first I hated the TV camera. I wouldn't say I've gotten used to it, or even that I'm perfectly comfortable with it, and for sure I haven't grown to love it, but at least I've learned to ignore it.

My girls are different. Donna hates the TV camera, although she's better on camera than she realizes. My older daughter, Brittany, simply loves it, and she's far better on camera than I will ever be. My younger daughter, Caroline, does not love it. I don't think she's yet grown to hate it because she hasn't been subjected to it that much, but she doesn't like it. So it was a bit unfortunate that the timing was such that Caroline's first African hunt needed to be filmed. Fortunately, there weren't any disasters, or even any problems.

Mornings were really frosty up in the Natal hills. I tell people to never underestimate how cold it can be in the mornings and evenings, but this particular morning was well below freezing.

Caroline, Mark Haldane (far right), and I with Caroline's common reedbuck. Haldane uses the Baynesfield concession primarily for bird hunting. Big-game species are limited, but it's a great area for exceptional bushbuck and reedbuck.

Our cameraman was our old friend Matt Young. Long of hair and beard and stereotypical of a Montana mountain man, he is a keen hunter himself, and not only highly professional with the camera but also extremely patient. If he's assigned to the shoot, even Donna will grudgingly acquiesce: "Oh, if Matt's going to film, then it's OK."

Anyone who thinks outdoor TV looks like wonderful fun should do a couple of hunts in front of the camera: Extra levels of complexity and difficulty are unavoidable even under the best of circumstances. "Best of circumstances" would certainly include a South African plains game safari, which this was to be—lots of game, lots of opportunity, reliably good weather. However, "best of circumstances" also includes a camera-experienced hunter working together as a team with a cameraman who is not only skilled but also familiar with the hunter, and vice versa.

Conrad Evarts and I have filmed together for more than a dozen years; we each know what the other is thinking and most likely to do. Matt Young and I haven't filmed together quite that much, but we have done it enough that we're still a good team, and we don't have to worry about what the other is doing. Brittany was joining us and would trade off some shots with Caroline, but the intent of the safari was that Caroline was the primary hunter, with Donna and I taking opportunities based on the girls' generosity. Brittany is always a pro on camera, and has filmed with Matt a number of times, so there was no potential problem there. Caroline had been on camera before, but never with Matt. Africa was brand new to her, as was our big, bearded camera operator. Intimidating for a seventeen-year-old? You think?

This hunt was put together by my friend, Mark Haldane, who I mentioned in earlier chapters. Although I hunted with him multiple times in Mozambique, Haldane is actually based in Natal. In most African situations I prefer to hunt with someone who grew up in the country where I'm hunting. Nonresident professional hunters may be just as good (and sometimes are better), but as a journalist I've always figured there was more to be learned from the local guys. In Mozambique, though, this is almost not an option. Between independence and their long civil war, Mozambique was effectively closed from about 1973 to the late 1980s, and almost none of the professional hunters who were there in 1973 returned to try again. So, hunting in Mozambique today is dominated by outfitters and professional hunters, like Haldane, from neighboring South Africa, with a sprinkling from Zimbabwe and elsewhere.

By the time these lines are printed, Haldane will have been hunting in Mozambique for more than a quarter-century, but, like many others, he retains an operation in

I don't think I've ever seen a better area for common reedbuck than Haldane's Baynesfield concession. Nice rams like this were commonplace, and if you looked around a bit there were some monsters.

Carl van Zyl and Caroline with a nice gemsbok bull. She really stretched the barrel of that 7mm-08 on this one, taking this bull at 305 yards.

South Africa as well. Unusually, however, his primary operation in his native Natal is bird-shooting safaris. No, we weren't focusing on birds, so our plan for hunting here was a bit different. We'd start in one of his primary "bird areas," hilly farm country northwest of Durban. There isn't a lot of species diversity there, but the area has exceptional bushbucks and common reedbucks and, with luck, a few other species. We'd spend a few days there, and then fly from Durban to Port Elizabeth, where Carl van Zyl of John X Safaris would take over the hunt. At that time I didn't know Carl, but because this was a normal rotation for Haldane's plains-game clients, a recommendation from Mark was plenty good enough.

I hadn't been in Natal for many years—properly now KwaZulu-Natal—and I had forgotten how beautiful it is—tall timbered hills and fertile valleys. It truly was perfect habitat for bushbucks and common reedbucks. Kudus are present and occasionally a troop of elands comes through, but other than a number of gray duikers, the only game we actually saw were bushbucks and reedbucks. We saw plenty, but in ideal country we were looking for the exceptional, so it was the afternoon of the second day before

The animal Brittany wanted most was an Eastern Cape kudu, so she got first crack and took this excellent old bull. Despite much effort, this turned out to be the only chance we had at greater kudu.

Caroline took her first shot in Africa. (That was fine with me. I didn't want it to be *too* easy—but, understandably, Caroline was getting a little antsy.)

Much of the country could be glassed from ranch roads, but there were some hidden pockets along a streambed visible only from a timbered ridge on the far side. So, in the late afternoon when it was the perfect time to sight bushbucks, we hiked along just inside the timber so we could glass into those hidden valleys. Funny how it works: Combine the right place with the right time, and things happen fast! We hadn't gone very far when we saw a bushbuck ewe in a tiny green clearing surrounded by thick stuff. It was June and the bushbuck rut was on, so we maneuvered just a bit and sat down. Moments later a ram stepped out, nearly black with long, sharp horns.

I'll be really honest: Caroline hadn't done quite all the homework she might have done. She wanted a zebra (which would happen) and she wanted a kudu (which would not happen), but she wasn't sure where the bushbuck fit into the scheme of things. Me, I was excited: More than thirty-five years earlier, a bushbuck had been my own first African animal. That's happenstance. For most of us the bushbuck is an animal that sort of grows on you, and it is almost never at the top of the wish list for a first-time African hunter. Now it's one of my favorites, but maybe it's just as well that Caroline had no idea how spectacular this ram was. Time for Dad to keep his mouth shut!

Mark had her sit down next to a stout pine, sticks in front, the tree offering a solid anchor to lean against. The ram was about a hundred and fifty yards away, not a hard shot, but not an easy one either. He was circling the ewe, so the angle was terrible . . . and then he stopped, broadside, and Caroline's little 7mm-08 dropped him with a central shoulder shot. A beautiful ram, perfectly shot, a great start—and a slightly bemused hunter who still wasn't sure exactly what she had.

We weren't up in the mountains, but we were in tall hills and June is the beginning of winter in Southern Africa. The next morning was one of the coldest mornings I remember in Africa, heavy frost, temperatures probably in the high teens. With whitetails we pray for such a morning, but most African antelopes are fair-weather creatures, and although we almost froze to death we saw very little until the sun started to warm things up. Finally Mark glassed the black horns of a very good reedbuck—just the horns—in some tall reeds far off across a flat. We initially tried a direct approach, but the valley dropped a bit, and although I'm sure we got in range, we couldn't see the reedbuck.

So we backed off, thinking he'd moved—but he was still there, standing like a statue. The next ridge was beyond him, maybe too far, but that seemed the only possible answer. A huge circle brought us in above him, a bit over two hundred yards. But now he'd seen us and was staring at us, only his head and horns visible over the tall reeds. Tough shot, but Caroline had been to the SAAM shooting school and felt

It's pretty rare to see porcupines out during the day. Donna wanted an African porcupine for a long time, so when we ran across this one she wasted no time.

Caroline's last animal of the trip was an excellent black wildebeest, which she missed once and then stalked again with success.

she could do it, so I backed off and Mark talked her through it: "Right under the chin, Caroline," he said.

The reedbuck dropped to the shot and we did our high-fives, but the shot was just a bit to one side, so when we approached the buck jumped up and headed toward the ridge we'd just vacated. Caroline was startled, and in that tall grass she's too short for a possible shot. The buck was beyond two hundred yards and still moving when he finally gained enough elevation for her to see him. I figured we'd have some tracking to do, but she was on him now, and when he cleared some tall grass, she rolled him, a beautiful shot.

With the day warming up a bit, the game was starting to move. On the way down out of the hills we spotted two bushbuck rams on a little finger ridge, one a real dandy. It was Brittany's turn, but she gave the shot to Donna, and we made a quick stalk. By then they'd moved into tall, dry grass, and between cover and the roll of the ridge she could barely see them, but we waited it out and she made a lovely shot with her .270. This was not Donna's first bushbuck, but definitely her best. The next day Brittany got a very nice reedbuck, an animal she hadn't taken previously. We tried hard to get Caroline a duiker, but they're tricky and it didn't happen—and then it was time to head south.

Carl van Zyl's "home place" is Lalibela, a beautiful "Big Five" estate. Located near the huge Addo Park, it's used for game viewing as much (or more) than hunting, and the lodge there is a huge complex, and one of the very finest lodges I've ever seen on the African continent. I have a feeling the ladies wouldn't have objected if we'd stayed right there, but we were treated to Lalibela for just a couple days on either end, spending the majority of our time over the mountains on the edge of the Karoo, near Graaff-Reinet.

We did do some hunting on and around Lalibela. Our first day there Carl took us to a concession northeast toward the coast. I think this was probably a super area, for we saw a lot of game, including kudus, waterbucks, nyalas, blesboks, impalas, and more, but on that particular day the wind was whipping thirty miles an hour and more, so the game was spooked. I'm surprised we saw as much as we did. Carl had asked Caroline what she wanted most, and her immediate response was, "A zebra!"

So that was our mission, and on a windy day like that it seemed a mission impossible! Finally, late in the afternoon, we spotted a small herd feeding in a (sort of) protected valley. The right side of the valley offered some cover, so we made a slow and careful stalk along game trails through the brush and then crawled out to the edge. Carl had judged it perfectly. We were about a hundred and thirty yards from zebras that were still feeding along contentedly, totally unaware.

The next problem was which one, since they were belly-deep in low brush. This took some study, as it often does, but finally Carl was sure—or sure enough. We were sitting, with thick Addo thorn making a low roof over us, so I broke the sticks down for a sitting position and passed them forward to Carl.

I heard him pointing out the shoulder chevron, and as her zebra turned broadside I held my breath. The shot was perfect, and the stallion ran twenty yards and tipped over. Zebra kills aren't always that simple or that clean . . . I know because I've spent long days tracking wounded zebras. I have huge respect for them, and I can assure you the 7mm-08 is not a big gun on an 800-pound stallion. But neither is the .270—they're really much the same.

A week later, back at Lalibela and on our last day, Donna got another turn. As she will say, "No girl has enough zebras." On that last day she absolutely flattened a big stallion, dropped it right in its tracks, with a 130-grain bullet from her .270. To my thinking this suggests two truths, if not actually proving them: First, where the

Back at Lalibela they had some Xhosa dancers on the last evening. They were much better at the drums than Caroline and I.

shot is placed counts much more than what the shot is placed *with*; second, while I'm not convinced that women shoot better than men, I am certain they pay attention better. When the PH says, "See that 'V' on the shoulder? Shoot him there," women seem much more likely to listen.

In between the two zebras we went west, over the Cape Mountains to another of Carl's concessions on the edge of the Karoo. This was another really cool area with big, beautiful hills and broad valleys. The camp wasn't quite as fancy as Lalibela, and it was smaller, with individual chalets of native stone. From the yard we could glass gemsboks all day, and kudus every now and then.

We actually glassed Caroline's gemsbok from the yard, a couple of bulls working their way along a low and very distant ridge. We were able to drive a thousand yards and cut the distance a bit, and then we worked our way down a dry streambed, paralleling them with the hope of converging on them a bit. The parallel part worked just fine, but when we crawled up out of the streambed, the bulls were still on the ridge, and just over three hundred yards out. Too far for Caroline, too far for a 7mm-08—but the first bull was really, really good, and they had no idea we were anywhere in their world. Also, they were now moving along very slowly, so we had plenty of time.

We'd climbed a near-vertical bank to a little shelf, so I passed Carl a couple of daypacks and in a couple of seconds he set up a good approximation of a benchrest. *Cool!* Caroline knew what a gemsbok was, and knew she wanted one. She also knew the shot was a bit far, but if Carl shared my concern he, like me, was keeping his mouth shut. Settled into her perch, she adjusted the rifle this way and that. Working the rangefinder, I gave her the distance and suggested she hold high on the shoulder, just below the hump—at that distance she'd have about ten inches of drop. The bull stopped on the crest, just above some jumbled rocks, and was skylined at 305 yards . . . and at the shot, he dropped like a rock.

By now it was Brittany's turn, and maybe past a bit, so that put her first up for kudu. We traveled a couple of hours in the dark to a different area, a big, open area of big hills and mesas and brushy valleys. In the half-dark we climbed a low, flat-topped butte and set up to glass on the far side just at sunrise. It was a good spot, and Carl had it dialed in. In beautiful golden light a group of bulls worked their way along a brushy draw right below us. Only one was really mature, and Brittany shot him well.

These were, of course, Eastern Cape greater kudus. At this stage there aren't a whole lot of southern animals that Brittany hasn't hunted, but this was one of them. Any greater kudu is a special animal, and while the Eastern Cape kudu is usually smaller in the horn (not necessarily in the body), it makes up for it with a long, luxurious cape. Brittany's was a beauty, but we could still see a lot of kudus moving through brushy patches far across the valley, so we hustled and got some photos so that Caroline could have a turn.

I really expected we'd get her a kudu, but although we saw a lot of cows and young bulls, we never saw another mature bull. Well, I figured we still had the evening, but that didn't happen, either. Just before dark we saw a spectacular bull, surely well over fifty inches, huge for this breed of kudu, but he was a half-mile away and moving. A quick move to cut him off failed . . . he vanished completely. We kept looking until the last day, but we never saw that bull again, and we never saw another mature bull. For sure there were plenty around, but it's a big country and sometimes certain things just aren't in the cards. As Jon Sundra once wrote, the greater kudu is an animal you're always looking for, and even if you're not, when you see one you'll stop to take a look.

At the tail end Caroline shot a nice black wildebeest after several abortive stalks. I traded places with Matt Young, and he shot his first African animal, a blesbok.

Zebras dusting themselves at Lalibela.

You'll note that, so far, I hadn't had a turn. That's a bit unusual for me, but on this particular hunt I didn't even take a rifle and didn't intend to shoot. But I did get one turn. On Father's Day the girls announced it was my turn, so I took Caroline's right-handed, short-stocked CZ 7mm-08 and sallied forth.

Carl and I quickly found a bachelor group of hartebeests, and there was one really big bull in the group. The first stalk failed. We really should have given up, but now we were sort of committed. So we followed him up one big ridge and down the next, and we finally caught up to the herd a couple hours later.

Now I had to be careful. Brittany, Caroline, and Donna had all shot really well, and it would be a long plane ride home if I messed up. Carl and I crawled up behind some big boulders and I found a good rest. Now we had to find the right bull, not so easy because hartebeests look much alike. Carl found him, then I did, and we agreed we were on the same page.

The hartebeest took the little bullet hard and vanished over the ridge with his buddies, but when we walked up, they were gone and he was there. After that I never considered taking another turn. Sometimes it's better to quit while you're ahead.

Chapter Nineteen

Namibia's Escarpment

I'm not sure why this is, but Namibia isn't known as a mountainous country. Even so, the country is studded with mountains. Some ranges, like the Erongo, are significant. Other ranges are smaller, and there are a surprising number of lone, isolated mountains, like Mount Etjo where Jan Oelofse operated, and where his company continues. Perhaps more surprising, Windhoek itself lies on a high plateau; the city's mean elevation is nearly 5,600 feet and surrounding ridges are quite a bit taller. The high country continues for some distance in all directions, but to the southwest, at a distance of about two hundred fifty kilometers, the rocky ridges drop abruptly into the sands of the Namib Desert, forming an escarpment as defined as the south wall of the Zambezi Valley.

Donna and I were hunting in the rocky hills above the escarpment with Mare van der Merwe and his family at African Twilight Safaris. This is harsh, arid country, but magnificent in its own way, and although the species diversity isn't great, what's there is fantastic. Mare's family ranch is huge, something over 100,000 acres, bordered by equally large properties, and in this part of Namibia no one has yet thought of game fences (thank God).

We were there in September. At certain times of the year—not then—Mare told me he gets a large migration of elands, gemsboks, hartebeests, and zebras coming out of the Namib. We didn't see any elands, but we saw quite a few gemsboks and hartebeests, certainly enough that a hunter could find one if it was important. But I wouldn't call those species fantastic or plentiful, at least not at the time of year we were there.

Some things were fantastic, plentiful, and spectacular: I've never seen a better place for Hartmann mountain zebras; I haven't seen a better place for big greater kudus in many a year; and I've never seen a place anywhere near as good for klipspringers. Springbok and steenbok numbers were also exceptional, and although the country is a bit dry for them, there were plenty of warthogs around.

We weren't there for plains game, however. We were there for a leopard . . . but, come to think of it, we weren't supposed to be there at all; we were supposed to be up in the Caprivi. It was a gun-company hunt, specifically with my friends at Kimber, so please take no hint of ingratitude. Honest, gun company hunts, especially to Africa, don't come along all that often, and they're appreciated. Donna and my accountant wish there were more! At this point in my life, however, time is a major factor and getting to Africa under any circumstance is not, so the hook was Caprivi, a legendary area I hadn't visited, always wanted to, and eventually would—but not this time.

Kimber's safari was with Jamy Traut, a great operator, and in the way these situations are dealt out—sort of like a hand of cards—I was supposed to hunt a leopard. But Jamy didn't get the Caprivi leopard permit he expected to get, so I was sort of subcontracted to African Twilight, which had a leopard permit available. Business-wise, this was not a good deal, as we never saw the Kimber folks, and we only saw Jamy at the beginning. We spent the first night and day with Jamy and his family at their Panorama ranch south of Windhoek where Donna shot a nice gemsbok, and then we were whisked off to African Twilight.

Jamy Traut at the "braai" *on his Panorama estate south of Windhoek. The original plan was for Donna and me to go up to Caprivi with Jamy, but because he didn't have a leopard permit, we hunted with African Twilight Safaris, and our first night was the only time we saw Jamy.*

For me, though, it was a great deal because I saw a beautiful slice of Namibia that I'd never seen before, and probably wouldn't have visited otherwise. Unfortunately, we weren't there at the right time. So instead of creating suspense unnecessarily, I'll get it out there up front: I never got a leopard, never saw a leopard. But it wasn't because leopards weren't there. These rocky hills produce some of Namibia's biggest leopards. I saw photos, I saw trail cam photos, and I saw the tracks.

The first order of business was to get a mountain zebra for leopard bait. These rocky hills are their natural habitat and they're plentiful. Hunting them in this country is a real mountain hunt and a great experience.

It also wasn't for lack of expertise; van der Merwe is a very good leopard hunter and has a lifetime of experience protecting his livestock. He doesn't get beaten often, but we got beaten. I'm not a pessimist, usually the opposite, but when whatever experience I have tells me things aren't going my way, I'm also a realist. We had leopards feeding—sort of—which is why I saw tracks and trail-cam photos. But the cats—three or four different toms—would hit once and not return. So we baited, and re-baited, and master . . . never mind. Needless to say, every time a cat hit, we'd sit the next evening, but we never had a return customer.

With a pattern this consistent, it appeared to me we were beaten nearly from the start. That sounds pessimistic, and maybe it is, but we played out the string and kept our baits going, checking them, and, of course, putting up a blind and sitting every time we got a hit. As I said, Mare van der Merwe is a competent and experienced leopard hunter; he was distraught, and I believe his story that I was one of very few clients to fail on leopard.

At the midpoint of the hunt we needed more zebra for leopard bait, so it was my turn. I hit a big stallion just at sunset, fortunately with a .375. He made the top of the ridge and died right there.

I think the explanation for the failure is simple: It was September, and it was too late in the year. The cold winter was over and it was starting to warm up. The cats weren't as hungry, and the warthogs and springboks were dropping their young, so natural kills were easier. Also, these are ranch leopards, persecuted for generations, and they're touchy. Late in the season is never good, but in wild country with sparse prey, September isn't so bad. Here, in ranch country, we were just too late in the season, and the best techniques in the world weren't going to change that.

We were there for a leopard hunt and it wasn't our intention to do much other hunting. Also, between baiting, checking baits, building blinds, and sitting long hours there isn't time to do much else. But as it became increasingly clear that things weren't going our way, we managed to hedge our bets just a bit.

Mountain zebras provided the leopard baits. Zebras are always challenging, but hunting the Hartmann mountain zebras on their native turf is always a great, sort of a mini-mountain, hunt. Donna took the first one, spotted in a group far up on a big ridge, a couple of miles away. Because of the wind, a direct approach wasn't possible, so we made a long circle on foot and came up above them. For a zebra, the distance of about

250 yards was pushing it with Donna's .270, but there was no way to get closer. So she lay down over packs, and although her zebra needed a finisher, he was anchored.

Midway through the hunt, we needed another zebra because we got yet another hit on a bait that appeared red-hot. It was not; the leopard never returned, but we had no way to know that. We needed a zebra *that day*, but that can be a tall order. We glassed a herd far up on a ridge, with just enough cover for a direct approach. We had a lot of ground to cover and we hustled as best we could, but when we got there the group had moved through a saddle onto the next ridge, and the shot was about 275 yards. I was carrying the Kimber Caprivi in .375, and on the one hand, it was good because I had plenty of extra power. On the other hand, it was not so good because that's a long shot for a .375!

We'd made the climb because we needed the zebra, but by that time the day was finished. I set up on sticks and took the shot. It felt good, and the big bullet made a solid *whack*, but the zebra turned and ran with the group, headed for the top of the ridge and out of sight before I could shoot again. Now I figured I'd really done it . . . dark was coming fast, and over the ridge was a near-bottomless canyon. We needed that zebra, and I figured I'd blown it.

With dark coming fast now, we followed a faint trail to the ridgetop, hoping to find where the herd topped out. We were expecting that we'd be back at it in the morning, but when we reached the ridgetop, my zebra was there, sitting upright on the exact crest of the ridge, stone dead. Now we had bait and could put it out in the morning.

The "Christmas tree" marking on the rump is a distinguishing feature of Hartmann mountain zebra, to my eye the most beautiful of Africa's several races of zebras.

We had to pack the zebras Donna and I shot off the hills. Donna's zebra had to be packed off the hill in pieces, so to save time Mare went back to the road and brought the Toyota in as close as he could. Once the zebra was loaded, he took us out by a different road, and along the way we saw one of the best greater kudu bulls I've ever laid eyes on. It's impossible to say for sure he was sixty inches, but he probably was, and if he wasn't he was awfully close. For sure he was a lot bigger than any kudu I've ever taken, and he was looking at us over some jumbled boulders from about eighty yards away.

Exactly why I didn't shoot him—or tell Donna to shoot him—is unclear to me. Our only real option was to step out of the truck and shoot, and I feel that's a very poor way to shoot anything, especially a magnificent animal like a greater kudu. But it was a gift from Mother Nature, and I kicked sand in her face. We weren't hunting kudus, and we didn't even consider shooting. The focus was leopard, and more than a week would pass before it occurred to me that maybe we'd better do some other hunting or the story would be awfully short.

Thus, our hunt for kudus sort of evolved as my hunt for a leopard devolved. Throughout Southern Africa, kudu hunting isn't what it used to be, which makes my decision not to shoot all the more regrettable. In Namibia a series of rabies epidemics

We weren't yet in kudu hunting mode when we saw this giant from the truck, about eighty yards away. It's impossible to say for sure, but with the first turn just outside the ears, a good second turn, and long tips, this bull is very close to the magical sixty-inch mark.

Donna and Mare van der Merwe are all smiles over Donna's kudu. At first glance he looked huge, but kudu are tricky to judge, and once shot we weren't really sure what he would measure. Later he turned out to be fifty-seven inches around the curl, a great kudu and a very good call.

have reduced the population in most areas. South Africa has a different problem: With the current prices being paid for high-quality breeding stock, any big kudu spotted is helicopter-darted and taken to auction rather than hunted. Mare complained that he'd lost a lot of kudus, but from the first day we saw more kudus than I've seen in a long time. The problem is that initially we weren't interested, but we should have been.

Needless to say, when the decision to do some kudu hunting was made, we tried to find that bull again, but it's big, rough country and we never got another glimpse. We did see a lot of nice bulls, and I eventually took a very pretty bull, but not the big one. We'd seen the bull I eventually shot slip off into a shallow, brushy

African Twilight's area is one of the best places I've ever seen for klipspringer. In general their distribution is very spotty in Namibia, but here we saw some almost every day.

canyon, and I thought it would be cool if I could get the drop on him. We actually went past him, but he couldn't stand it and broke sixty yards away. Using the .375 again, I swung with him and flattened him. Honestly, he was no monster, but he was a very pretty bull. He was also my best kudu in quite a few years, and I was perfectly happy.

Now Donna was being difficult. She insisted that she'd only take a kudu if it was bigger than any other kudu she'd taken. Her best at that time was fifty-three inches, a wonderful greater kudu. I thought we could do better, and so did Mare, but how can you be sure? Kudu bulls are the devil to judge, and very few give you the kind of time that big boy gave us. We kept looking for him for Donna, and although mine was a very nice bull, I probably sort of "settled" so that maybe she would have a chance at the big boy.

We couldn't find him, but late in the hunt, not far from where we'd seen the big one, we ran across two mature bulls in a sand riverbed. One was a nice, normal kudu, maybe fifty inches; the other was a lot bigger. He wasn't the big one, but he was a very fine bull with a perfect shape and good curls. In short, he had *everything*. We drove past and stalked back, and the bigger bull still looked big. But now, with Donna on the sticks, we had a problem: "Are you sure it's *that* big?"

Aw, geez, how can you be sure? Total length lies in the curve and the curl, not in the width or the height, and nobody can be *sure* until the tape is applied. She was shooting a Kimber .30-06, and the clock was ticking—he started to run just as the shot went off! The bull lurched into the brush, but she'd hit him well, just behind the shoulder, and we found him quickly, down and dead.

Now I was worried. Without his little buddy beside him, he was still a gorgeous kudu . . . but he didn't look quite so big. Donna was happy and didn't ask, but I was afraid our excitement had led to a fair amount of ground shrinkage. Later that afternoon Mare and I slipped out to the trophy shed and put a tape on his horns. Fifty-seven inches! That's not only an awesome kudu, it's bigger than any kudu I've ever shot.

We were nothing if not persistent, and I still hoped we would find a leopard before we had to leave. We kept checking baits until the very last, but at the tail end even the intermittent hits stopped. At a convention eighteen months later, somebody showed me a picture of a big leopard from Mare's place, and I assume that's one of the leopards that taunted us.

So even though a leopard would prove elusive and we would continue checking baits until the end, we were done but just didn't know it. Our hunt, however, was not quite done. Springboks weren't plentiful, but quality was spectacular. I shot a dandy, but I think the real capper on the hunt was Donna's klipspringer. That's an animal she hadn't had a chance to hunt, and I never expected she'd get one in Namibia. Although they have plenty of perfect habitat—rocky hills and *kopjes*—distribution is spotty; moreover, the "klippie" is sort of a special animal there, with limited permits just like the Damara dik-dik. But in this particular area there were lots of them, actually more than I've ever seen anywhere else, let alone in Namibia. Mare had a permit, so, time away from the uncooperative leopards permitting, we kept our eyes open and eventually we saw a really nice male with a female.

At certain times of the year the area gets a big migration of springbok and gemsbok from the Namib. Numbers weren't high while we were there, but there were some very nice springbok; I took this excellent ram on the last day.

One of the great things about Africa isn't just the variety of game; it's never knowing what among that variety is going to provide the shiniest memories. We followed the pair up over some rocky tops, and at some point Donna got a quick shot and missed. Now the hunt was on, and we stayed with them over a couple more rocky tops. Eventually Mare saw the female, so we got a little closer and Donna set up on some rocks.

Mare was certain the male was still there. I was not, but filed it under the heading of "listen to your PH." He was right. After a little bit the ram stepped up, totally out of nowhere, and stood next to his mate. Donna pasted him perfectly, and although that wasn't the end of the safari, that's one of its best memories. That, and the brightly colored little adder I almost trod upon on the way back to the truck. . . .

CHAPTER TWENTY

KALAHARI LION

This hunt took place in 2013. The world has changed a lot since then, and our small lion-hunting world has turned upside down. At this writing, the regrettable demise of Cecil the Lion took place about a year ago. The Zimbabwe government has not pressed charges against the hunter, which I think is entirely appropriate, and the charges against the outfitter were dropped. I doubt we will ever know if the hunt was fully 100 percent legal (although I'm fairly certain the American hunter was, if not clueless, blameless), and there will always be differences of opinion on the ethics. No matter where you stand, however, it was extremely regrettable, and both the hunting community and Africa's lions are paying a heavy price.

At this writing Americans have not been allowed to import legally taken sport-hunted lions for several months. Whether we ever will again is an open question. Another legal issue that has arisen is that, somewhat arbitrarily and definitely against international and scientific consensus, the U.S. Fish and Wildlife Service decided to divide Africa's lions into two subspecies: 1) Central and West African populations and 2) the rest of the continent. The former, again arbitrarily and without the agreement of the international body, CITES, is considered endangered by U.S. authorities; the latter is considered threatened.

You'll get no argument from me. The African lion is threatened, primarily by habitat loss and human encroachment. I happen to believe that *carefully regulated* sport hunting is not only good for the lion, but essential, because it places very high value on an animal that is, otherwise, simply an extremely dangerous nuisance to rural Africans. The American safari market is by far the largest in the world, so the inability to import legally taken lions has, in essence, devalued them, and this is not good. Regrettably, lions from Benin, Burkina Faso, Cameroon, and the Central African Republic are unlikely to ever again be importable into the United States despite the fact that these countries have been conservative in quota and have done a reasonably good job of managing lions in the remaining habitat.

Equally theoretically, at least at this writing, there should be a permit process for lions from East and Southern Africa, or at least from certain countries and areas across this vast region. Such a permit process has been in place for leopards since the 1980s. It has worked just fine, and the leopard has continued to thrive. So, maybe . . . but, also at this writing, one of the big unanswered questions is what will happen with South Africa's captive-bred lions.

South Africa's lion situation is extremely complex. There are genuine breeding populations in the major parks, and also on some of the larger private properties. Whether there are any genuine "free-range" lions in South Africa is another question. But there are certainly "born in the wild" lions, and there are "captive-reared" lions that are introduced, not only for hunting, but also into game-viewing estates. This business of hunting introduced lions is not new.

Lions breed extremely well in captivity, and by some estimates there are just short of ten thousand lions in breeding operations in South Africa. The purpose of these operations is to support the tourism industry, both hunting and photographic. I have generally been against the concept of hunting captive-reared lions, but, understand, I started hunting in Africa in a different time when a lion permit was fairly standard on a fourteen or twenty-one-day safari. Success was far from assured, even back in the 1970s, but I had my chances. Regardless of how the permit thing eventually shakes out, it's extremely unlikely that I will ever hunt another lion. Again, I had my chances, and most of them came along before hunting a wild lion became the highly specialized, controversial, and incredibly costly endeavor that it is today.

As the day heated up, the tracks started to wander; obviously the lion was looking for a shady patch to lie up in, and we lost the tracks several times. It was during one of these lapses when the lion roared. . . .

The lion was close and angry.

So, from my pedestal, it's been very easy for me to look down on the hunting of captive-reared lions, especially since I knew very little about it. Some years ago I hunted briefly (for other game) with a South African outfitter who was heavily invested in lion hunting, and during the hunt we had some frank discussions. I fully understood that, although not inexpensive, these captive-reared lion hunts offered a lower-cost alternative, thus allowing more hunters to experience a lion hunt. I also understood that some hunters do these hunts purely because of cost, but others do them after partaking in two or three unsuccessful lion hunts elsewhere.

This gent gave me some other arguments to consider. He believes the South African lions take pressure off wild lions elsewhere, and this may be true. He also showed me the regulations—they vary by province—and this hunting is regulated. By law there are minimum periods a lion may be released before a hunt is conducted. By law, at least in the Northwest Province, baiting is not allowed and the hunt must be conducted on foot. One more thing I hadn't thought about: If the practice is stopped, as many hunters, nonhunters, and antihunters alike would prefer, what exactly is going to happen to those nine-thousand-plus lions in captivity?

My curiosity was up, and I realized that I was mentally condemning something I'd never seen and knew little about. That's not good journalism. We talked about me observing a couple of these hunts, but my friend was terribly injured in a vehicle accident the next year and we never put it together.

Fast-forward a bit. Donna wanted to take a lion, and the only way we could possibly afford it was a South African lion hunt. Also, even then the urgency was building. It's been clear for some time that importation of lions was going to change, and not for the better; moreover, the Cecil incident fell right into the hands of the antis and created a perfect storm. But that's now. In 2013 I still had no desire to do a South African lion hunt for myself, but I had a great desire to see one done.

We shopped around quite a bit, eventually deciding we'd be better off to stick with friends. Corné Kruger of Namibia-based Omujeve Safaris told us he did lion hunts on a big property in South Africa's Kalahari that was pure tracking. With him we would be hunting lions that had been in the wild for at least six months. I never got a chance to do a tracking hunt—back then Botswana lions were way above my pay grade—so tracking in the red Kalahari sand sounded awesome.

Donna was joined by a doctor friend, Heather Smith, who would also be hunting. I was along as a pure observer. We flew into northwestern South Africa and drove for about six hours. Bradley Augistin of Sans Souci Safaris picked us up and we talked lion hunting most of the way. One of his hands was in a cast—he'd been badly bitten by a lioness a couple of weeks earlier. He had gotten off very lucky—the lioness was shot off him just as she got his hand in her mouth. That reminded me of something I'd heard several times: These lions are not less dangerous than wild lions—they are perhaps more dangerous because they have little fear of or respect for humans.

A young eland bull near camp. A herd of elands came into camp every evening. Perhaps they felt safer there?

Accommodations were excellent with a well-appointed central lodge, full of good Kalahari trophies, and private rooms in outlying brick buildings. Corné

Heather Smith flattened this really beautiful lion on the second mock charge. It was a very exciting hunt.

couldn't make it down from Namibia for the hunt, but we were joined that evening by Omujeve's Japsie Blaauw, a great young PH who you'll hear more about later.

The place was classic Kalahari: fine red sand, shepherd's trees, and patches of thornbush. First off we checked the rifles. Donna brought a Proof Research .338, plenty of gun for a lion. Heather didn't bring a rifle and was issued the ranch's .300 Winchester Magnum, to my thinking a bit light. Guns all good, the ladies decided Heather was up first, and we headed out to look for tracks . . . and look for tracks . . . and look for tracks.

A very few really good trackers can follow lions on hard ground *sometimes*, but generally it takes soft soil to hold the imprint of a cat's paw. Kalahari sand is ideal for capturing tracks, but determining the age of a track in dry sand is a special skill; tracks last a long time, so the age is determined by windblown leaves and other debris in the track. On that first day it didn't matter because we never found a fresh track. Obviously this was a big place; we rarely retraced our steps, and although we did see the boundary fence, I think we only saw it once.

Mind you, being skeptical of this situation, I was paying attention. Bradley insisted that the lions present, though all introduced, had been there for some months. OK, understood, but what shocked me was that Bradley told me that, immediately after release, they watch their lions for a few days. So far no lion had taken more than three days to make a natural kill. The prime candidates for lion meals there are gemsboks, kudus, and wildebeests; clearly that offers a major testament to Mom Nature!

He said, further, that their "grid" of roads excludes a lot of country, so it isn't unusual to take two or three days to find a fresh track to follow. In Heather's case it was day three, after covering a whole lot of miles that, eventually, got pretty boring, just like all cat hunting. Per Bradley (and I say "per Bradley" because I can't know for sure, but have no reason to question it), they have a couple of small prides operating on the property. The track we found, however, was a lone male. Whether kudus, gemsboks, lions, or whatever, there are old tracks everywhere; the trackers showed me *why* these were fresh: clean edges, no sand, no leaves. The tracks were made that morning. We left the vehicle and took the spoor.

The track ran straight and true for several kilometers. This lion was not hunting, not seeking water, just moving. Then the track started to meander and was temporarily lost when we jumped the cat. I saw him moving to our left at a couple hundred yards, a fantastic lion—but now we pretty much had to start over. We tracked into midday, and although it was still winter, the day was warm. Sooner or later the cat would look for shade, and when he did the track wandered and circled, and was again lost. The trackers cast left and right, and we stayed put.

Because I was carrying only a camera, no rifle, this had already been a different kind of lion hunt for me. Donna was carrying a rifle, but this was Heather's lion, so we were just along for the ride. While the trackers were looking for the spoor, I took the opportunity to step off a few yards to answer a call of nature. That's where I was when the lion roared.

This is a very clear track from Donna's lion. He is obviously a very big male, but tracks this clear and sharp aren't common in Kalahari sand.

I'm not sure who levitated, but in an instant Donna was beside me, and we were in a tight huddle with Heather and crew up front. Aside from the fright, I learned something interesting in that scary moment. The lion was close, but at close range the nature of the sound is such that it was impossible to tell where it came from . . . at best there was a vague

Donna's lion didn't have as long a mane as Heather's, but it was the largest-bodied lion I have ever seen. She used a Proof Research rifle in .338 Winchester Magnum, not always legal but a very good choice for lion.

direction, but nothing more. Perhaps intimidation is part of the lion's hunting tactic; I was intimidated, for sure!

The lion was in a thick patch of bush about fifty yards from where we were standing, and eventually we spotted him because of his lashing tail. Bradley and Japsie took Heather forward a few steps and got her on sticks, and as the tail lashing became more urgent, I was pretty sure we were going to wear this thing. The tail stopped, he came at us with a deep growl, and then, fortunately, he pulled up short, a mock charge. He came forward once more, emphasizing his point, and on the second go Heather was ready and shot him straight in the chest, just under the chin. He dropped to the shot and never moved—so much for my assessment of proper cartridges!

Needless to say, it was a gorgeous lion, and perfectly shot. Hunting was over for that day, and it's entirely possible we started a bit late the next morning, looking for Donna's lion. Same deal, it took a couple of days to find a fresh track, and it was late in the morning of the second day when we found another huge track.

Heather's lion had taken us more than six miles. Donna's lion didn't take us quite that far, but it got interesting early. We'd been on the tracks for a couple hours, going slow, when the wind did nearly a 180, changing from quartering to us to straight behind us. Well, at that stage it was not an issue because we had no idea where the lion had gone, so we continued to track. Shortly the tracks began to meander; clearly the lion was looking for a place to lie down. Then the tracks lined out again, moving fast from

Heather and Donna relax and take their boots off after a long day. The ground is fairly level, but it isn't easy walking in the sandy soil.

the point where the lion had been standing when the wind changed.

We found some shade and sat down for a half-hour or more to let the lion and the wind settle down. Until this point we'd been tracking an unaware lion, but now he'd clearly smelled us, so the longest stretch of tracking lay ahead. No worries . . . he'd need to lie down before we did.

So we tracked for a couple more hours, and the track led us into an open meadow. I was behind and didn't hear what was said, but I saw Japsie's body language change as he moved Donna forward and set up the sticks. Me, I'm still looking for the lion, but, of course, I'm looking in the brush on the far side of the clearing. It never occurred to me to look *up*! The lion was in the fork of a huge dead tree, ten feet off the ground, looking at its back trail and, thus, directly at us. It was very strange!

Donna shot him out of the tree. She hit him well as the .338 is plenty of gun. But strange now became eerie, for this lion refused to die. In one of those short times that seems an eternity, he eventually gave it up. Donna still has nightmares about those yellow eyes staring at her when she moved up for the finisher. Heather's lion perhaps had the better mane, but Donna's lion was an amazing brute, the biggest-bodied lion I've ever seen.

So that's a straightforward account of two South African-style lion hunts. It was a good experience, made better by the fact that we knew exactly what the story was. The biggest part of this issue is that too many operators are still selling these hunts as something they are not. Some hunters still tell the story sort of like this: "Things were slow for several days, and then a lion moved in from Botswana." Sure, and I'm Peter Pan! Given an honest seller and a willing buyer, I no longer have a problem with these hunts. I still don't want to do one for myself, but remember, I've had my chances, and I neither need nor want to take another lion. But I want you to be able to dream of hunting a lion, so I hope the permit process proceeds as it should.

Chapter Twenty-One

Arly

"More Americans have walked on the moon than have hunted in Burkina Faso," said my friend Arjun Reddy. At that time he was probably right—very few Americans have hunted in this West African country, and not many more had ever heard of it. Thanks to that sad hotel terror attack in 2016, more people have heard of Burkina Faso today—what a way to get on the map!—but it's always been there. When I was in school, the name of the country was Upper Volta. Maybe that rings a bell, but it's far too colonial in connotation, so in 1984 the name was changed to Burkina Faso. This translates to "land of upright people," meaning *honest* rather than *tall.*

The country sits west of Nigeria, south of Niger and Mali, and northwest of Benin. It is, thus, sub-Saharan Africa, arid country, but south of the great Sahara and north of the forest zone. The game is similar to that found in northern Cameroon and northern C.A.R., except there are no Derby elands (but probably more roans). The hunting areas in Burkina Faso are in the easternmost corner; the hunting areas in neighboring Benin are in the northwest, so, essentially, they come together, with exactly the same species and similar conditions. I think more Americans have hunted in Benin than Burkina Faso, and there is little reason to hunt in *both* countries—although I might.

The entry to the Arly camp showed a good map of Burkina Faso. Our hunting area was in the southeastern corner, along the edge of Arly National Park with the Benin border just to the south.

On the surface, maybe it sounds like there's no reason to hunt *either*, which may be why so few Americans have. Both countries are well within the French sphere of influence, with primarily French outfitters, and primarily a French clientele. More American hunters are "collectors" than Europeans, and neither country offers major indigenous rarities; there are no bongos and no Derby elands. There were, however, a couple of westernmost races of antelopes I didn't have: nagor reedbucks and West African kobs.

Perhaps more interesting is that it is an exotic location, a place relatively few people have visited, and yet it's an extremely inexpensive destination. Daily rates are reasonable, as are government trophy fees. For most of us the primary quarries will be buffaloes (the smaller West African savanna buffaloes) and western roans, the largest race of roans. This region offers the most reasonable opportunity on the African continent to hunt buffaloes and/or roans.

I can't tell you which is better, since I haven't hunted in Benin yet, but I can tell you Burkina Faso was *really good!* Donna and I were at an SCI fundraiser in New York when we ran into Arjun Reddy. He'd just come back from a hunt with Arly Safaris in Burkina Faso and was raving about the amount of game he'd seen, and he had the pictures to prove it. I was hooked, so I set us up for a hunt there the following March.

Arly National Park lies on the border between Benin and Burkina Faso, with the hunting area adjacent to the park. The safari camp there is "joint use," a large facility near the park entrance that can house photographic traffic for Arly or hunting clients along the boundary. Chalets are blessedly air-conditioned when the generator is running. The staff is competent, friendly, and well-trained; the cuisine is decidedly French and very good.

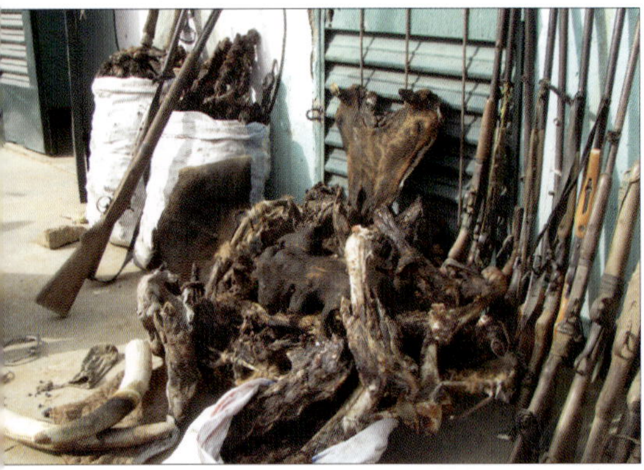

As is the case in so much of Africa today, poaching is a serious issue. This is some of the meat, ivory, and illegal firearms confiscated by park rangers during the 2013 season.

Burkina Faso lies well north of the equator, but it's a warm country, with short winters and springs and long, hot summers. We were there in mid-March,

The nagor reedbuck is a small bohor reedbuck only huntable today in Benin and Burkina Faso. This was an animal that I really wanted and hadn't hunted, so for the first few days Arjun Reddy and I focused on this small reedbuck, eventually finding a very nice one.

when midday temperatures were already rising into the low 100s. As with most dry climates, the temperature swing between midday and midnight is significant; mornings were pleasant, but the days heated quickly and early evening hours were still sweltering. Thus, the air-conditioning units in the chalets were just plain awesome, and so was a large and gorgeously clear and clean swimming pool in the center of the camp. Hunting days are short in that climate; most mornings we'd get back to camp between ten and eleven, and go straight into the pool. While the generator didn't run all the time, the staff wasn't sparing of it. Most afternoons we could take a nap in air-conditioned splendor, and then head back out around four o'clock for a late-afternoon hunt.

Our professional hunter was Ismael Compaore, brother of the safari company's owner. He proved extremely competent, a good judge of trophy quality, and an amazing eye for quickly reading the terrain and planning a successful stalk. Like most folks there, he spoke French plus his own tribal tongue. This was no problem for hunting, and in any case we had two English speakers on hand, a white guy named Tony Dagman, serving as camp manager, and Larry, a young local fellow whose English was excellent.

But I regret not being able to have detailed discussions with Ismael because his "thing" was lion hunting, as was his father's passion before him. When I was there, his company got only two permits per year and were invariably successful. At this point in his career Ismael had guided clients to twenty-nine lions; his late father more than fifty. The legend of these lions is their bodies are large but their manes are short, but this is not uniform. Ismael showed us photos of some truly spectacular lions, and I would have liked to have talked to him more directly about lion hunting.

The hunting was quite simple and extremely productive. This was partly because we had a good PH and a great tracker named Palamanga, but also because there was a lot of game in the area. As I gathered, the hunting concession was a long slice of country along the park boundary. In the afternoons we'd sometimes drive a considerable distance, then work our way back, but in the mornings we would often hunt straight from camp. At that time of year there was more water in the concession than in the adjacent park, so there was plenty of game movement back and forth.

We didn't encounter buffaloes every day, but probably every other day and a few times in herds of two hundred and more. We saw small groups of roans every day, likewise sing-sing waterbucks. Reedbucks and kobs were plentiful. Harnessed bushbucks were scattered, but we saw quite a few. Western hartebeests were present but scarce; I think we saw brief flashes of two small groups, but we weren't hunting them so we didn't worry about it. Strangely missing, however, were pygmy antelopes. Western bush duikers and red-flanked duikers occur, but we

The swimming pool at the camp was clean and absolutely clear, and it proved to be a real blessing when we got back from our morning hunt. By eleven A.M. *temperatures in March were well over 100 degrees F.*

caught brief flashes of the former and never saw the latter. Warthogs also occur, but we saw few.

Ismael leads Donna on a stalk for her roan. The roan is probably the most common large antelope and we saw plenty . . . but it takes some looking to find a good bull.

To some extent I put this seemingly odd mix down to an amazing selection of predators. We never actually saw lions, but we weren't looking for them. We heard them roar frequently, and we saw fresh tracks every day. Obviously buffaloes were their primary prey, but we saw leopard tracks and Ismael captured photos of a big male with a trail camera.

It's interesting to look on the map of Africa and appreciate just how far west Burkina Faso is, and yet it has lions, leopards, and, big surprise, one morning we saw a female cheetah with half-grown cub! Another big surprise: We saw lots of elephants, sometimes as many as a hundred in one day. My understanding is the majority of Burkina Faso is pretty much devoid of wildlife, and certainly we saw nothing on the long drive from Ouagadougou (pronounced *Wah-ga-doo-goo*) . . . but in this corner of Burkina Faso, the country is clearly doing a good job of managing its wildlife. As a reward, the United States has now devalued their lions . . .

I had taken most of the animals present in the area on hunts in Cameroon and C.A.R., so Donna and I were splitting the safari: She would take the roan and hoped for a harnessed bushbuck; I wanted a reedbuck and a kob; and both of us had a buffalo on license. This plan put Donna up first for buffalo, and it was the second or third day, just breaking dawn, when we ran into a group of buffaloes shortly after leaving camp. Only slightly spooked, they moved off into the bush, but we had to wait for enough light before we could follow.

A half-hour later Palamanga showed us the buffaloes, dark forms in trees ahead. I dropped back and Ismael took Donna and cameraman Matt Young on a slow, perfect approach. The buffaloes were on the other side of a grassy watercourse just feeding. Donna set up on sticks and in a couple of minutes a nice bull stepped out. Through my binocular I saw the bullet hit the shoulder, and although the bull was long gone before another shot was possible, I wasn't worried.

Except this buffalo hadn't read the script. We followed him through a long, hot morning and jumped him twice, but Donna never got another shot. We followed until noon, and past noon—and by then it was beastly hot, 130 degrees Fahrenheit. Truthfully, we pushed it too long; the heat was getting to all of us, and Donna was getting ill. Heat exhaustion is nothing to mess with, and at that point we had no choice but to break off the pursuit. We found her buffalo a day later, dead, and I found the bullet hole in the shoulder, pretty much where I thought it was and where it should be. Who knows, odd things happen sometimes, but the real message was to be careful of that equatorial heat. It was a couple of days before she was more or less back to normal, and I don't think she felt right the rest of the trip.

Hunting buffaloes is always important to me, but the one animal I wanted most was the nagor reedbuck. This is an area where you can run into any of the animals present at any time, so it isn't exactly correct to say we concentrated on this, but we did put a priority on trying to find a good one. I wasn't in on the conference that classified African animals; to my eye the nagor reedbuck is visually indistinguishable from the Nigerian bohor reedbuck to the east but, hey, I don't make these rules, and, after all, this pretty little antelope was a major reason, *er, excuse*, for me being there.

Great pains are taken to recover animals whole, then they're taken back to camp where weights and measurements are carefully recorded. We know for certain this roan weighed 297 kilograms, or 653 pounds; it was a very big antelope.

Securing one was not difficult. Ismael knew where to look, primarily in areas with long grass, typical of all reedbucks. We saw quite a few females and a couple of small bucks, but when a female and a young buck jumped up near the track and bounded away, they were followed by a really nice male.

The smallest of the kobs is the West African kob, which is very common in this area. This is a fairly good representative of the race.

We dismounted and made a half-circle, finding the big boy standing in tall grass a couple hundred yards from the road, looking back. I was carrying Donna's Blaser .270, and we were a bit too close to set up sticks. Taking a couple of deep breaths, I took the quartering-to shot offhand at maybe eighty yards, anchoring the buck nicely in his tracks.

By now Donna was feeling a lot better, so we put a priority on getting her a roan. These were western roans, largest of the roans, easily the most common large antelope in the area. We saw at least a few every day, but seeing roans and finding a good bull isn't exactly the same. We got a glimpse of what seemed a really good bull, but a careful stalk failed and we never saw him again. A couple of bulls looked good from a distance, but not so up close, so we passed. Then, one bright midmorning, from a low ridge, we glassed a beautiful bull working his way along a streambed.

Ismael and Palamanga put their heads together. I would have made a circle; they felt we could drop into the streambed and there would be enough cover for a direct approach. Fortunately, I kept my mouth shut because they were right, and I probably would have overshot the bull and given him our wind. Palamanga led us carefully and slowly into dead ground, and then increased the pace, obviously intending to cut the bull off. It worked except that, at less than a hundred yards, all a tall person—like Palamanga—could see were thick, curving horns traversing the skyline. I could see part of the horns; Donna, six inches lower, probably couldn't even see that.

My West African savanna buffalo was taken from a bachelor group that had both red and black bulls in it. We think this was the largest, and definitely the darkest.

But we had the wind and we had the roan's course and direction, so Ismael carefully moved us up a few yards and set up the sticks. The roan crossed the streambed forty yards ahead of us, but was blocked by brush. Then he walked up a low, open rise, and Donna got the shot at sixty yards. She was using her .375 and hit him hard, then again, and he was down in the open, a great roan and one of Africa's very special antelopes.

The West African kob is visually indistinguishable from the Central African kob of Cameroon and the C.A.R., although historically the horns are a bit smaller. Although found only in small groups, the kob is probably the most common antelope in the area, essentially replacing the impala in the savannas of Central and West Africa. Getting a nice one was more a matter of when than if, but late one evening just at dusk I took a very nice one, so you could say my safari was complete . . . except for a buffalo.

There were plenty around, so it's an overstatement to say we had trouble, but we weren't closing the deal very well. For two hours one morning we worked a big herd of a couple hundred. There were good bulls in there, but we couldn't sort one out. Eventually they moved across a watercourse that marked the park boundary, putting them off limits. We tracked another group of bulls, and they also led us to the boundary. It was getting late in the hunt when we found fresh tracks of three bulls.

We took the tracks at 6 A.M. and bumped them the first time about 7:30. There were actually four bulls, one very red and the others black, just bits and pieces in really thick stuff. I genuinely thought we were going to get a shot, but they saw us first and clattered off. At this point it was still nice and cool, but it was starting to heat up, and it was a whole lot hotter when, three hours later, we were still on the track. These buffaloes aren't poached, and we hadn't bumped them all that badly, so I don't know what was on their bovine minds, but they kept walking, straight and true, and we kept following.

The ground was baked hard, but Ismael and Palamanga held the tracks beautifully for three straight hours. We'd come through a belt of thick stuff, an ideal place for the buffaloes to lie down, and probably an impossible place to get a shot. Then the country opened up, and there, like a gift, were the buffaloes on the far side of a sparse glade. They were about a hundred and fifty yards away and we had the wind. We watched them for a moment, and for the first time we realized there were *five* bulls, four black and one red, in a tight little knot. I'd had the red buffalo in mind, but by far the best bull was one of the black ones, much better horns than his fellows. Using a big termite mound for cover, Ismael duck-walked us to about seventy-five yards, and then we stepped to the right and he put up the sticks.

As if on command the largest bull, the black one, detached from the group and walked slowly to the right, behind another termite mound and then in the clear. I was shooting an Aimpoint red-dot sight on my Montana Rifles .375, the first time I'd used such a sight on a buffalo. The bright red dot was amazingly clear on the black shoulder. The first shot looked good, felt good, and obviously hit hard—but then a strange thing happened.

It was a bit of a chore to get the vehicle to the buffalo and get it loaded whole, but we know the weight was 471.6 kilograms or 1,038 pounds—about right for a big bull of this West African savanna race of buffaloes.

Upon receiving the bullet, the bull turned and ran directly toward us. I don't think he was really charging, but who knows? For sure he was headed straight at us! With the TV camera rolling, I suppose I could have let him come a bit farther, but at this point reflexes kicked in. He closed a bit, and then I put the red dot on the center of his chest, stopping him with the second shot and dropping him with a third shot to the neck.

It took a little while to get the truck in, but there were procedures to follow. In Burkina Faso, whenever possible animals are loaded *whole* and taken back to camp. Weights are taken on a good scale, along with horn and body measurements, and all data are carefully recorded.

We often hear that the largest race of African buffaloes, the southern Cape buffalo, is a "ton of black fury." Although I've never weighed one whole, I'm pretty sure I've never seen one that weighed a ton; fifteen hundred pounds is a lot more like it for a really big bull. But as you progress westward across the continent, they get smaller. The Nile buffalo isn't as big, and the Central African savanna buffaloes are smaller than the Nile. These West African savanna buffaloes are smaller yet, although considerably larger than the true dwarf forest buffaloes. With this one, a big bull with excellent horns, I can say that the exact, precise weight was 471.6 kilograms—1,037.5 pounds—which is pretty much in line with what the references say a big bull of this race is supposed to weigh.

Our only failure, if you could call it that, was that Donna didn't get a harnessed bushbuck. We saw three or four nice rams and made some stalks, but each time they eluded us in tall grass and thick bush, and there was never a chance for a shot. That's OK; maybe that's an excuse to go back sometime, and I wouldn't mind at all, but if I had it to do over again I'd go a bit earlier in the year before the heat gets so brutal.

All in all, Burkina Faso is a hidden gem. Firearms clearance in Ouagadougou was the quickest and easiest I've ever experienced. The hotel there was clean and comfortable—and *not* the same one that was the target of the 2016 terrorist attack. The drive to camp was a long day, but the countryside was pretty and we were in an air-conditioned vehicle. The camp was fine and the food excellent—and its clean, cool swimming pool was a huge bonus. The game was plentiful and visibly undisturbed. This country is far off the beaten track and the hunting industry is small—but they're doing a good job.

CHAPTER TWENTY-TWO

BACK TO THE VALLEY

We'd had an exceptionally tough buffalo hunt. This isn't particularly unusual in the Zambezi Valley in June. The cover is still thick and green, making it relatively easy to close on buffalo—but extremely difficult to see them and sort the herds. Now we were down to the afternoon of the ninth day, our penultimate, and we finally had a chance. A big herd had come across the sandriver from Dande, working its way along a system of hills and gullies.

At a distance we'd seen a couple of nice bulls in the herd. Using the terrain well, PH Mike Payne had gotten us not only ahead of them but also above them, so we could look across a *korongo* and see them working their way along the opposite hillside. It wasn't my buffalo; Chad Allen had purchased the hunt at SCI. The auction package included my company, a dubious benefit perhaps offset by a Blaser R8 .375 that was also part of the deal. So I stayed with the trackers, able to see a few buffaloes while Mike and Chad worked down a brushy finger, looking for a clear shot.

Dry sand riverbeds are a major feature in the Lower Zambezi. There are usually some pot holes that hold water almost throughout the season, and the soft sand is an ideal medium for picking up fresh tracks.

Midday lunch break in a shady spot on a sand river, typical of Zambezi Valley hunting.

About an hour of light remained when I heard the shot, and I was sure I heard the *thunk* of the bullet striking. For sure I heard buffaloes snorting and running everywhere, so I went down the finger to Mike and Chad, the former staring intently through his binocular, the latter still standing, rifle ready over sticks. Mike pointed out where the buffalo had stood, about ninety yards across the gully . . . and to the thick stuff beyond, where they'd just glimpsed a buffalo moving.

Like me and our trackers, Mike had heard the hit, and the reaction had looked good. The herd was long gone, so we assumed the single buffalo was Chad's, and that it was hit. We never saw it again and heard nothing more, but with light starting to go, we waited as long as we could before sliding down into the streambed and clambering up the far side to see what we could find. There was no blood and no indication of a hit, but with the light going, blood would be hard to find. Believing it was a good hit, we walked to the truck in last twilight and went back to camp in good spirits.

Next morning, in the clear light of day, things looked a whole lot different. There was no blood anywhere, so we went back to where Mike was certain the buffalo had stood. Yes, we found the place where we'd last seen the buffalo, but instead of a buffalo we found a stout sapling with a fresh bullet scar, nearly cut in half. So far our detective work had been good. "OK," we said, "if that was *here* and the buffalo stood *there*" . . . so we took a few steps . . . and hidden in the grass, we found a rock centered by a bullet.

Now we had to bring in the game scout, show him the sapling, show him the rock, show him where the buffalo had stood, and show him the couple of running tracks we could find. We all had heard the bullet hit *something* solid, but that isn't always definitive. To my mind, though, the forensics were definitive.

The stick deflected the bullet, and the impact on the rock was too low to have hit anything. Lack of blood also isn't always definitive, but put it all together, and it appeared the bullet had passed under the buffalo's chest, struck the rock just behind, and spooked the bull enough to cause a reaction similar to a hit. Our game scout agreed, and the hunt could continue. Good thing, because on the walk in we'd heard buffaloes. The herd hadn't gone five hundred yards, so even though it was now late on the last morning, we were far from done.

We were in Chewore South, one of five Designated Safari Areas that make up what's called the Lower Zambezi complex. In the years when I was filming the *Tracks* series and hunting with Chifuti Safaris, I spent time in all of them: Sapi, Chewore North and South, Dande North and South. Of them I would have judged Dande North and Chewore South to be the best for buffalo, but I hadn't been back in the Zambezi Valley for

At this particular time we had difficulty finding buffalo tracks, but the Lower Zambezi is a great place to track dinosaurs. These petrified and extremely clear dinosaur tracks are a famous landmark in Chewore South.

Plains game is always scarce in the valley, but on this hunt even impala seemed scarce and unusually spooky. Chad Allen managed to take a good impala ram midway through the hunt . . . and that's just about the only opportunity we had.

several years, and that can be a long time in Africa. We'd hunted together many times, but Mike Payne was no longer with Chifuti; he'd gone out on his own with Leon Du Plessis and established Save Safaris in the northern part of the Save Valley Conservancy. Chifuti was no longer the concessionaire in Chewore South, and, technically, we weren't even supposed to be there.

The auction hunt was to be conducted on the conservancy, but the game department was playing games and hadn't issued the permits. To his credit (and undoubtedly at great expense), at the last minute Mike changed venues, getting us clearance to do the hunt in Chewore South.

At first I was delighted. Just a few years earlier it had been a place where one might see a thousand buffaloes in a week. Even then, though, we'd started to worry. We could see lots of buffaloes and plenty of bulls in the herds, but this is among few places in Africa today where I'd consider lions overpopulated.

It was the late Ian Gibson, whom I've talked about before, who pointed this fact out to me. "See how few calves you see in the herds," he'd told me once. "We're headed for trouble here."

He was right. In 2010 and 2011 the herds were still big, but calves were rare, picked off by lions. Now, in 2014, it was possible we were seeing the results. It was also possible that it was just early and green, and equally possible that there was better grass to the east or west. Whatever the reason, or combination of reasons, we had one of the most difficult buffalo hunts I've ever experienced in the valley. We didn't encounter buffaloes every day, but that isn't unusual. In total we saw enough buffaloes, probably eight or ten small herds—but not a single one had a mature, hard-bossed bull among them.

We also saw very little sign of bachelor bulls, *dagga* boys, and this wasn't like the valley I remembered. There was a small group, three or four, hanging around along the Chewore. We tracked them twice, both times into incredibly thick stuff, both times we were close to getting a shot when midday eddies gave us away and the buffaloes hightailed it for regions unknown. There were a few other tracks that went the wrong way, meaning across the boundary, but the lack of bachelor bulls added to the lack of bulls in the herds was disappointing.

Of course, the majority of the buffaloes could have been elsewhere at that particular time. On the fifth day Chad's buddy, Rick Carrol, who was hunting with Leon Du Plessis, got into a big herd along the boundary with Dande North and shot a very nice bull with little difficulty. Still, we saw lots of signs of predators—lions, hyenas, wild dogs, and more leopard tracks than I have ever seen in the valley, including a couple of really big tracks.

It would have been an awesome time to hunt leopards, but we weren't hunting leopards, and if we were, we'd have had a tough time finding bait animals. We were seeing "enough" buffaloes, but we were seeing almost no plains game. Impalas, usually plentiful, were scarce and jittery. We encountered a handful of kudus, and we saw a bit of zebra sign . . . and in ten days, that was about it. In part, of course, this was also because of the time of year: It was too thick and too green for glassing, there was lots of water in the bush, and the valley never has a real concentration of plains game anyway. It's impossible to reach a fair conclusion, but it wasn't the Chewore South I remembered.

It was now midmorning on the last day. I think Chad's "miss" crushed us all after so much effort, but it happens. I've missed two buffaloes because of unseen sticks, and hit another with a bullet that struck a branch, keyholed sideways, and hit

Chad Allen and I are standing in front of an exceptionally large baobab tree in Chewore South. A tree like this is many hundreds of years old.

two feet left of where I was aiming—fortunately it went in the center of the neck. So no big deal, except why *now*? I'll say this for Chad Allen and Mike Payne—they kept smiling, and we kept trying.

So now the herd was moving ahead of us and the wind was dead wrong. We thought they were still on our side of the boundary, but close, so we couldn't afford to spook them. Mike took us off the tracks and back to the truck and we made a couple of wide loops, ensuring that they hadn't crossed out of the concession and trying to pinpoint their location without giving them our wind.

By now it was midday, hot and still. We hadn't seen fresh tracks for a couple of hours, but we thought the herd was probably resting in a flat of thick bush just up from a sandy channel. So, with the wind right, we walked across the hot sand, up a shallow bank, and through a patch of long grass.

The grass thinned fifty yards from the riverbed. To our left were three or four palm trees, and beyond a small clearing lay thick thornbush where we thought we would find the herd. Mike's tracker was in front, followed by Mike with his Krieghoff

Camps in the Zambezi Valley are never fancy, but always comfortable. In Chewore South we had "Botswana-style" tents with en suite shower and toilet in the rear.

Chad Allen (left) and Mike Payne with their amazing last-day buffalo, taken in a full and absolutely unprovoked charge. While I say "unprovoked," the buffalo had recently been mauled by a lion and was understandably not on his best behavior.

.470, and then came Chad who was still carrying his double .470 because, after all, we'd started the morning expecting to follow-up a hit buffalo. I was trailing behind, rifle slung, along with Chad's buddy, South African PH Francois Rudman, who was, like me, just along for the ride. Francois was carrying Chad's Blaser.

As we stepped out of the grass, a buffalo bull rose from the shade of the nearest palm tree, probably not thirty yards from us. He rose facing us, shook his head once, and immediately launched a full-out charge. As the buffalo accelerated, everything else slowed down. I can still see it in slow motion.

Mike's tracker ducked and vanished, looping back to the right and, thus, giving an opening for a shot. Chad took a half-step left, Mike a half-step right, and they stood shoulder to shoulder. By now the buffalo was less than twenty yards and closing, head up, black muzzle and black horns gleaming in the sun, totally magnificent.

By this time Francois and I both had our rifles off our shoulders, but we never raised them. This was not our show, and things seemed eerily under control. Amazingly, calm but direct, I heard Mike say, "Take him, Chad. Take him now."

I don't think the instruction was needed. A half-second later Chad's first barrel centered the buffalo full on the chest, followed instantly by Mike's first barrel. Ten thousand foot-pounds of energy turned the buffalo away, then ten thousand more to the shoulder, the third and fourth shot sounding as one. The bull was down, ten yards in front of us.

Only then did we hear the other buffaloes, disturbed by the commotion. The herd was directly ahead of us, close—this old bull had chosen to lie down on our side of the herd, and in a few moments we understood why he had charged. A lion had tried to pull him down, maybe three or four days earlier. His tail and right hip were deeply lacerated and his penis sheath was badly torn, the wounds deep and suppurating. One could theorize that the lion had taken him from behind, lost its grip, and slipped underneath. It didn't take much imagination to figure out why the bull was irritable or, why, as we approached, he'd figured: *That's enough of that!*

CHAPTER TWENTY-THREE

THE GOLDEN ORYX

Honest, it wasn't the unusual golden color phase of gemsbok that took me on this hunt; in fact, I didn't even intend to take one. In part it was business, in that I'd agreed to accompany the buyer of a hunt auctioned at SCI, something I try to do once or twice a year. Mind you, *I* certainly wouldn't pay extra for my company, but it's a ploy that seems to add value to a donated hunt. I didn't really have to do this particular one, but it sounded interesting. Over the years I've spent a lot of time in Namibia, but never in the south. So when Barry Burchell of Frontier Safaris asked me to join this hunt in southern Namibia, I immediately agreed.

Barry Burchell actually lives in the Eastern Cape northwest of Port Elizabeth, but he and his family have two large ranches in Namibia. The northern property is near the southern boundary of Etosha National Park; the southern "farm" (their term) is near Keetmanshoop, some three hundred miles south of Windhoek. This semidesert country lies between Namibia's two great deserts, the Kalahari to the east and Namib to the north.

Weaver bird nests are a fairly common sight in Namibia. These little birds gather in large colonies, and eventually the weight of their nests will break down the tree.

As might be expected, the area is great for Namibia's desert game: gemsboks, springboks, hartebeests, kudus, wildebeests, elands, and more. But while the golden oryx wasn't my motivation, it was part of the auction package, and on this ranch, these animals are the Burchell family's pride and joy. The golden oryx breeding program was started

Barry Burchell and I after my shot on a beautiful gold oryx bull. The 140-grain bullet from the .264 hit perfectly and exited, but I was surprised that the bull ran as far as it did before expiring.

years ago by Burchell's late father, Fred Burchell. In recent years, when "color phases" have become highly valued by game ranchers in both Namibia and South Africa, what neighbors once thought folly turned into a marvelous investment.

The gemsbok is normally fawn-gray, with black and white underparts and facial masks. The golden oryx has no black at all; the colors are essentially muted with the body color a pale tan, which looks yellowish in sunlight. The markings that should be black, including the face mask, are a darker tan that is very golden. I saw one mounted life-size in Dick and Mary Cabela's trophy room and remarked on how beautiful it was. For a few moments as I stood looking at it, I was stumped as to exactly what it was, which doesn't happen very often.

That said, I'm not really into the color phases of various African antelopes. Oh, sure, years ago I took white and black springbok and a white blesbok, all fairly common today. Although I've seen them and they're beautiful, I have no interest in the copper springbok and black impala, and much less in the numerous spotted and brindled "this and that" being bred today. I'm in agreement with SCI in its decision to call a halt to the addition of new "color-phase" categories. Of course, if I were a

A snappy double on very nice springbok. I didn't expect to take two, but the first ram went down so fast that the group didn't run, and Barry pointed out a second ram.

game rancher who had a unique herd, and if other game ranchers wanted to buy them at exceptional prices, I'd love them to death.

The golden oryx, however, is a bit different. Like all the color phases, it's an uncommon and recessive gene, but it does occur in the wild and has been known for centuries. The first historical reference was made near Swellendam in the Western Cape in the 1700s, describing an antelope that looked like a "roan antelope with gemsbok horns," a good description of the golden oryx. They are not as reddish as the roan, but closer in color to roan than the typical gemsbok. In 1965, one of the guys I worked with on the Weatherby committee took two on open ground near Meridan, Namibia—just a bit north of the Burchell ranch.

As the story goes, Fred Burchell saw a few of these oryxes on his ranch, and over time managed to capture a few more in the neighborhood. Theirs is a huge 100,000-acre spread, so this has not been an intensive breeding program in small paddocks. No herds are pure, and the gene remains recessive, but over time, with more golden oryxes of both sexes, there have been more golden offspring. They are extremely distinctive in a herd, and plentiful enough that a few can now be captured and sold annually, and a handful of older bulls can be hunted.

The hunt was purchased by my friend J. C. Bell and his family, who were trying to get their Global Sportman's Network off the ground—but the draft choice for the hunt was J.C.'s niece, retired Marine Warrant Officer Jill St. John. Although new to hunting, St. John is somewhat famous in our small Marine Corps world.

Warrant officers are typically in narrow specialties. In the army, the majority of helicopter pilots are warrant officers, or WOs. Marine Corps chopper pilots are commissioned officers, while our WOs are in technical specialties such as communications, maintenance, ordnance, and so forth. It's an awesome program: Young non-commissioned officers, usually sergeants or staff sergeants, apply and if accepted, go to school and are warranted as WO1. There are four more ascending pay grades; Jill retired as a Chief Warrant Officer Four, "CWO4," about equivalent in pay to a major with the familiar form of address being "Gunner." *Nobody* messes with a Marine Gunner in his or her specialty!

Typically warrant officers are not assigned to command, but they certainly can be, and in the chronically shorthanded Marine Corps world, they often are. That is where Jill's claim to fame comes into play. In Iraq she was in charge of a headquarters unit, but we still pride ourselves on every Marine being a rifleman first. So when things went to s--- (forgive me, but that's a common Marine phrase), she was the first female officer to lead ground troops in combat. By all accounts she did very well, but unfortunately got badly injured by an IED in the battle of Fallujah and was eventually medically retired.

I first met her uncle, J. C. Bell, at Mark Haldane's Zambeze Delta Safaris in Mozambique in 2012. That was J.C.'s first African hunt, but he got hooked and has returned several times. Jill went with him on another Mozambique hunt a year later, but I wasn't in camp, so although I'd met her at a convention I didn't really know her, but I most certainly knew *of* her. As I said, she was relatively new to hunting, but was also hooked on Africa. With the Marine Corps crossover we had a lot of common ground in multiple worlds, so it was a good group—made even better by Barry Burchell, a good guy and good host, and always full of fun.

The camp itself was also excellent, with private chalets marching along a knife-edge ridge and with a circular, central *boma* of unique and clever design. The outer part was walled against wind and chill. Inside was a roofed ring with bar, tables, and cooking area, but the center of the roof was open to the sky, allowing a sheltered campfire. A year later I would discover that this design was a miniature of the *boma* at Burchell's main camp in the Eastern Cape.

Namibia is ranch country, so, as in much hunting on the American plains, a windmill tower offers a good vantage point for glassing.

I suppose we could have started with other game, but Burchell is very proud of his golden oryxes, so he wanted to go after Jill's oryx first. As I said, they're not in separate herds at all; most herds will have a few. But that's breeding stock. What Barry wanted was to find older bulls wandering on their own. On vast acreage with lots of rocky hills and brushy canyons that's not especially easy, but he and his trackers knew generally where to look. Midafternoon on the first day, we found the perfect bull, older and with worn horns, wandering on a big flat by himself. Barry took us on a long stalk, and we caught him in some taller brush at the base of a low, rocky ridge.

Jill made a good shot, but not quite good enough; an hour later we caught up again, and this time her golden oryx stayed down for good. Up close it was really a gorgeous animal, and when Barry kept insisting that I should take one as well, I quit resisting!

I suppose there were some first-day jitters involved there—we are all subject to them. Over the next few days Jill shot a half-dozen more animals, mostly with more difficult shots, and all were perfect. She was using a McMillan .300 Winchester Magnum. It had a big scope on it, not bad for this semidesert country, but in general we all agreed it was too much scope for African hunting. Even so, it worked well, and there's no doubt that a fast .30-caliber is one of the best choices for plains game, provided the shooter can handle it. Although a petite woman, she handled it very well.

Me, I took a different approach. When I was a kid I had a .264 Winchester Magnum and I thought it was magic. Also, as a youngster, I remember reading a story by Col. Charles Askins entitled "The .264 Winchester Magnum in Africa." I think it was about a Kenya hunt, and I remember that he shot a lot of plains game with it and extolled its virtues. A burglar got my .264 in 1980 before I had a chance to take it to Africa.

Jill St. John recalls her shot on this jackal as her best of the safari. It was dark and the jackal was some distance away, so I have no idea how she pulled it off, but it was perfect.

Often recalling that Askins story, I'd always wanted another one. Somewhere I came into one of Parker Ackley's rare *left-handed* Santa Barbara Mauser actions, and a good Obermayer

Jill made a good shot, but not quite good enough; an hour later we caught up again, and this time her golden oryx stayed down for good.

6.5mm barrel. Serengeti Rifles put them together into a left-hand, 26-inch-barrel .264. Expecting open ground, which we surely had, I figured it would be perfect for this kind of country. For bullets I was shooting a combination of old Winchester Power Points, the original .264 load, and new 140-grain Hornady InterLocks in handloads. Performance of both bullets was super, but in retrospect I'm not sure the 6.5mm was a perfect choice.

One day we went way off to the north where Barry told us there were lots of springboks. Jill shot first, taking a very nice ram, and then I took a turn. We found another group and made a stalk over rolling ground. My ram went down so fast that, spooky though they are, the rest didn't know what had happened. Another good ram stepped out, and Barry suggested I'd better take that one as well, so I did. It also went down in its tracks.

The springbok has a lot in common with the pronghorn: similar size, vaguely similar in appearance, and very similar hunting conditions. The .264 is a big gun on springbok, so it's no surprise these two dropped so fast. However, as the safari progressed, I started to see a difference. In the main I was shooting well. A zebra and "regular" gemsbok went down with one 140-grain bullet each, but, in a head-to-head comparison, they didn't go down as quickly as I thought they should have, and certainly not as quickly as Jill's animals shot with a 180-grain .30-caliber.

The first time this thought struck me was on my own golden oryx. We were driving through a rocky valley when we saw him run off to the left and go through a low, rocky saddle. Barry pronounced him good—meaning an older bull—so I grabbed the rifle and he grabbed sticks, and we hustled up into the rocks to the right of the saddle. As expected, the oryx had dropped into the next valley and stopped in some brush on the far side, looking back. I got on the sticks, and in a few seconds the oryx walked clear. He was, maybe, a hundred and sixty yards away, and it was all very simple. I shot him carefully toward the back of the center of the shoulder.

Both Barry and I were certain of the shot, but the gemsbok wasn't impressed. He ran hard to the right, and although I expected him to tumble at every step he kept going, running straight and strong and out of sight. The blood trail was wide and clear and simple to follow, but it led us three hundred yards down the valley . . . and then it turned left and went up through the rocks toward another saddle. He didn't make it quite that far; we found him just short of the pass, piled up in midstride, and hit perfectly.

One animal proves nothing, for every animal reacts differently upon receiving a bullet, and gemsboks are tough. Over the years I've taken, and seen taken, a lot of African plains game dropped cleanly with milder 6.5mm cartridges, with the .270, and with 7mms from the 7mm-08 and 7x57 on up. On the other hand, I've used .30-caliber cartridges more than anything else. Provided I did my part, I've always been pleased with the decisive results. I'd wanted to take the .264 to Africa for many years. It worked well, but my bottom-line instinct was that I'd been right all along in choosing—and recommending—a .30-caliber for the general run of plains game.

You aren't going to starve in Barry Burchell's camp!

This was brought home once more toward the end of the hunt when I most certainly did not do my part. I had a blue wildebeest quartering toward me, and I was

This mountain zebra stallion was the largest animal I took using the .264. It worked fine, but after a last-day near-disaster with a blue wildebeest, I finished the hunt thinking the 6.5mm was a bit on the light side for the full run of African plains game.

trying to hit the point of the on-shoulder. Sometime later, when we finally got him, we discovered that I'd wobbled quite a bit, hitting just inside the *off*-shoulder.

The blue wildebeest is, in my opinion, one of the toughest antelopes, and at possibly five hundred pounds, he is also very large. A wounded wildebeest can also make for a very long day. Thanks to some excellent tracking, we recovered this one and learned that a poor shot—mine—was the cause for the chase. Bullet weight and energy don't make up for poor shooting, but I'm convinced the drama would have been shorter had I used a 180-grain .30-caliber bullet.

Jill continued to shoot well. I think she would tell you that her best shot was on a jackal, her first nighttime hunting experience. It was very good, good enough that, with the chance she had, I'm not sure how she did it. I reckon her best shot was on her second springbok, another very fine ram. We were on a point, and the ram was standing on a flat below us at something over three hundred yards. She crawled forward, rested the rifle over a boulder, held a bit high for the distance, and simply flattened him. That was one of those (many) times when I was really glad it wasn't my turn to shoot!

That's a wonderful thing about hunting African plains game: In a compressed time period you get multiple opportunities under a variety of conditions and your confidence improves dramatically. Jill was not inexperienced, but she was better, faster, and more confident at the end of the hunt than at the beginning. I've seen this with both of my daughters and with Donna . . . and, if I think back, I saw it in myself many years ago.

CHAPTER TWENTY-FOUR

HORSES, DOGS, AND CATS

Today South Africa is the epicenter of the safari industry, hosting perhaps 40 percent of all hunting safaris continent-wide. This is a major shift in my time. When Kenya closed hunting in 1977, there were only a handful of operators in South Africa and a small fraction of the wildlife that exists today. South Africa's safari industry exploded in the 1980s and 1990s, but even when the industry was in its infancy, Johannesburg was the gateway to Southern Africa, not always the most direct but often the simplest way to reach Botswana, Mozambique, Namibia, Zambia, and Zimbabwe.

I figured this out early on, so even when there was comparatively little going on in South Africa, I would often stop there for a few days on the way to or from a longer hunt in another southern country. The first such foray was in 1979. I was en route to Rhodesia, and I stopped in South Africa to make a short hunt with Gary Kelly specifically for a nyala.

Most of the wildlife we encountered paid little attention to the horses, exhibiting pretty much the same nonchalance I've seen when on horseback in the American West.

I'm thus a little nervous when asked how many African safaris I've done. On the one hand, I've now lost count; on the other hand, I'm not sure a short "stopover hunt" should be considered a safari. If we include separate African hunts in unique locations with different operators, the total is now well over a hundred . . . but I can assure you I've bought a whole lot fewer

Ant Baber and I are pleased with this really beautiful southern greater kudu, which we hunted on horseback. This one is definitely not a giant, but it's a fully mature bull in the mid-fifties. It's the kind of kudu that, in today's Africa, is pretty hard to pass.

round-trip tickets than that. As the gateway to Southern Africa, and because South Africa's game list, thanks to incredibly varied habitat, is longer than any other African country, a lot of these short hunts took place in South Africa. Over the years there have been many, but the following four vignettes highlight some memorable hunts.

Kudu on Horseback

Although I've taken quite a number of nice greater kudus, I have never taken a monster. Actually, as I recounted in chapter nineteen, Donna has taken a bigger kudu than I ever have, by one inch, at 57 inches. I keep looking, but after repeated rabies outbreaks in Namibia and skyrocketing live-capture prices in South Africa, the odds of me ever taking a kudu approaching the Holy Grail of 60 inches have declined. Even so, hope springs eternal, and the greater kudu is always an animal of special interest to me.

Operating from his Ant's Nest lodge, Anthony "Ant" Baber has good kudu country in South Africa's Waterberg Mountains, well north of Johannesburg and south of the Limpopo Valley. I knew him from several SCI conventions, and he's a great guy. He eventually proposed a hunt I couldn't refuse: a kudu hunt by horseback only, with a reasonable chance for a very big bull.

Horses were my dad's thing in life, so I'm no stranger to them, but the one little detail I overlooked was that my experience is with western saddlery, and in South Africa they ride English. No matter where you are, a great way to see the country is from horseback, but at the end of the first day my thighs were aching and I was rubbed raw in some sensitive places. The terrain was foothills and tall ridges, not steep stuff, and the trails were good. I did fine absent a saddle horn, but it would take longer than I had to get conditioned to the unfamiliar gear.

A horse is a wonderfully quiet and unobtrusive vehicle for reaching good glassing spots. Impalas and other antelopes paid us little mind, but we saw relatively few kudus. I'm not sure why; this part of South Africa is very good for big kudus, and I was there in June when the rut should have been in full swing. It was probably just the simple fact that kudus are always difficult, big kudus more so, and you have to be in the right place at the right time. No matter—despite my sore backside, the country was beautiful, and riding was a different way to see it.

Early on the third day when it was still cold and sunlight was just starting to warm the ridges, we glassed a bull tending some cows. He was far down the next ridge and a great distance away, but for sure he was fully mature, and he looked *big*. Given the time-distance factor, I doubted we could close, but the wind was good. So we rode across the valley and up the ridge, then on along the ridge for a few hundred yards, where we tied the horses and began an approach. The stalk was neither long nor challenging, but after two days in that unfamiliar saddle, I could barely walk!

The kudu had been in sunlight on a slanting bench at the end of the ridge. We moved along the top for maybe a quarter of a mile and the bench came into view across a low saddle. Amazingly, horns glinted in the sunlight—the bull was still there, feeding, about four hundred yards away. Tall and wide, he was a perfect kudu, fully

When I arrived in Johannesburg for the brown hyena hunt, my rifle had arrived but my duffel bag with ammo did not. That's Benand Els on the left in the Pretoria Safari & Outdoors store, getting ready to load up some .264 Winchester Magnum handloads.

Tino Erasmus and I are happy with this gorgeous brown hyena. Although not importable to the United States, the brown hyena is relatively widespread and increasing in numbers in Southern Africa. This one was mounted life-size for the Safari & Outdoors store in Pretoria.

mature with good turns and long tips. At that point we knew he was not a giant but he was a very good bull in the mid-fifties. Right or wrong, I made the call: If I could get a shot, I should take it.

Moving carefully now and using cover, we gained a hundred yards. The bull was still feeding, only partially visible in low *mopane* scrub. At this point our ridge dropped into the saddle, so if we moved closer, we'd lose sight of the bull. With the brush ahead of us, it was impossible to tell when—or if—we might regain visibility. I was shooting a Ruger single-shot in .375 Ruger. Three hundred yards is a long poke for any .375, but it's doable if I could get steady enough. I tried a boulder, but it was too low, so I leaned into a couple of saplings, got fairly comfortable, and waited for an opening.

The white side-stripes were visible between trees, and after a couple of minutes the shoulder came clear. I held a few inches below the withers for the distance, and the hit sounded good—but the kudu was instantly *gone*, completely out of sight. After watching for a few minutes, we headed that way to look for blood. We were still looking when we stumbled over the kudu, stone dead behind a low outcropping. In size he was exactly what we'd thought he was, but he was a particularly gorgeous kudu, and I think I made the right decision.

A BROWN HYENA

In the Atlanta airport near the departure gates used by South African Airways there is (or was) a U.S. Fish and Wildlife display of wildlife prohibited for import. It includes ivory, of course, a spotted cat, of course, . . . and a very sad mount of a brown hyena. This is totally inexplicable to African and American hunters alike. The brown hyena is clever and nocturnal, but relatively common and definitely increasing across much of Southern Africa. It is not and has never been considered endangered by CITES, but for unknown reasons has been included under the U.S. Endangered Species Act since the law was written. No one knows why, and the only theory I have is that some biologist involved in creating the act forty-odd years ago happened to like brown hyenas.

So it's not an animal that can come into the United States, but by the first decade of our brave new millennium I'd taken just about every huntable species south of the Zambezi, and I was running out of excuses to return. Two species remained on my list: brown hyena and serval cat. I'd tried for both a number of times and failed miserably. The serval was really more of a random thing. They occupy a broad range, so dozens of times I'd been in areas where they occur and, although always looking, I'd never had a chance at one.

The brown hyena was different. In both South Africa and Namibia I'd spent a number of nights sitting over baits that brown hyenas—according to trail cameras—were hitting. I never saw one, but once, in Namibia, Dirk de Bod and I were sitting for a huge dog hyena—according to tracks and trail-cam photos—when we heard him coming. Disturbed guinea fowl told us of his progress along a streambed, and he was close. Then I felt a puff of breeze kiss the back of my neck, and that was that. In the morning we found his tracks coming in . . . and, just short of the bait, his running tracks going out. This near-miss made it sort of personal.

Tino Erasmus's home and safari headquarters, about three hours north of Johannesburg. Set on a well-shaded knoll, the home is a classic South African hunting lodge.

When I took the brown hyena very quickly, we had some time to play. We shot a couple of impalas to keep the leopard hunts going and had a really good bird shoot for guinea fowl and francolin.

I was doing a book signing at the excellent Safari and Outdoors store in Pretoria when I met avid South African hunter Benand Els. He took me to his house, and I was enthralled. He had the most marvelous collection of Southern African trophies I've ever seen, at that time almost complete, and spectacular in quality across the board. Of course, his trophies included a huge brown hyena and a monstrous serval. When hunting any animal, there's an element of luck, but it's also a matter of being in the right place at the right time. Benand knew his country and its game; he told me that for a brown hyena I needed to spend a few days with Tino Erasmus, and for a serval I needed to talk to Charl van Rooyen.

First we hatched a plot to get the brown hyena with Tino Erasmus. By that time Benand was managing Safari and Outdoors, so I went straight from the airport to the store where Tino was planning to pick me up. I had my .264 from the previous chapter; it arrived nestled nicely in my gun case, but my duffel bag didn't show.

I took this very good black wildebeest with a Musgrave .375 H&H. The distance was severe for a .375, but we'd spent some time on the range and I was confident. I held a bit of daylight over the backline, and the big slug dropped in and took the animal down cleanly.

A good gun shop is sometimes a special blessing! They didn't have any .264 Winchester Magnum ammo, which didn't surprise me. They did have loading dies, new Nosler brass, and 6.5mm 130-grain Nosler AccuBonds. So, right there at the store reloading display, they whipped up some handloads. I bought trousers, socks, gloves, a shirt, and a jacket, and Tino and I headed north.

Between the time we spent loading ammo and the three-hour drive, it was late afternoon when we reached Tino's beautiful headquarters and met his awesome family. We had a quick bite, and dusk was approaching fast when we went to the range. Amazingly, Benand's handloads were precisely "on" at a hundred yards, about the same as my own 140-grain loads.

I had now traveled some forty hours and was exhausted, but a full moon was rising early and Tino had a big brown hyena feeding. He suggested we should head for the blind, and although I would have preferred some sleep, I agreed. It wasn't far, but dark had fallen by the time we got there, so we organized things by feel. Tino pointed out the bait, which was barely visible in the rising moon. I adjusted the rifle on a rest so that it was set on the bait, and through the scope I could make out the smelly mound. In the poor light it looked far, but was probably eighty yards away. Then we settled in to wait, me expecting a long, cold, and sleepy ordeal. The previous night, per the trail cam, the hyena had come at midnight, and that was a long time away.

Barely a half-hour had passed when Tino nudged me. I could see through the scope that a large animal had come out of thick bush to the right and was standing in the moon's shadow to the right of the bait.

Tino whispered, "I think it's a bushpig."

Later he told me this was based not on visual identification but because it was simply too early for the brown hyena to show.

The animal walked into pale moonlight, and I realized that a bushpig did not have a long, bushy tail. Tino recognized the brown hyena in the same instant and squeezed my arm. The cross hairs were already on its shoulder, and although the form was blurry and unclear, I thought the animal turned slightly, quartering away. I also thought the cross hairs were right behind the shoulder when the trigger broke and the flash blinded me.

The animal ran to the right, a hit most uncertain (at least to me). We waited a little while, heard nothing, and then we advanced to the bait while Tino's tracker brought up the vehicle behind us. Using flashlights, we looked for blood at the bait and found none. Even in the dark we could see a couple of obvious game trails leading off to the right, so the tracker and I started a serious search for blood, a few inches at a time, while Tino cast ahead. Twenty yards in he found a big and beautiful brown hyena, hit perfectly behind the left shoulder. This particular quest was over. Since the brown hyena cannot be imported into the United States, mine resides with Safari and Outdoors, mounted life-size as such a gorgeous animal deserves.

As instructed, I'd planned to spend a few days. At that point I didn't know Tino Erasmus; I just knew he'd pulled off a long-awaited miracle. I'm glad I had the time to get to know him better. He's not only good at strange night hunts for hyenas and bushpigs but he is also one of the best leopard hunters in Southern Africa, with an incredible track record on South Africa's large-body but extremely clever cats.

The night of the brown hyena we celebrated for a little while, and then I slept long and hard. The next day we had a wonderful afternoon. We shot guinea fowl and a few impalas for leopard baits, and the following day we went up into the Waterbergs to freshen some leopard baits and check trail cameras. His baits were incredibly well-sited, likewise his blinds, and there were big leopard tracks all over

One must be in the right place at the right time for difficult animals, as well as have a bit of luck. I had looked for a serval cat for thirty years, yet it took Charl van Rooyen but two nights to find this beautiful serval for me.

the place. Like all South African operators, his problem is getting permits, but he's a guy I want to hunt leopards with someday.

A Visit with Musgrave

Along the road we met my friend Andre van Dyk, publisher of South Africa's *Wildlands* magazine, and Tino handed me off. We took a fascinating tour of the Musgrave gun factory in Ermelo, in Mpumalanga. Musgrave is a great old South African brand, rescued from oblivion by Frikkie du Plooy and moved to his J J Wapens shop in Ermelo. At this time they were still making all their rifles on refurbished Mauser 98 actions.

I suppose a "gun-factory tour" is a bit off the subject for this book, but here's the deal: Even though I'm left-handed, so they don't do me much good, I love the classic Mauser action. The original Musgrave firm accumulated a huge store of Mauser actions, and when Frikkie purchased the remnants, he got the entire inventory. I have never seen so many original Mauser actions in one place.

Sooner or later, of course, the supply will dry up, and they'll have to source or make another receiver, but I was extremely impressed by the work they were doing with the great old Mauser actions. Obviously, they needed polishing and truing-up, and then du Plooy's team added good American Timney triggers, top-quality barrels, and excellent stocks.

We took a couple of them to the range. I was shooting a .375 H&H, and the accuracy was simply awesome. The next day we went looking for a black wildebeest, which is probably not the most ideal game for a .375. The closest we could get was something over three hundred yards, so I held a bit of daylight and essentially dropped a bullet into his shoulder. Fortunately the big bullet dropped in with extreme authority, flattening the animal. It was a very fine black wildebeest, and only the second one I've ever taken.

THE SERVAL KING

Given enough time in Africa and plenty of luck, many hunters eventually take servals in chance encounters. Despite cumulative months in areas where these gorgeous little cats live, I've only ever seen one. It was in the Rungwa region in central Tanzania in 2010 where servals are quite common, and, knowing that I wanted one badly, Michel Mantheakis and his team were always on the lookout. We actually saw one for a brief instant, going about five hundred miles per hour across a narrow burned strip. And that's it.

So, in accordance with Benand Els's instructions, I got hold of Charl van Rooyen. Charl hunts on the boundary between South Africa's Mpumalanga and Limpopo provinces, with concessions in both. Although relatively widespread, servals are now on special license only in a couple of provinces—Limpopo, as I recall, but not Mpumalanga to the south. So we started our hunt with a trip to the game department, where I was issued a license.

Servals tend to like grassy areas and are often found around agriculture. They prey on small mammals up to the size of duikers, but birds are their primary quarry. Now, let's be clear: Charl is not exactly a serval specialist, no more than anyone else,

I glassed this really good southern mountain reedbuck at long range and eventually stalked up to it at less than fifty yards.

but some of the country where he hunts is ideal habitat, and he gets the farmers whose land he hunts on to leave them alone. By paying attention—scouting and listening to reports—he usually knows where a few servals are hanging out, and he hunts them sparingly, only a couple a year. In this fashion, Benand told me, he is usually successful—and expects to be successful. By my standards, this makes him the Serval King!

Like many of Africa's smaller predators, servals are usually hunted at night where legal, and we planned this hunt carefully for the dark of the moon, when cats tend to be more active. Charl knew where a serval was hanging out, and I hope he knows I believed him . . . because the first night was a total bust. This didn't surprise me because, although the moon conditions were perfect, it was a gusty, blustery night, and *nothing* was moving. We saw a few hartebeests, a couple of eland cows, and that was about it. Charl was disappointed; I think he expected to take one the first night. Me, I'm used to failure on tough stuff that I really want. Tino Erasmus's magic trick with the brown hyena was an exception in my world, hardly the rule. So I wasn't surprised, and we had other nights ahead.

It only took one more. The next evening we went after a different cat, reported by a farmer to be frequenting some fields at night looking for mice. We saw not one but two right away, just eyes moving through too tall grass. I suspect it was a female with a near-grown kitten, but it could just as well have been a big male with a female. Doesn't really matter because they were in thick vegetation, and we never got a clear look, either for identification or shooting.

I figured that was that, but we kept looking, and a couple of hours later Charl picked up eyes in an open field. This one was alone, and the CZ .375—the only rifle I had that trip—made a resounding *whack*. Honestly, though, in the dim light I never saw the cat clearly until we walked up to it. Without question the serval is the most beautiful of Africa's small cats, and this was a big one. God bless the Serval King!

With time left over, Charl showed me some of his country, a really delightful mix of lush valleys and tall ridges. The area is good for a wide range of plains game and South Africa's disease-free buffaloes, but it's especially good for mountain reedbucks. I hadn't shot one in quite a few years, so that's where we focused our remaining time.

There were plenty, but we passed several and had failed stalks on a couple more—and then Charl glassed a real monster up on a knife-edge ridge. As I said, I only had a CZ .375—I was headed from there to the Zimbabwe hunt with Chad Allen and Mike Payne. With buffalo loads and a low-power scope it was fine for short-range night hunting, and, as I'd expected, the big bullet did very little damage to the fragile serval. But it is *not* an ideal choice for mountain hunting, especially not for a small antelope presenting a small target.

This reedbuck cooperated well. We watched him bed with a couple of ewes just below a rocky point and made a long climb on the backside, coming up above him. From the point we couldn't see him at all, so we started down, and I got the shot at forty yards, just horns and a bit of backline showing above the tall grass. By far this was my very best mountain reedbuck, a wonderful bonus to a short but perfect South African hunt.

Chapter Twenty-Five

Blaauwkrantz . . . Thirty Years Later

In forty years I've seen a lot of changes in African hunting, certainly not all of them for the good. In South Africa, however, much of what has happened to hunting and wildlife is good. Back in 1985, when I first hunted in the Eastern Cape with the late Lew Tonks, things were just getting started. Over the mountains in the Karoo, Bowker & Scott had been in business for a long time, but that's semidesert country. If you wanted an Eastern Cape greater kudu, the best—and one of the only—places to go was Arthur Rudman's Blaauwkrantz, in the heavy coastal thorn north of Port Elizabeth. We had a perfect kudu hunt back then, and we tried without success to get a Cape grysbok.

Blaauwkrantz was quite a lot smaller then, and so were the Rudman children. A few years ago Russell Lovemore and I went to Blaauwkrantz for just an evening to hunt bushpigs with Eardley Rudman, long since grown up. François Rudman, also long grown up, was with Mike Payne, Chad Allen, and me when we hunted buffaloes in Chewore South in 2014. I'd promised Eardley before, and I promised Francois then, that I'd come see them and see how Blaauwkrantz had changed. We did that in July 2015.

An appropriate comment might be that I don't know why I stayed away so long, but that wouldn't be altogether true. I know exactly why, and it has nothing to do with Blaauwkrantz or the Rudman family. Some of us find a great place and keep going back. Others, like me, continue to seek new horizons. I've been few places that I wouldn't like to return to, but it comes down to time and resources, and there are a lot of great places I'll never get back to. But, trust me, it's not personal! So a full thirty years passed before I returned to spend a few days at Blaauwkrantz.

Of course it had changed. The lodge was much expanded. Arthur and Trinette were, forgive me, a bit older, but then so was I. These days Arthur Rudman is mostly handling the farming side of the family business. Sons François and Eardley run

We were looking for Eastern Cape kudu, always the Rudmans's specialty, when I spotted movement on a brushy hill. It turned out to be an excellent bushbuck, nearly black with good horns. Off sticks, the shot was really difficult, but somehow I made it work.

the majority of the hunting, along with daughter Zani and her husband, Philip Dixie. And Blaauwkrantz has gotten a whole lot bigger. Rudman was early into the wildlife game in his part of the Eastern Cape; he did well and invested wisely, buying up adjoining properties as he could. Blaauwkrantz—which means "Blue Cliffs," a reference to its oddly bluish outcroppings—is huge today, and more or less contiguous, running not quite to the coast, but from coastal plain to tall ridges.

Since I'd gone there thirty years earlier for Eastern Cape kudu, that had to be my main goal again. I also wanted to hunt bushpigs the way Eardley does it, and basically enjoy the country for a few days. François and Eardley tag-teamed me, and that was fun, for I remember both as boys, and they remember me. Just kids thirty years ago, they both are now excellent and extremely experienced PHs.

I started the hunt with Eardley. First we checked the rifle, an accurate left-hand Kenny Jarrett in .300 Winchester Magnum, stoked with some of the first of Hornady's

The Rudmans raise goats as well as game, and both jackals and caracals are a constant problem, so part of their long-term success is aggressive predator control. While I was there, Blaauwkrantz's predator control team was taking inventory.

then-new ELD-X bullets. That went well, no adjustments needed, so we headed west just after sunrise, looking for kudus in brushy ridges. It was a slow morning for movement; we saw just a few cows and calves, and it was nearing midmorning and warming up when we hiked over a ridge to glass a brushy valley.

Although the sun was just right to catch the glint of kudu horns, we didn't see any, but while we were looking I caught movement in thick bush on the far ridge. For just a moment a good bushbuck ram walked into view, and then vanished again just as quickly. I told Eardley, but in a sea of green thorn it took forever for me to figure out exactly where I'd seen it. Finally, I figured it out, and we both focused on the distant spot where I was sure I had seen the ram.

Eardley saw him next, stepping between two bushes, and then he was gone again. Confirming a good ram, I ranged the spot—about three hundred yards—and got on the sticks, now trying to find that certain spot in a blanket of brush. The ram stopped to feed, partially visible, and I finally got on him. At that distance, on that size animal, it was tricky, but the bushbuck dropped to the shot.

We were so busy congratulating each other we almost didn't see the ram get back up! I missed with the second shot, connected with the third, and then we had to figure out how to find it on that thick hillside. We did, and it was a very nice ram. Although often overlooked by the hunting fraternity, the bushbuck is one of my favorite African antelopes.

HUNTING WITH THE HOGFATHER

The bushpig is common and widespread in South Africa, but it is primarily nocturnal and tricky to hunt. A daylight encounter can happen any time, but the two most common techniques are hunting with hounds and baiting. Typically neither is particularly selective. Dogs follow scent and bay the first pig they can; on bait it's often too dark to be absolutely certain, so you shoot the biggest pig and hope for the best. Since bushpigs are generally considered a nuisance, this is not a problem, but it takes a bit of luck to get a decent boar.

Eardley Rudman, uniquely among his peers, is so fascinated by bushpigs that his family nicknamed him "Hogfather." For several years now he's made a study of targeting big boars, using multiple bait sites and using trail cameras to sort them out. As I wrote, a few years earlier Russ Lovemore and I hunted with him, and, well, we shot sort of a "minimalist" bushpig. Eardley was embarrassed. I wasn't upset—it was just too dark, with passing clouds covering the moon, and there was no way to be sure of what we were looking at. This time, however, Eardley was determined to get us a big boar.

He'd been checking his trail cameras and watching the wind and the moon. The first evening we sat watching a bait in sort of a natural amphitheater, with a half-circle of open ground and the thick brush that bushpigs love above and to the right. The setup was perfect, with good visibility after moonrise, but the wind turned fickle. About ten o'clock we saw two big pigs approach the bait. They were shadowy forms but clear enough, and I thought we were in business. Then, halfway across the narrow opening, they caught an eddy of scent and turned back like the Hounds of Hell were after them. Frantic crashing through the brush sounded for a long time, and then silence. It was pretty clear we were done for that night.

Hogfather Eardley Rudman is setting up a shooting rest in the blind. Bushpigs are widely hunted over bait in the Eastern Cape, but Rudman is unique in that, using multiple bait sites and trail cameras, he actively targets big boars and has unusual success.

I took this big and extremely colorful bushpig boar with Hogfather Eardley Rudman on the second night of my hunt. I got to wear the boar-tooth necklace, and my name goes on the roster of successful bushpig hunters.

No worries. Hogfather had plans B, C, and perhaps D in place, depending on the wind. The second night we set up in a narrow valley with thick brush all around, but this time the wind was steady, coming down the cut. Trail cameras had shown two big pigs, an obvious boar and either a big sow or smaller boar hitting the bait, but with thick brush so close there would be little warning when they came in.

That's how it happened: The pigs came silently out of deep shadow about an hour after full dark. I'm not sure if Eardley heard them, saw them, or—as the Hogfather—*sensed* them. I know that, although I was sitting perfectly still and watching the dark mound of the bait pile, I heard nothing, saw nothing, and sensed nothing until Eardley touched my arm.

The rifle was set solidly in two sets of sticks and the scope was on the bait, so I leaned forward to the scope. The moon was still low and the bait in shadow, but through the scope I could see two forms, one behind the other.

Eardley whispered, "The boar is the one behind. Take him when he comes clear."

Exactly how he knew this is unclear to me, but, after all, he's the Hogfather, not me. Later he told me he could see the "warts" on the snout, but I'm not sure I believe him. To my eye the pigs were about the same size, and in that light there was no way I could see warts! I could see the two pigs separate slightly, the one in front moving right, opening up the shoulder of the pig behind, so I held on the center of the shoulder. At the shot I was blinded by the flash, unsure what had happened.

The pig was down in its tracks, and it was, indeed, a big boar. This is an underrated animal, especially if taken fair and square in natural light. That night I got to wear the boar-tooth necklace, and I got on the Hogfather board. A couple of days later, François and I took a nice warthog, thus earning me a place in history on the Blaauwkrantz "ham slam" list.

A DOUBLE ON EASTERN CAPE KUDUS

Since the very beginning of South African hunting, we have separated out the Eastern Cape greater kudu because, although it is similar in body size, it is smaller in horn and more luxurious of cape than the southern greater kudu to the north and northwest. By nature I'm more of a "lumper" than a "splitter," so I've never been crazy about the separation between Eastern Cape, southern, East African, and Abyssinian greater kudus. The western greater kudu of central Sudan, southern Chad, and parts of the C.A.R. is at least a third smaller, but the rest, when speaking of average to good specimens, are visually indistinguishable.

I have to admit, however, that this separation has played well for the Eastern Cape kudus. Since they are smaller in the horn, they have not attracted undue attention from the game breeders, and the healthy climate of the Eastern Cape has helped them resist diseases that have ravaged kudu populations elsewhere.

In this I suppose things have come full circle. Much of Hemingway's *Green Hills of Africa* (1935) is devoted to his quest for a kudu; ultimately he was successful. Likewise much of Robert Ruark's *Horn of the*

The trick to finding greater kudu in this thick thornbush is to get high and glass thoroughly and patiently. There are lots of kudus out there, but spotting them is difficult.

The Eastern Cape greater kudu has smaller horns than the southern greater kudu, but the markings are striking and the coat is long and luxurious. Thirty years ago Blaauwkrantz's area was one of few places where this kudu could be reliably hunted, and it's still a very good place.

Hunter (1953) is devoted to his quest for a kudu, and ultimately he was unsuccessful. Over the years I've theorized that they were simply hunting in the wrong place.

Since the great rinderpest epidemic that swept the continent from the 1890s to early 1900s, East Africa has been unreliable as a destination for taking a greater kudu. Contrast this to Southern Africa. In my time, the greater kudu has been one of the more common large antelopes in Southern Africa, with success relatively certain on a seven- or ten-day hunt. This has now changed.

Disease, primarily rabies, has ravaged much of the region, as has live-capture for the game-breeding market. Throughout their range a mature southern greater kudu bull is no longer a sure thing, and if you're successful, watch your wallet, because prices have skyrocketed. The Eastern Cape greater kudu, though a few inches smaller on average, has avoided these problems. Undoubtedly, things will change again but, today, in 2016, as these lines are written, the Eastern Cape is Africa's greatest kudu hunting grounds.

It was the Eastern Cape greater kudu that drew me to Blaauwkrantz thirty years earlier, so, of course, I wanted to reprise that hunt. The third evening of my kudu hunt with François Rudman found us walking along a tall ridge, hoping to catch a kudu moving down into the valley below. We found a group of bulls on a little hogback to our front, maybe seven hundred yards away, and at that distance a couple of them looked pretty good. Climbing back to the top, we looped around to come in above them, but they had vanished. Theorizing that they were working their way down to feed in the valley below, we dropped on down so that we could see the bottom. The light was starting to fade, but the valley was full of kudus!

Too little light remained to properly judge horns, so François marked an older bull by obvious body shape, and we hot-footed it down the ridge to the valley floor. At 250 yards he set up the sticks, and when the bull stepped out, I shot him. I thought I'd aimed just behind the shoulder with the bull quartering away, but with the shot I lost sight of him, and in an instant there were kudus running everywhere for cover, but mostly back up the ridge. One bull ran straight toward us, and I was convinced this was the bull I'd shot at. For an instant François thought so, too, but he stopped me in time and as this bull scrambled past us at less than twenty yards. Then we moved forward, quickly finding my bull, an old, emaciated kudu with wide curls and seriously worn tips.

I was happy, but François thought we might do better, so the next morning we headed west to where there were deep ravines cloaked in the impossibly thick Addo thorn. The morning was clear and sunny, and I'm sure we were a mile away when François caught the glint of a kudu horn on a thick hillside. Much time passed while we scrambled this way and that to get a better view of the right draw, and in that thick bush I thought it impossible to get a closer look, let alone a shot. I was wrong. It took us the best part of an hour later and we were now on the next ridge over, but we saw the same kudu horn glinting in the sun. The bull, meanwhile, was feeding on a choice thornbush, its body hidden.

He was not a huge bull, but Eastern Cape kudus are not normally huge. The turns of his horns were good with the tips nearly parallel, and it was a mature bull. François set up the sticks, and then we waited for a long time, seeing horns, then nothing, and

I'm flanked by François Rudman, left, and his dad, Arthur Rudman, good friends and a great South African hunting family. Those three mounted kudus behind me are truly exceptional for Eastern Cape kudu, some of the very best from decades of game management.

then horns again. Eventually he stepped between two bushes and offered a shot. It was short of three hundred yards, but still a long poke off sticks.

Taking a careful breath and a more careful hold, I got the shot off, and again lost the kudu in the brush. We waited a long time, all the while seeing no movement. We then moved across and found him down ten yards from the shot. He was a perfect Eastern Cape kudu . . . and about the same size as the one I shot thirty years earlier.

Recovery looked harder than it was. We got some help, and there was an old ranch road on top of the ridge. After making four challenging shots in as many days I should have quit while I was ahead and passed into Blaauwkrantz legend. But, no, I'm not that smart. That evening, I blew an easy shot at a very nice impala, and it's only a miracle that we recovered it before dark.

Chapter Twenty-Six

Rhino at Otjiwa

In my time in Africa I've seen the rhinos come and go, and go and come. It depends on which rhino we're talking about. When I hunted on Mount Kenya in 1977, black rhinos were still plentiful, at least up there where tall-tree forest gives way to dense bamboo. Every day or so we'd hear the distinctive snort and a rhino would crash one way or the other, often straight toward us. We'd quickly find a stout tree to get behind and watch it crash past and away. At that time I could have

On a leopard safari with Russ Broom in 1992 we came out of a leopard blind in the dark and ran straight into a black rhino—long after rhinos were thought to be gone from the Zambezi Valley. We scattered like quail and had a hard time getting reoriented in the dark.

In Southern Africa the black rhino has been saved from extinction, at least for now. There are no free-range populations, and the new wave of poaching places them in danger once again.

had a rhino permit very cheaply, but in Kenya a thirty-five-day safari was required for a rhino license, and that was impossible for me.

I am still amazed at how quickly the black rhino vanished. In Zambia's Luangwa Valley in 1983 we saw one, and that was the last black rhino I ever saw in wild, unfenced Africa. But it wasn't the last trace. We saw tracks and dung in the Selous Reserve in 1988. Amazingly, after all the warfare and all the poaching, in 1989 Roger Whittall and I saw the fresh tracks of a lone rhino bull along the Zambezi in Mozambique, south of Cabora Bassa. And in 1992 Russ Broom and I came out of a leopard blind in the dark and ran straight into a black rhino. This was in the Binga area south of Lake Kariba in Zimbabwe's Zambezi Valley, a place and time when black rhinos were thought to be gone and the few survivors darted and relocated to safer areas. There is, however, no mistaking that distinctive *whoof* and the crashing that follows. We scattered like quail, and had a helluva time getting rejoined and re-oriented in the dark.

Since then, of course, I've seen a number of black rhinos in parks and private reserves, and it's always a thrill. With protection they have been making a comeback in Southern Africa, but it is unlikely that a single black rhino walks in any genuine free-range situation anywhere on the African continent.

The white rhino is the same—no longer a free-range animal—but its story is different. Although it is probably more docile by nature, the white rhino's primary vulnerability is that it is a grazer, more a creature of open ground than the browsing black rhino. The northern white rhino was already depleted at the time of the Roosevelt safari in 1909, and despite relocation attempts from zoo populations, it is almost certainly extinct in the wild. The southern white rhino was considered extinct in 1900, but fortunately that was wrong. A small population was discovered in Natal in the 1920s, and South Africa's first parks were created to protect these survivors. By the 1950s the Natal parks were overpopulated. "Operation Rhino" relocated white rhinos to new areas.

Limited hunting for white rhinos was reopened in the 1970s. This controversial move opened up new habitat. With potential for revenue, private landowners were now willing to host nucleus herds, and although the rhinoceros is a very slow-breeding animal, over time the growth became exponential. The rest is history: In 2008 the population was estimated to exceed twenty thousand individuals, and for the moment the white rhino was considered out of danger.

But let's back up for just a moment. Under the U.S. Endangered Species Act, in the 1970s Americans were not allowed to import legally taken white rhinos. This kept the prices very low. When I first hunted in South Africa in 1979, the trophy fee for a white rhino was about the same as for a nyala, five hundred dollars. Then the CITES treaty allowed importation, and prices skyrocketed. I took a southern white rhino near the Palala River in northwestern South Africa in 1986. At that time I had to add a zero to that original five hundred dollar trophy fee, and although a lot of money for me

I am in the study of the late Dr. Ian Player, a few weeks before he passed away. Player deserves much credit for the salvation of the white rhino. Never a hunter himself, he became a staunch supporter of regulated sport hunting because of the value it placed on "his" rhinos.

at the time, that was a very good price back then. By today's standards, it is laughably low. Add another zero and perhaps double it today!

It is arguable whether the larger but less aggressive white rhino is properly a full-fledged member of the Big Five. My friend, colleague, and superb writer Tom McIntyre takes the purist's view that it is not, an intermittent argument we've had for thirty years now. In the old days, when Africa's dangerous game was first grouped, the leopard, because of size, was not included and "Big Four" was the common term. In those days, when the white and black rhinos were both hunted, no distinction was made between the two. Later the leopard was included and the Big Four became the Big Five. SCI makes no distinction between black and white rhinos in awarding its Big Five "pin." To blur things even further, the African Professional Hunters Association added the hippo to this last group, so now we have the "Big Six." When SCI added the Nile crocodile, we now have the "Dangerous Seven."

In 1986 I was probably the only living outdoor journalist with some claim to having taken the Big Five. Yep, it's all a bit silly and doesn't make much difference, but I've always been glad that I took a white rhino when I did and when such a safari was affordable. I've also become very glad I took one *where* I did. The Palala River country was the site of an early translocation of white rhinos, and the rhinos were wild and unfenced. My white rhino was probably among the last taken that was genuinely free-range. It also almost certainly contained the last free-ranging roans in South Africa, and I was lucky that during my hunt on the Palala River, we ran into a sizable herd of these antelopes.

W. P. Barnard demonstrates the dart gun Ray Puckett and Donna will use. Powered by a .22 blank, it propels a dart with accuracy to, perhaps, twenty-five yards, but even at that range the trajectory arc is getting steep.

So now let's fast-forward to 2008. The southern white rhino was flourishing, and at least in protected areas in Southern Africa—Namibia, South Africa, and Zimbabwe—the black rhino was recovering quickly. Then began the disastrous new wave of commercial poaching that con-

After several hours of tracking, we can see Donna's rhino, napping in dense thorn ahead. It is still much too far for the dart gun, so it's my place to stay back while they gain a few more yards.

tinues to this day. In October 2014, shortly before his death, I had the honor to conduct what was perhaps the last formal interview granted by Dr. Ian Player. Player started as a game ranger with Natal Parks and worked his way up through the ranks to become head of Natal Parks Board. As a young man he was a leader in Operation Rhino; the rhino became his life's work, and he is properly credited with a primary role in saving the southern white rhino.

As a game ranger he was no stranger to the rifle, but he was not a hunter and was outspokenly opposed to reopening rhino hunting. In time he saw he had been wrong. Hunting opened privately owned habitat to rhinos, and Player eventually gave almost full credit to the hunting community for the rhino's recovery. In that last interview he restated this, but by this time the poaching losses had escalated dramatically, and he was watching his life's work crumble.

Although he told me, "The death of just one rhino doesn't please me . . . it doesn't please me at all," he understood fully and had long accepted that placing economic value on the rhino had become its salvation. At the end he was strongly advocating opening legal markets for rhino horn. Range nations have significant stores of rhino horn from natural deaths, recovery from poachers, and dehorning. This last, regrettably, is of questionable value; today's poachers will often kill a dehorned rhino simply so they won't ever waste time tracking that rhino again.

Player believed that CITES could and should create a monitored international market, thus undercutting the black market and eliminating the incentive for poaching. Further, he believed that horn from living rhinos, which regrows fairly quickly, could be harvested as a renewable and sustainable resource as part of that international market. Since his death, South Africa has unilaterally authorized trade in legal rhino horn, but international (CITES) action is required to make this meaningful.

At this writing selective hunting has been the primary legal means of placing value on the rhino, and today's prices for a surplus, nonbreeding or "problem" animal are astronomical. We certainly couldn't afford to hunt a rhino today, but, realistically, even if we could, losses of rhinos from poaching continue to escalate, so legal rhino hunting is once again becoming questionable. Yet there must be a way to place value on these animals; otherwise, neither African governments nor private landowners can afford to keep them and try to protect them.

The other option has been the "green" or darting hunt. Of the many things I have been wrong about in my life, this is one of them. Although an unpopular view that I mostly kept to myself, my view was the "dart-and-release" concept was a step down the slippery slope of "catch-and-release" hunting. Also, realistically, tranquilizing is not a perfect science, and it brings unnecessary risk to the animal. So my opinion was that if a species was endangered, it should be protected; if there was a sustainable surplus, then it should be hunted.

With the rhino fully asleep, the full team moves in. There is much to be done—blood samples, inoculations, microchip implant, and more. The rhino can only be down twenty minutes before the antidote is administered, so timing is important.

As with lions, I could be smug about this since I'd had my chance . . . and, since placing value is what it is ultimately about, it was OK in my mind if hunting a rhino had become an unaffordable dream.

This thinking became complicated by the fact that Donna, who has

Donna and W. P. Barnard with "Donna's rhino," an older cow that, surprisingly, turned out to be pregnant. Five minutes later she was back on her feet and lumbered away, none the worse for wear.

come to love hunting, really wanted a rhino to complete her Big Five. It was complicated further by the fact that rhino darting had changed. Although it placed value on the animal, and no matter that precautions and insurance were part of the deal, first South Africa and then Namibia made it illegal to dart a rhino just so one could have a photograph taken. Today rhino darting can only be done legally for genuine veterinary purposes, and only a licensed veterinarian can administer the tranquilizer. (I'm very much OK with this position.)

We were at an impasse in Donna's quest to complete her Big Five when my friend, fellow Kansan, and fellow African addict Sean Scott offered a way. One of the outfits he arranges hunts for is W. P. Barnard's Otjiwa game ranch in northcentral Namibia. They have an excellent breeding herd of white rhinos, and it turns out that, in any captive situation, periodic veterinary work is required to administer anthrax and other immunizations, along with implanting tracking chips, collecting DNA samples, and more. Ideally a rhino should have a trip to the vet every couple of years, but with veterinary and helicopter time, this is unaffordable for most landowners who have rhinos. The "green hunt," now otherwise illegal, could perhaps be done legally in a way that allowed hunters to pay for this work.

The hunter would track a rhino, stalk in close, and administer a "vita-dart" with vitamins and immunizations, followed, as legally required, by a veterinarian administering the actual tranquilizer. We called it a "veterinary darting," done as an experiment in 2013. As I said, right or wrong, I'd been opposed to the "green hunts." To some extent I was not wrong because in some instances the same poor rhino was being darted over and over, certainly placing value on the animal but also creating unwarranted risk . . . of addiction, if not death. On the other hand, I'd never actually seen such a hunt done, so although I was deeply skeptical, Sean's concept of such a hunt for legitimate veterinary purposes was irresistible.

It turns out it was one of the best things we've ever done. I didn't know W. P. (pronounced in the Afrikaans "Vee Pee") Barnard, but we had many mutual friends, including my primary Namibian mentor, Dirk de Bod. Barnard proved a really good hand, and his Otjiwa operation proved a real gem, well-developed with very good game. Over the years I'd driven past his gate a number of times on the way to the Etosha region. It's a big area, with a lot of flat thornbush plus several ranges of rugged hills, ideal for Namibian plains game and good country for the white rhino. The lodge sits atop a rocky knob, gorgeous in itself, and magnificent for its view.

While Donna had a very specific goal, I was on this hunt purely as an observer. Generally speaking, I'm not very good in that role, but I was extremely curious, both from personal and professional standpoints. In this regard I was fortunate. Another Kansan, Ray Puckett, also an experienced African hand, came into camp just after us to dart a rhino, so I'd get to observe two of these strange operations. We were also really fortunate in W.P.'s choice of veterinarian, Dr. Mikhail Lambert Roux. An extremely experienced South African vet, he's darted hundreds of rhinos but, equally important to us, he clearly loves his work and was extremely patient in explaining what he needed to do and how we would go about it.

The safari camp at Otjiwa sits on top of a rocky kopje, a beautiful place.

That's where Donna's luck ended. She had to go first! The dart gun was a modified .22 bolt action with a scope, the heavy dart

These are white rhinos at Otjiwa, and if they were black rhinos, we would not be this close! Without question, the white rhino, though larger, is less aggressive than the black variety.

propelled by a .22 blank. We took a few shots with a practice dart, both to verify zero and to become familiar with the gun. The trajectory was fairly flat to maybe fifteen yards, and then it started to drop like a rock. Theoretically a thirty-yard shot might be possible, but it seemed to me she needed to be quite a bit closer than that to be sure of shot placement.

The rhino herd on Otjiwa is about twenty strong, a good-size private herd. W.P. had identified three or four rhinos that needed attention, so it was a matter of which track we could find, and which rhino we could close with. From there, at least initially, it was just like any other hunt. We tracked one bull for hours, but the wind kept giving us away, the rhino kept moving ahead of us, and we were unable to close. We backed off and regrouped, found another track, and implemented Rhino Plan B. Now into the heat of the day, this one, a thirty-year-old female, also took us through sandy thornbush for a couple of hours before we found her lying down in thick thorn.

Depending on how you look at it, here's where being an observer was either very good or very bad. The rhino was in very thick stuff, and the dart must have a clear path. They would have to get very close for a sure shot, but "they" didn't include me. So, barely able to see the gray battleship of rhino through the thorn, I stayed back about sixty yards with the trackers and watched the show while W.P. and Donna closed, one careful step at a time. I was dying . . . and Donna was about as excited as

I've ever seen her, certainly as pumped as she'd been after making a six-yard shot on her Botswana elephant.

One slow step at a time they closed to sixteen yards, found a small window in the thorn, and I heard the muffled *whap* of the blank cartridge. Then they stood very still while the rhino crashed off. With the vita-dart administered, W.P. got on the radio, and Dr. Roux came in with the helicopter and administered the tranquilizer, then backed off and waited for it to take effect.

OK, let's understand: The hunt and the stalk were not necessary. The helicopter is necessary so the veterinary work can be done quickly, minimizing the time the rhino is down, but obviously the tranquilizer could be administered *first* from the air, then all the rest. No matter which way it is done, the expenses remain the same: The owner still has to pay the costs of the helicopter, veterinarian, medicines—for twenty rhinos, ten times per year. The concept is to place value on the rhinos, and the difference is, of course, that the "hunter" pays a bit to offset the cost of the operation. Donna—and then Ray Puckett the next day—had the opportunity to stalk in close to a rhino and make the "shot." It was plenty exciting, a real rhino hunt, and what followed was simply amazing.

The rhino remained on its feet for several minutes after the tranquilizer was administered and covered quite a bit of ground. We retreated to the truck and followed the chopper, converging about the time the rhino went down. Dr. Roux put a wet towel over the rhino's head to keep her calm as she went to sleep, and poured water over her to keep her from overheating. He had been firm from the beginning: "After she's asleep, we have twenty minutes, then I have to administer the antidote."

He worked quickly, implanting a microchip, drawing blood, smearing antibiotic ointment on some thorn scratches. At the same time W.P. took horn measurements of "Donna's" rhino. A few quick photos and then Dr. Roux, watching the clock, administered the antidote. We backed away to a safe distance, and in just a minute the rhino lumbered to her feet, groggy at first, and then, seemingly insulted by the whole affair, she lumbered off none the worse for wear. It was an incredible experience and the next day, with Ray Puckett, we would observe it again. I hesitate to say it given how vociferous I was before, but with a prehistoric creature like a rhino that is now once again dwindling in numbers, we felt better about it than if we'd actually shot it.

CHAPTER TWENTY-SEVEN

ON THE FRONTIER

I've never been to a place in Africa I wouldn't like to see again. Well, actually, that's not altogether true . . . during the Second Gulf War I was headquartered in Kuwait, but we moved around quite a bit. I spent a few days in Djibouti, and I'm not particularly interested in going back there. So let me qualify that: I've never been to a *hunting area* in Africa that I wouldn't like to return to! There are some countries that are (or have been) open that I haven't been to, and in the nineteen African countries I have hunted, there are many areas and regions I haven't seen. There remain a few countries that still may open that I'd like to have a chance to see. Africa is a big place, however, and I've seen a lot of it, but no one will see it all.

Frontier Safaris's main headquarters sits on a tall ridge with a commanding view of great game country. The round building is the boma, *enclosed on the sides and open in the center so a wind-proof fire can burn regardless of weather.*

Frontier Safaris isn't hunting buffaloes on its place yet, but someday it might. The outfit has a very nice herd building up, and this breeding bull is truly spectacular.

Over many years and many safaris one can usually find excuses to return to a favored place. There may be some special race of gazork that has eluded you, and after that there's always the chance to find a better one. Eventually even these excuses wear thin, and you're left with the simple fact that you return to a place *because you like it*, and perhaps that's the most valid excuse of all. In terms of "collecting"—a word that I hate when applied to hunting—I have absolutely no reason to return to the Eastern Cape. There is nothing there I need to improve upon, and nothing there that will give me an extra point for the Weatherby Award, which, after a decade as a nominee, I recognize I may never win anyway.

There are other places I would like to return to, but many of them are beyond my means, as are some of the places I haven't been. Ultimately, however, good hunting in good country with good people offers its own excuse, so I returned to South Africa's Eastern Cape yet again in both 2015 and 2016. In 2015 I started at the Rudman family's Blaauwkrantz, as recounted earlier, then went on to a place I'd never been, Barry Burchell's "home range" at his Frontier Safaris, a bit more than two hours northwest of Port Elizabeth. This was another SCI auction hunt that I agreed to accompany; this was in 2015, and it was so much fun that I agreed to do it again in 2016. In that year I started at Barry's Frontier Safaris, then finished by spending a few days with my old friend J. P. Kleinhans on his own "home range" east of Port Elizabeth. I spent more than a month hunting in the Eastern Cape, and in all ways it was wonderful.

In 2015 our auction winners were Charlie Goodwin and Joel Thiesen. Joel brought his son, Blake; Charlie brought his whole family—his wife, Sarah, their three young children, and his dad, Larry Goodwin. This was a first safari for both families, and thus a most important occasion. Donna joined me on that hunt, and it was marvelous in so many ways. First of all, there was no agenda, no grand quest. It was just see it, enjoy it, plan a stalk if you like, or not.

On some days I hunted with Donna; on others she went out by herself and I rode along with Charlie or Joel. At night we gathered at Barry's *boma*, a huge structure with protected walls and roof around the perimeter, but with the center ceiling open to the stars. This was great because on those cold Eastern Cape winter nights, you could enjoy a warm fire, but be protected from wind with most of the smoke escaping.

Donna took this superb Cape hartebeest with a very nice long shot from her LAW in .270 Winchester. It dropped straight down in its tracks.

A huge herd of blesboks on a big ridge at Frontier Safaris. Carefully managed for many years, this is one of the best-stocked areas I've ever seen, with huge acreage and a wide variety of habitat.

Charlie and Joel had acquired a major package of game along with the hunt, and they kept the skinning shed busy. Donna and I didn't dull many knives, but we had a great hunt. This was one of the first outings for Hornady's ELD-X bullet (Extremely Low Drag – eXpanding) bullet. Extreme long-range shooting at game is not my thing, but I was interested to see how this bullet would perform on substantial game. So I shot a blue wildebeest, no problem, and I had one of the longest, most frustrating—and most *interesting*—hunts ever for a zebra.

A small herd of zebras were feeding along a brushy watercourse. We worked our way in on the ridge above them, and from that angle it was almost impossible to be certain which one—if any—was a stallion. I think we were on them for three hours, maybe more, before the animal we thought was the stallion turned away in a small opening, clear enough to see his testicles. I shot him as he swung broadside.

One awesome afternoon we made an incredible double on hartebeest bulls, both at considerable range. There were four bulls, two of them very good. We'd worked our way along a ridge above them and found a perfect boulder to use as a rest. Donna was up first, and at that moment we had no plan to take one apiece. Hers dropped to the shot and stayed down, and the rest milled, so we switched places on the boulder and I shot a second excellent bull. Mine didn't exactly go down on the first shot . . . it's a good idea to avoid competitions with female hunters. They will usually win.

Daughter Brittany, who was at that time living in Johannesburg, came in for a couple of days. We were filming, and it's such a game-rich area I figured we'd get at least a couple of animals on camera with Britt . . . but it just didn't happen. At last light, on her last evening, she took a wonderful blue wildebeest bull. That was the only shot she got, but she did it perfectly and her wildebeest went right down.

As I said, there wasn't any grand quest involved. Donna was pretty much in the same boat because, although the game list in this area is pretty long, she'd taken just about everything the area has to offer on previous hunts. After a couple of days of looking around, she decided her number-one animal would be a nyala. She had a decent bull from Mozambique, but was hoping to find a better one.

Although nyalas don't naturally occur this far south, they were introduced a long time ago and have done well. They're plentiful throughout much of the Eastern Cape today, and Barry has a lot of them on his place. That said, my impression is that the nyala is naturally more of a tropical animal, and I think the best horns usually come from warmer country—Zululand and Mozambique. But, while a monster would have been welcome, the goal was a nyala in the upper twenty inches with a good lyre shape to its horns.

Our elder daughter, Brittany, joined us for just a couple of days, and those weren't especially lucky days. Just at dark on her last evening the only shot she got was at a big blue wildebeest. She got a good one.

Charlie Goodwin made a really nice long shot on this blesbok with a rifle I've never before seen in Africa: a Browning chambered to the .243 Winchester Super Short Magnum.

This shouldn't have been a tall order, but it proved to be. I have no idea how many young and "almost-big-enough" nyalas we saw and passed on, but surely several dozen. One afternoon, back for lunch, we glassed six bulls on the steep slope below the lodge, none quite big enough. So that particular quest failed, and I really didn't have anything special in mind.

Everything, however, was extremely special for both the Thiesens and Goodwins, and they did very well. Joel and Charlie both took excellent greater kudus, and pretty much the works on down from there. They were also luckier on nyalas than we were. Joel got a very nice bull, as did Larry Goodwin. The nyalas were there; we just weren't lucky.

On the last day I got sidetracked by a really nice waterbuck. We were hunting with Barry's son, Scot, just seventeen years old that year and already an accomplished PH. He took me on a brilliant stalk, and we should have gotten a shot at forty yards, but at the last second a nervous cow spooked, and they ran over the ridge in a group. That should have been the end of it, but we dropped over the edge and caught them on the far side. I hit the bull but not well, and after a bit of cat-and-mouse, I managed to finish him at something over four hundred yards.

It was such a fun hunt that I agreed to a similar auction package for the following year, 2016. This time our "victims" were Steve Gieseking and Lloyd Gettemeyer.

Steve came solo, while Lloyd was accompanied by his wife, Debbie, and their two daughters. Steve and Lloyd are hunting buddies, and while Steve had hunted in Africa a couple times previously, it was a first safari for the Gettemeyer clan.

Donna needed to use the time to see her dad in Florida, so my younger daughter, Caroline, came with me. This couldn't possibly have worked out better. The older Gettemeyer daughter, Morgan, was twenty, the same as Caroline. The two girls hit it off immediately, and, of course, both were big hits with the young PHs in camp. Caroline and I hunted with Scot Burchell, now eighteen, and I was again impressed at how great a PH he is, and not just for his age. Obviously he's hunting on the family property so he knows it perfectly, but he's calm and confident, and he inspires confidence . . . and is already an exceptional judge of trophy quality.

Once again there was no grand quest for me. I was using Hornady's ELD-X again, and again in a .300 Winchester Magnum—my left-hand Jarrett—but I was

Caroline, my younger daughter, joined me at Frontier in 2016. Her first animal, on the first day, was a really nice blue wildebeest, cleanly taken with her little 7mm-08. That's Scot Burchell with her, a really fine young professional hunter.

using a 200-grain ELD-X instead of the 180-grain bullet I used the previous year. Years ago I often "upgraded" to a 200-grain, .30-caliber bullet, but recently I've thought (and written) that today's bullets are so darn good that there's no reason to go heavier than 180 grains in a .30-caliber. I'm not sure that's wrong, but I am sure that this 200-grain bullet hit extremely hard.

I shot only three animals on the hunt, but all three were big and tough, and all three were taken with one shot each. A very big blue wildebeest and a zebra stallion each dropped in its tracks, literally flattened . . . something you don't see often with either species. The third animal was a nice eland bull, and no .30-caliber is a big gun on eland. We glassed a group of six bulls feeding on a ridge 800 yards away. Scot marked them well, got the wind right, and led me on a perfect stalk. We got right in the middle of them, and I had a fifty-yard quartering-away shot.

The bull took the bullet hard, but ran with the group and was instantly out of sight. I have a lot of respect for eland—or, for that matter, anything that big—so I was a bit worried, and more worried when we couldn't find a drop of blood anywhere. Scot left his tracker to try to pick up spoor while we cast ahead on the tracks of the group—and found the bull down and done about eighty yards down the ridge.

Mostly, for us, this was Caroline's hunt. It was just her second time in Africa, and the area held a lot of animals she'd never hunted—and some she'd never seen. We brought her infamous Ruger 77 in 7mm-08, stocked in the hottest pink laminate you've ever seen. She was shooting Hornady's American Whitetail load with 139-grain Interlock bullets, a plain-Jane, "vanilla-ice-cream" load, but devastatingly effective at the modest velocity of the 7mm-08.

She opened the ball game with a blue wildebeest, a very tough animal that I have a lot of respect for, and, obviously, the 7mm-08 is a small cartridge for this animal. Scot spotted the herd just at dawn, up on a ridge not far from camp. There was a very good bull by himself on the right-hand side, so we ducked into the brush and made a fairly direct approach. Scot got Caroline situated on the sticks, about 130 yards from the wildebeest, and he later noted that her barrel was dead-steady when the shot went off. The hit looked really good, but the bull ran hard to the left, as did the herd.

The group reappeared on the next hillside a quarter-mile away, and we were pretty sure Caroline's bull wasn't with them. Seeing the hit, I'd bet money he was down—but exactly where and how far was another question. So we walked to where

I didn't do much shooting on either safari, but in 2016 I was really excited by this eland. Scot Burchell took me on a perfect stalk, and I shot the eland with my Jarrett .300 using 200-grain Hornady ELD-X. Although it's not a big gun for eland, its performance was perfect.

the wildebeest had stood, quickly finding running tracks to the left. Another twenty yards and we almost stumbled over his dead carcass.

Caroline continued this performance with monotonous regularity: hartebeest, blesbok, impala, springbok, warthog . . . no problems. The animal she wanted most was the kudu that had eluded her on the previous trip, and this again proved a challenge. Getting a kudu would be a matter of luck even though there were plenty around. The kudus were just coming into the rut, and Steve and Lloyd both shot theirs in the first few days. Scot and I, however, couldn't seem to make it happen for Caroline.

We saw lots of immature bulls . . . and one morning we saw a monster. We were working our way up a narrow road along a ridge, steep and brushy on both sides. Scot's tracker, in the high seat behind, stopped us frantically, pointing ahead. Getting out quickly, we got rifle and sticks and moved forward a dozen yards to a slight dip in the road. Just off the road a hundred yards away stood the best Eastern Cape kudu I've seen in many years, maybe ever. Scot got Caroline on the sticks, but the roll of the terrain was such that she was a bit too short, and all she could see was horn tips. It was frustrating because Scot and I could see the bull clearly—but there was just no way Caroline could get a shot.

The kudu calmly walked away into the brush, *gone*. A hundred yards above us, the hillside was open, but below that the brush was lush and green, as was the valley below. We spent the rest of the morning trying to locate that bull, and we tried on several other occasions as well. He never showed himself again, but he was there—a month later a hunter I know sent me a photo of him. His son had taken him, and the whole camp was excited. For sure that was the kudu of the season, but the hunter couldn't tell me what he measured because they never put a tape on him, an extremely ethical concept that, unfortunately, is all too rare today.

We had several days of high winds. No animals like wind because it baffles their senses, but it bothers some species more than others, and it made kudus especially hard to find. On perhaps the fifth or sixth day we caught a calm, sunny afternoon, and the kudus were on parade. As usual they were mostly younger bulls, but we made a stalk on two bulls feeding together. Neither was quite big enough, but one was going to be a giant, deep curls and long horns. His tips were still pointed out; he needed another year or two. Caroline could have shot him and few would have known the difference. I knew what he was—and wasn't—but I kept my mouth shut. Scot, a young PH anxious to please, but equally anxious to do the right thing, said no.

We were glassing a series of ascending ridges, working our way along what they call the Up and Down Road. I think we saw more than a dozen bulls in a couple of hours, probably thirty kudus. Sunset was approaching fast when we glassed two last bulls, feeding along contentedly. One was clearly young, but the other was mature. He had done all the growing he was going to do. The tips weren't perfectly parallel and he was no giant—but he was certainly mature. The wind was good, and I thought we had enough daylight to close on him. I think Scot was of the mind that we had some days left and might find a bigger bull. To my thinking it was Caroline's first (and long desired) kudu. A first *any animal* not only doesn't have to be a monster, but perhaps shouldn't be.

We were on a ridge, glassing these bulls halfway up the next ridge at maybe five hundred yards. I think Scot had in his mind to pass and he was the boss, but he made the tactical error of asking "*Oom* (Uncle) Craig, what do you think?"

Caroline and Scot with her Eastern Cape greater kudu. The kudu was her most-wanted animal, and we looked at quite a few immature bulls before we found this one.

Well, maybe he wanted approval because it wasn't a huge kudu—but what a great setup. Pointing to some thick cover just below our crest, I said, "I think we should slip into those trees and work our way down—we should be able to get fairly close."

We set up at the base of our ridge, just 150 yards from the kudus, but only the smaller bull was visible, working his way up the far ridge. I was a few steps behind, staying out of it. Although the bigger bull was obscured, Scot could see him moving behind some trees. He got Caroline on the bull, and when the kudu stepped out at two hundred yards, she fired, dropping him in his tracks. This was unusual. I figured she had hit a bit too high, and was worried that he might get back up—I lost the biggest kudu I've ever shot at to a similar scenario. Scot figured the same, so he had Caroline shoot again, but it was totally unnecessary. The kudu had dropped to a perfectly placed shoulder shot, and no second shot was needed.

Morgan and Caroline hunted together on several outings, and I went out with Steve and/or Lloyd a few times. Caroline spent most of the rest of her hunt in search of a nyala, and for us it was a repeat of Donna's hunt the previous year. Well, not exactly . . . we actually saw three or four really nice bulls, but at the conclusion

Steve Gieseking was truly charmed on this hunt, running into one great animal after another. I was with him when he took this truly excellent waterbuck.

of our stalks, either they had vanished into the brush or it got too dark. So it was the same in that no shots were fired at nyalas.

They were definitely there, however. On the second day I was out with Steve and his PH, Jason. We were on the rimrock above a deep canyon, glassing two kudu bulls way up the ridge on the far side. Jason's tracker happened to look left and saw a very big nyala bull feeding in thick bush down in the bottom. We made a quick lateral stalk, and, of course, the bull wasn't visible when we got in position. But he had to be there, and after an interminable wait, he stepped into a small opening and Steve shot him.

That was sort of the way Steve's hunt went: All the animals he wanted stepped out and seemingly surrendered to him. It started with an exceptional bushbuck on the first day, quite possibly the single most difficult animal in that area, and continued throughout the hunt. I was also with him when he shot a truly exceptional waterbuck.

Things are rarely exactly equal when two buddies hunt together, so it was perfectly normal—though no doubt a bit frustrating—that Lloyd had a much more difficult hunt. But, like Steve, he filled his twelve-animal package without great difficulty, along with some spares. Caroline and I had our timing a bit messed up and we left a day before the rest of the group, so, unfortunately, we missed seeing Morgan's spectacular 40-inch gemsbok bull, a great gemsbok anywhere and a monster for the Eastern Cape.

Before we left, however, Caroline acquired a nemesis. It wasn't the nyala because she never really had a chance. Instead it was a waterbuck. At last light, she missed a giant. I wasn't there, but by description it was bigger than any waterbuck I've ever taken. We looked all day the next day, and unfortunately it wasn't a perfectly clean miss . . . we found just a few drops of blood, quickly fading to nothing. Probably a grazing hit, who knows, but we couldn't find it, and it was never found. Although a bit hard to swallow, it's not a bad thing to recognize that this, too, is part of hunting.

J. P. Kleinhans picked us up at Frontier Safaris at midday. J.P. is an old friend, but I'd only hunted with him in Mozambique, meaning that I'd never seen his home operation in the Eastern Cape. Like Barry and Liselle Burchell, J.P. is a member of

Caroline's bad luck on nyala broke at the last minute. We spent the last weekend with our friend J. P. Kleinhans at his place. He took us for a "little drive," and he showed us a group of more than a dozen nyala bulls—an amazing sight. We think this was the largest, but who knows? Caroline made a fine shot in failing light and had her nyala.

In 2015 Donna was looking for a nyala, and in 2016 Caroline was looking for one. We saw bunches of young bulls like this one, but at Frontier the big boys never gave either of them a chance.

our Endorsed Outfitters group, so I thought it was important to spend a couple of days with him and his wife, Natia. My intent was not to hunt, but J.P. had other ideas. His area is lower and warmer, with a lot of very thick thornbush, ideal for nyalas and bushbucks.

On the drive over Caroline recounted her victories and her trials and tribulations, so we went out that evening to "look at some nyalas." Just at dark we had a group of thirteen nyala bulls and a few females feeding below us, less than two hundred yards away. J.P. spread the sticks low so that Caroline could sit behind them and get steady, and then the hardest part was sorting out the biggest bull. Most were youngsters, of course, but there were three or four shooters, and we finally agreed on the best of the bunch. The next trick was to stay focused on him while the light faded and while they mixed back and forth. Finally he stepped clear, and Caroline shot him perfectly on the shoulder, a gorgeous nyala. I'm glad she'd spent quite some time looking for nyalas with Scot, else she might think it's an easy animal . . . and the nyala most certainly is not.

We also tried to fix the waterbuck problem, but that didn't quite work out. That's OK; it's always good to have *something* to go back for that you really, really want, and perhaps even better if it's an animal you failed to get earlier.

We had only three days, so we spent the last one in a lovely concession of tall ridges about an hour from J.P.'s place. It was my turn, and we were looking for a kudu. We found a very big bull far up on a steep, brushy ridge, and I set up at 450 yards, dialing the range. I think I could have pulled it off, although who knows . . . but he never stepped clear of the brush. When he didn't show himself, I was perfectly happy to call it a day. It had been a wonderful Eastern Cape safari, and probably not the last.

CHAPTER TWENTY-EIGHT

AT LONG LAST, CAPRIVI

Throughout most of my lifetime—and for decades before I was born—it was called the "Caprivi Strip." It is a strange extension of Namibia that runs generally eastward between Angola and Zambia to the north and Botswana to the south, extending 280 miles to the Zimbabwe border. Today this name is politically incorrect; it is now officially the "Zambezi Region" of Namibia. That sounds odd, because "Caprivi" has an African ring to it, like Serengeti and Kalahari. Except it is not. It was named after German Chancellor Leo von Caprivi, who negotiated its existence to create a corridor and, hopefully, a navigable waterway

Although one tusk was broken off near the tip, this is a spectacular old elephant, and especially good for Caprivi. Japsie Blaauw, a great young PH, did a perfect job.

Caprivi is the most open country I've ever hunted elephant in. The cowherds we ran into were mostly in open grassland,

between German South-West Africa (now Namibia) and German East Africa (now Tanzania). A small obstacle known as Victoria Falls made this a pipe dream, but the corridor remains part of modern-day Namibia.

It is a place I have long wanted to see, a gaping hole in my African experience. It was open to hunting briefly in the 1970s, before the long Angolan conflict made it untenable. I should have gone there then, when it was truly unspoiled. I did not, but as a young hunter I found it fascinating, a place where many of Africa's most interesting animals came together. Historically good for the entire Big Five, the area also hosts lechwes, sitatungas, kudus, roans, and sables, one of few areas on the continent where so many desirable antelopes can be found naturally in one place.

It was closed for many years, but it's been open for quite some time, and I missed some chances to hunt there. Joe Bishop went there on an elephant hunt with Dirk de Bod, but it was a time when I just couldn't go. In 2013, hunting with Jamy Traut, I was supposed to go to Caprivi, but a leopard permit wasn't available, so I wound up with African Twilight southwest of Windhoek. That was a great hunt, but I still wanted to see Caprivi.

In 2015 I finally went to Caprivi for one last elephant. That's my story and I'll stick to it—for now. I've done enough elephant hunting, and although the pursuit and the approach are wonderful and hunting is essential for management, I've always felt a lot of remorse when I've taken an elephant. Maybe if I had any clue where I could look for a much bigger bull with some chance for success I'd try, but I really don't.

In my time in Africa elephant hunting has changed a lot. Elephant hunting was already closed when I hunted in Kenya in 1977, but we saw huge herds of elephants—including some very good bulls—on the open Tsavo plains. Kenya closed hunting altogether a few weeks later, and in just a few years most of Kenya's elephants were gone.

naking it relatively simple to make sure there were no mature bulls in the groups without disturbing them.*

In the 1980s, when commercial poaching was at its height, it seemed almost certain that elephant hunting would soon be a thing of the past. Fortunately, this was incorrect. The better protected southern herds were impacted little. Zimbabwe remained constant, Botswana reopened, and the ravaged herds of Mozambique and Tanzania began to rebuild. The limited elephant habitat in Namibia and South Africa reached carrying capacity, and Caprivi reopened. In the 1990s and early 2000s we were in a new era of elephant hunting, with lots of choices.

These lines are written in late 2016, and the pendulum has swung again. Africa is being ravaged by a new wave of commercial poaching, with populations falling almost everywhere. Elephant hunting is closed in Botswana, and Americans are no longer able to import elephant trophies from Tanzania or Zimbabwe . . . and haven't been able to import Mozambique ivory since 1990. At this writing there appears hope for legally hunted Zimbabwe ivory, but as of 2015 South Africa and northern Namibia had suddenly become the premier destinations for an elephant safari.

Caprivi has changed, too. The habitat remains excellent, but after numerous resettlement schemes there are lots of villages and lots of cattle, so room for wildlife has shrunk dramatically.

Our bull was clearly too big for the "own use" permit I had, but in addition to a broken tusk, he was limping badly on his right hindquarter, so the game department gave us the go-ahead. The poor animal had been stitched up the right rear with a burst from an AK-47, probably a week or so before.

Once the elephant was down, we sent word and villagers quickly gathered. Recovering the meat is extremely important in almost all modern elephant hunting, and absolutely essential in Caprivi.

As a geopolitical area, Caprivi is small—elephants can walk across it, from Botswana to Angola or Zambia (and vice versa) in a day. With Botswana's grossly overpopulated elephant herd just to the south, a quarter million strong, there is much elephant movement in Caprivi, but resident game is reduced to pockets. The quality of big buffaloes, roans, and sables is good—but quotas are, of necessity, small. So, in the main, Caprivi is no longer a "general bag" destination; the elephant quota is higher than for any other species.

I hunted with my old friends at Omujeve Safaris, brothers Corné and Nick Kruger, and Japsie Blaauw was my PH. It wasn't just a specialized safari, it was single-minded: I had a permit for one elephant bull, period. It was an "own use" permit, essentially a community meat quota elephant, with the nonexportable tusks going to the government and the meat distributed to the local villagers who are plagued by elephants on a constant basis.

There was a sharp upper limit on tusk weight, and all this was just fine with me for multiple reasons. First, my primary purpose was to see Caprivi, so any permit offered an excuse. Second, with closures and bans elsewhere, the value of Caprivi trophy elephant permits had justifiably skyrocketed; the nonexportable "own use" permits were a lot more reasonable. Caprivi has a lot of elephants, and a lot of bulls, but the average tusk weight is probably in the upper forty-pound range, with odds of finding a bull much over fifty pounds fairly slim. So, I reasoned, *you're not going to find the elephant of your dreams, so it's OK if you can't bring your tusks home.* Remember I said that!

Omujeve operates most of its Caprivi hunts in western Caprivi, not a huge area but well-buffered between Botswana and a couple of small national parks. At the end of the hunt, with a few days to spare, we spent some time there. It's a beautiful area of thornbush and grassland, with plenty of buffaloes, a lot of red lechwes and some other plains game, hippos and crocs along the Chobe River, and constant elephant movement.

My hunt was in a new conservancy in far eastern Caprivi, and the country was quite different. This area was also on the Chobe River, which is just a trickle in September, with Botswana's Chobe National Park to the south. This ensured constant movement of elephants and buffaloes back and forth across the river, but the area was mostly a sea of grass with just scattered pockets of cover.

This was a new concession for Omujeve, so they hadn't yet built a camp. Instead, we stayed at a tented tourist lodge a few miles up the river. The people were really nice and the camp wasn't very full, but I was amused that they put Japsie and me in the very farthest tents, so photographic guests wouldn't be disturbed by our comings and goings with rifles. Hey, around the bar and campfire everyone was very friendly, and it was really a lot of fun, but we tried to keep pure hunting conversation to ourselves!

It was sort of a park boundary hunt on steroids, since the Chobe National Park boundary was also the Namibia/Botswana border. We started by glassing the river, lots of cattle here and there and a huge herd of buffaloes on the Botswana side—but nothing on our side. Then we shifted to the dense tree lines to the north, several miles away across the sea of grass. There were actually lots of elephants there, and we worked several herds. They were mostly cowherds with calves, but there were a couple of young bulls. So, in the strictest sense of the meat quota permit, we could have taken a bull with little difficulty. But that's not the way the game should be played. Japsie and I didn't really want to shoot a young bull with potential; our goal was to shoot an older bull, perhaps with broken tusks or simply one with small tusks.

In the afternoon, when the tree lines didn't pan out, we returned to the river. Japsie had hunted in this area before, and had taken good elephants and buffaloes by being patient and watching the river boundary line. Patience is not my strongest suit, but I'm all for whatever works. He was right: As the afternoon progressed we saw a lot of elephants wa-

Some of the villagers brought their families when they came to help butcher the elephant. Japsie was prepared with a big sack of candy to hand out to the children.

tering on the Botswana side. Toward sunset, several small groups came across to our lush grasslands, but no bulls.

Every morning we'd pick up a local guide who represented the villages in the conservancy, and every evening we would drop him by his village. He asked around, and on the third day he had a report of a "big bull" hanging around a village to the southwest. We went down there and picked up a local herdsman. He took us to some nearby thickets, and we saw a small herd of cows. Nope, that wasn't what he was looking for, so we cast around in a big circle, checking footpaths. Japsie found a fresh track, but it wasn't large, so we pronounced it a young bull and went back to the river line. There it was the same deal as before: Lots of afternoon movement, but only small herds of cows came across to our side.

The next morning started with a feeling of *déjà vu*: That "big bull" had been around a village—close-by a cluster of huts—all night, and the villagers were afraid of him. This time our herdsman guide took us right to the elephant, which was standing in a five-acre woodlot surrounded by grassland. We spotted him from the truck, but it was too far and too thick for a look. So Japsie and I unlimbered, he with his .458 Lott and me with one of the new English-made Rigby .416s.

The wind was good and the bull was calm, so we got a really close look. Japsie looked long and hard, and perhaps longingly, but I knew instantly: This bull was too big! The right tusk was long, heavy, and perfect. The right tusk was also thick, but several inches were broken off short at the tip. He was an old elephant, hollowed and gaunt, and a great elephant . . . but too great to fit any "nontrophy" definition.

The last act was to pile wood on what little remained of the elephant and light a funeral pyre. Aside from appropriate cleanup, the theory among elephant hunters is that this prevents other elephants from knowing one of their brethren had died at that spot.

As we backed off, a stray eddy gave us away. The bull lifted his trunk in alarm, then spun away and started off. As he did we saw that he was limping on his right rear leg. He ran just a few steps, then slowed and walked slowly into the trees.

Omujeve's Corné Kruger was baiting for a big crocodile for another client. He wanted to make sure he had his trail camera just right, so he approached the bait at crocodile level—he did, however, stop short of chewing on the bait!

Back at the truck we held a conference. Our conservancy rep—who wanted the meat—was firm: The elephant was injured and had a broken tusk, so we should take him. Japsie was uncertain. Not knowing the precise rules, I had no opinion. Japsie Blaauw is a great young PH, and he did exactly the right thing: He got out the satellite phone and called the game department. Obviously we couldn't speculate on the nature or severity of the injury to the elephant's leg, but we had all seen that one tusk was broken off short, and that was unequivocal. It took a while, but the game department gave us the green light.

By this time we had no idea where the elephant might have gone, so we checked the perimeter of the woodlot. There were no tracks going out, so he was still in there. Now it was past noon, in the heat of the day, and the elephant should be calm and resting. We got ready again, this time deadly serious, got the slight breeze in our favor, and went into the trees just a bit ahead of where we'd last seen the bull.

There was no tracking; we were just a few yards in when we saw him dimly through branches, standing under a shady tree. Checking the wind carefully, Japsie led me in, angling for a side brain shot. We were still sixty yards out, too far, when the elephant suddenly walked away. At first I thought we'd spooked him although I didn't have a clue exactly how, but he walked a few dozen yards before stopping in another shady patch. We made a big half-circle to make sure the wind was perfect, came in again, and exactly the same thing happened. This time he walked almost to the edge of the grove, stopping with one tusk resting on a big anthill.

Our next half-circle took us back into the clearing, and then we used the termite mound for cover. At fifteen yards Japsie stopped and nodded, and then we started to side-step to the right to get the elephant in view. Yes, there he was, full frontal . . . but a big tree limb blocked the forehead. Inevitably the elephant saw us, not yet threatening, but concerned. He took a few steps toward us, and I took the frontal brain shot at twelve yards. Japsie followed up instantly, and although I ran up for a finishing shot, the bull was down.

He was a fantastic old bull, bigger than we thought—over sixty pounds on the left tusk, over fifty on the broken tusk. You bet I had regrets about not being able to take this, my last elephant, home—but no regrets about shooting him. The limp had been caused by a burst from an AK-47 into his right hip. The muzzle was obviously climbing in full auto because four or five bullets had impacted the hip solidly in a vertical line, and two more had made deep furrows as they skipped across his broad back, somehow missing the ridge of the spine.

The encounter had probably happened a week or so earlier. The entire hip was horribly infected, the bullet wounds oozing pus. His suffering must have been awful. This was actually a small-bodied elephant, more typical of Zambia elephants than the huge-bodied Botswana elephants. Undoubtedly it was his track we'd seen the day before and passed because most Caprivi elephants come from Botswana. In this part of Caprivi Zambia lies to the north, so my guess is he encountered the poacher somewhere in the southwestern corner of Zambia and fled south as far as he could. For the past few days he'd been holed up in this little woodlot, in too much pain to continue on to Botswana and relative safety. Whether he could have survived or not is unknown, but he had lost much weight and was in poor condition. Because of that, plus the widespread infection, I doubt he would have survived.

Word was sent, and in an hour or so more than a dozen men—some with their wives and children—converged on us to help with the butchering. It took until nearly sundown, then wood was piled on the bones and offal and the remains were burned. A Viking funeral pyre seemed in order for this old warrior, but the practical reason is to erase the evidence that an elephant had died here so that other elephants wouldn't suspect what had happened.

We saw a big herd of buffaloes across the river in Chobe every day, and one afternoon they were close enough for glassing. Some of the bulls were spectacular! With time remaining we went to Omujeve's main camp in the west where we saw quite a few elephants and more buffaloes. Again I was struck by the excellent trophy quality of the buffalo bulls.

After so many years of wanting to see it, I was a bit disappointed by Caprivi. There are lots of villages and hard-surfaced roads—to me it is not "wild Africa" anymore. But it is a great area for dangerous game, and I decided I'd have to return to take at least one Caprivi buffalo.

Chapter Twenty-Nine

The Bella Forest

On my first hunt in Liberia, as reported in chapter seventeen, I expended a lot of effort (and faith), but the hunt yielded little in terms of success. There was actually quite a lot of game up in the northwest corner near the Guinea border, but zebra duikers were seemingly absent, and although black duikers and water chevrotains were definitely present, I never had a chance at either. Obviously, I needed to try again if I could find the right area.

After that rocky initial season, guide Tony Henry scoured the countryside for months, talking to village hunters and walking along forest trails. Success improved, and in 2014 outfitter Morris Dougba reported that he'd found a really good area for zebra duikers, and all the other game. In December 2014 Ken Wilson, then Morris's agent, had a truly spectacular safari, easily the best of both competing outfitters since Liberia had reopened. Ken took a zebra duiker, water chevrotain, and what must surely have been the new world-record yellow-backed duiker. All omens were good, so Dr. Mike Adams and I booked for a fourteen-day hunt in March 2015.

On the second night I took an Ogilby duiker. Although not one of the more colorful forest duikers, it's a rarity and the first taken since Liberia reopened. This began a weird rotation of animals between hunting partner Dr. Mike Adams and me.

Then the devastating Ebola epidemic hit. It was pretty clear no safaris would be conducted, but rather than cancel prematurely, Mike and I hung in, waiting to see. In the late winter it just got worse; Morris

As unlikely as it seems, a day after I got my Ogilby duiker, Mike came into camp with a bay duiker . . . and another Ogilby. We were off to a very good start! That's Mike's guide, Amos, on the left.

cancelled the season and, amazingly, Ken sent us a full refund. On the one hand, I was pleased with the honesty. On the other hand, it didn't bode well; Mike and I would have been happy to let things ride for 2015, but whether there would be a 2016 season seemed in question.

In the aftermath of Ebola, American expat Steve Kobrine, Morris's only competitor, did not return to Liberia. One of Kobrine's clients took the first zebra duiker in modern Liberia, but by the time of the Ebola outbreak, the two outfitters were running neck and neck on this great prize. After things settled down, Mike Adams and I rebooked for March 2016, again for a full fourteen-day hunt. We didn't get the exact dates we wanted, but we would start our hunt in the dark of the moon, the period that veteran forest hunter and Weatherby winner Rex Baker believes is most critical. As our hunt progressed, the moon would be increasingly bright and eventually full. Whether this would matter remained to be seen.

I call Mike the Duiker King. It's no joke that he's passionate about the little antelopes. While a ten-day hunt is normal, he wanted extra days to give him the best possible odds. Me, well, I really wanted a zebra duiker and a water chevrotain. I figured this would either happen or not; for me the extra days might offer a better chance for a dwarf buffalo or a red river hog. I'm always an optimist in the planning stages. Going in, I was expecting *everything*!

Mike and I flew into Monrovia in the evening, checked into a grossly overpriced hotel, and had a late dinner with Rex Baker and Wilson Stout, who had just come in from Morris's camp. Wilson was over the moon: He had taken a zebra duiker, a water chevrotain, and a good black duiker. Rex had gotten a water chevrotain, the only animal he really wanted. He'd spent the rest of his hunt trying to find buffaloes and had failed—but he'd seen quite a few tracks. Up until that time in the season, Morris's clients were pretty much 100 percent on zebra duikers, a marvelous accomplishment for Morris and his team, and about 50 percent on water chevrotains. No one else had hunted longer than ten days, so the signs were obviously very good for our hunt.

Mike Adams brought in the first water chevrotain. I was happy for him, but at that time the camp was running about 50 percent on this great prize, so when he got one, I assumed I would not.

The new area was in the Bella Forest north of Monrovia. Beyond the coastline, Liberia's road network is just plain awful; it wasn't all that far to camp, but it was a solid half-day's drive with several questionable bridges that might or might not survive the next rainy season. We arrived in the early afternoon, greeted by guides Tony Henry and Amos and the redoubtable Franz Coupé.

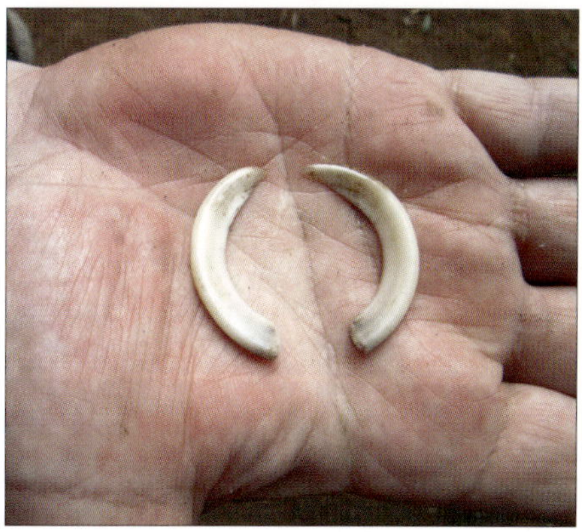

The water chevrotain is one of the fanged deer, thus related to Asian muntjac and water deer.

Tony Henry and Franz Coupé joined me to photograph my water chevrotain, taken just a day after Mike Adams got his. Most hunters would rate this as Liberia's second great prize after the zebra duiker, but I think the water chevrotain is really cool.

Franz, a genuine African legend, is a spry eighty-year-old working on his fiftieth season as a PH. He wouldn't guide for the small forest animals—that was Tony's and Amos's job—but he was there to help out and try to develop the buffalo situation.

Having Franz in camp was both invaluable and delightful. I'd never hunted with him, but I'd known of him for years. He knew *everybody*, and had guided an inordinate number of famous hunters during his long career. We traded stories for hours on end, and that's a very good thing because Liberian hunting is a matter of hurry up and wait, with long periods of heat and boredom.

Virtually all duiker hunting is done at night. The black duiker is somewhat diurnal, but most of the forest duikers and especially the water chevrotains are almost entirely nocturnal. It's common for hunters to insist on daylight hunting, but if you try to hunt both day and night you wear yourself out in just a few days. Trying to figure out how best to play it, Mike asked Tony and Amos on the first afternoon if, so far in the season, *any* animals had been taken in daylight. The answer was no, nothing in daylight. With two weeks to hunt we had a long haul in tropical heat, so we immediately decided to concentrate on night hunting; days could be spent scouting for buffalo and pig sign and napping as we could. That was the plan, but we'd soon find that our days would take a different turn.

Camp was far short of fancy, but adequate. Mike and I shared a thatch-roof rondavel, complete with bucket shower and a genuine flush toilet, with the reservoir filled by the bucket. The campsite had been mostly cleared and looked down on a running stream—a well-chosen spot. The dining and lounge area was off the kitchen, an open cement deck with thatched roof for shade—and I can assure you no campfire was needed!

That first afternoon we unpacked and checked the guns, and after that we sweated a lot while we tried to nap our way through the agonies of jet lag. The sweating wouldn't stop, but in a couple of days we became acclimated and the humid heat was less oppressive. At least that was true for me; Mike Adams is from Louisiana, and I don't think the climate bothered him nearly as much as it did me.

We'd brought all kinds of stuff: bug-proof tents and freeze-dried meals for spike camping; all manner of goodies to augment camp fare; mounds of composition books, bundles of pencils, and pounds of hard candy for the local school kids; and somehow Mike had managed to cram a full-size chainsaw into an extra duffel bag!

We used neither the tents nor the Mountain House meals. Spiking out was discussed, and might have been useful if we'd ever found fresh enough buffalo tracks to take action on, but we did not. All game was taken by simply walking out from camp on an extensive network of forest trails Tony and Amos had cut specifically for the purpose. Camp fare was generally plain—lots of rice and enough chicken that we started to grow feathers—but Morris had sent in a nice Liberian

Franz Coupé (left) and Mike Adams at the drying rack. With such extreme humidity, the only way to properly dry salted skins is to place them over a very slow fire.

Local villagers were harvesting palm nuts in a nearby forest. We used these nuts as well as salt to establish several bait sites for red river hogs. Such ploys are often irresistible, but although we had fresh tracks early in the hunt, nothing came in, and no more fresh tracks were seen.

lady to cook. She did a fine job with what she had to work with, and was a stickler for cleanliness: Neither Mike nor I had any stomach issues, which is saying a lot, considering the length of hunt, the hours, and the conditions.

The camp guns were mostly the same as I'd seen in 2013: three 12-gauge pump guns, an SKB, a Mossberg, and an old Winchester Model 25; a Model 70 Super Grade .458; and one addition—a scoped Ruger No. 1 in .375 H&H. All were somewhat the worse for wear after three rough seasons in the forest, but still perfectly functional. Mike decided the SKB fit him best, and I latched onto the Mossberg because of its ambidextrous tang safety. We each took a couple of "pattern board" shots to verify the hold, and we were ready to face the forest, or as ready as we were going to be.

These two shotguns had 3-inch 12-gauge chambers. Morris had a choice of Remington 3-inch shells with No. 2 shot or 2¾-inch shells loaded in Mali, apparently with No. 4 shot. Mike and I both started with the good 3-inch shells, but the distances were so short that I found them needlessly destructive, so I switched from Remington green to Mali red, and I think Mike did, too. The Mali cartridges are the only locally available ammo, so they are what all the local hunters use. We found them deadly and effective on the smaller duikers. They might have been underpowered if we'd run into one of the big duikers, yellow-backed or Jentink, or either a red river hog or giant forest hog—in Liberian-speak, "red pigs" and "black pigs"—but this never happened although Mike and I generally loaded a Mali red first, followed by Remington green in the magazine—with a scarce and precious slug load handy in a pocket.

Both shotguns worked very well. Over the course of the hunt Mike and I shot well over a dozen animals between us with an equal number of shells, the only glitch being that he encountered one misfire. The "system" of forest hunting at night was also effective. It worked like this: Tony and Amos, walking first with headlamps, were going to see things Mike and I couldn't possibly see. This was partly because they would be in the lead, but mostly because their "forest eyes" were a lot better than ours. When they saw something, whether a reflected eye or just movement, they would do their very best to identify the animal, and if it was something we were looking for, they would aim a laser pointer. Both Amos and Tony were very good at seeing game, identifying the species, and pointing it out. Under these circumstances, however, there is simply no way to properly identify the sex of these small animals in thick forest, let alone judge (or even see) the horns.

This is regrettable, but probably not the management sin it appears to be. The small forest duikers have a much shorter life span than larger antelopes, reach sexual maturity at a much younger age, and apparently breed at any time of the year. They are, thus, naturally very prolific, so management and sustained yield are probably more a matter of restricting the offtake rather than attempting a males-only harvest, which is actually impossible. Thus, on the rarer or more desirable animals such as zebra duikers and water chevrotains, either sex should be considered an equal trophy—and getting either one depends entirely on luck.

This being the case, although the Liberian license allows multiples, Mike and I judged it much the same as the situation with the royal antelopes in Ghana: The zebra duikers, at least, should be restricted to one per customer. At the tail end of the safari that was our recommendation to Morris, but that lay in the future. As we prepared for that first evening, we didn't know if we'd even see a zebra duiker, and many long nights would pass before that question was answered.

Camp food was far from fancy—a lot of chicken and a lot of rice—but our cook was very good and a stickler for cleanliness. None of us had any stomach issues, which is saying quite a lot in the forest.

After a couple of nights I got used to it, but that first night was eerie and weird.

For me the great prize of the trip was this ancient black duiker, more gray than black and with incredibly thick horns. Even with one broken horn, he's one of the largest ever taken.

Tony walked first, scanning constantly with his headlamp. I stayed as close behind as I could without bumping him, my LED headlamp dimmed to cast just a small pool of light at our feet. I walked with my head down, constantly watching for snakes (which, fortunately, were never seen); and for sharp *punji* stakes left from cutting the trail (these were not prevalent, but common enough to create a hazard). Although much cooler than the midday heat, the air was still warm and close. I could almost hear myself sweat. After a half-hour my shirt was soaked; after an hour my trousers were wet and heavy to the knees.

The walking was slow and steady and generally not difficult, and I don't think Tony missed much. In some cases the trails led along streambeds, especially good for water chevrotains; in other cases, it went up and down surprisingly tall ridges. On some really steep spots vine "handrails" had been laid, so we could literally pull ourselves up hand over hand, or let ourselves down in the dark with some measure of safety.

That first night we left camp just at dark and walked about three hours, seeing absolutely nothing. At some point Tony asked what I thought. I *thought* I was tired, but what I said was, "Tony, there's nothing moving; we're wasting our time." Obviously this is what he thought, too, which is why he asked, so we circled back to camp by another trail. The trail network was extensive and well-laid out, but in the dark almost every inch looked much the same. Once in a while I'd recognize a stream crossing—often a vine bridge—or a distinctive tree or handrail, but I seriously doubt I could have ever found my own way back to camp.

On that first night I was fairly sure I recognized a trail intersection, and in a short time I saw the glow of camp lanterns through the trees. Franz was waiting up for us, but Mike wasn't back yet, so we enjoyed the first of several late-night trips down Africa's memory lane. Mike came in an hour or so later, also empty-handed—not an auspicious start.

Things changed on the second night, at least for me. I don't think we were 600 yards from camp when Tony's body language changed . . . a bit later I knew exactly what was happening, but at that moment I could see nothing, so I had no idea. He stopped, staring, then moved forward a few steps and stopped, headlamp stationary. Although clueless, I had enough sense to be ready. Tony's laser pointer went on, and as I raised the shotgun I saw movement for the first time, a reddish animal turning away just as I fired.

At this point, as I'd been instructed, I remained still so Tony could keep his bearings while he dove into the bush. A few seconds later I lost sight of him, and then he called for help. The animal—I still had no idea what it was—had fallen over a steep bank into the stream below. I hustled into the forest, found the bank with Tony below, and reached down to give him a hand. At this point I asked, "What is it?"

Triumph in his voice, he said, "Ogilby!"

I was shocked, but he was right. It was an Ogilby duiker, a medium-size reddish duiker, not especially beautiful but most uncommon. The SCI record book describes it as one of "the least-known forest duikers." This was the first Ogilby duiker Morris's outfit had taken since they started operations—an incredible gift.

Since they were known to occur in this area, Mike and I had talked about Ogilby, but we agreed we were most unlikely to get one. Again Mike got nothing that night and, as the resident Duiker King, he was happy for me but couldn't keep from turning green with envy. By headlamp we took the stomach out, filled the cavity with ice, and hung the animal up for skinning in the morning . . . and, in the sober light of that next morning, we realized that our daily routine had just changed.

Although rural Liberia has a hunting culture, it is all meat hunting, with almost no history of sport hunting. If there's no sport hunting, there's little need for taxidermy. Three years earlier I'd worked with Tony on skinning for taxidermy; he understood it fully and had a good hand—better and more patient than mine. There was, however, no "designated skinner" in camp. Only Tony really knew how to do it, but it was unreasonable to expect him to guide *and* skin. Although he previously had been managing the camp and sometimes cooking, he couldn't guide and shoulder the responsibility for all these other jobs.

Mike Adams is a great skinner—far better than me—and, of course, Franz has a lifetime of experience. So we started working not only on my Ogilby duiker, but also on previous hunters' trophies in order to see if we could salvage them. Absent refrigeration, trophy care isn't easy, and in extreme heat and humidity it's very touchy. From that point on something came into camp just about every night, so trophy care became a half-day job; mornings were spent skinning, salting, and drying over *very* slow fires, and training some of the guys so Tony could concentrate on hunting.

Duiker King Mike and I both realized that getting an Ogilby was an incredible fluke, and there was no way he was also going to get one. He took it pretty well, but I felt awful; I wanted a zebra duiker and a water chevrotain really bad, and I think the black duiker is exceptionally attractive, but I'm not even a duiker prince. If I could have given the shot to Mike, I would have.

Between the lack of sleep and the heat it's hard to be certain what happened when, but my notes say that on the third night I shot a Maxwell duiker. This wasn't an animal I was looking for—I had taken a very good one on the previous Liberia hunt—but despite best efforts, identification isn't always perfect. On that same third night, Duiker King Mike Adams shot an Ogilby duiker—bigger than mine! Three years and no Ogilby duikers, then two in two days. We had a happy camp that night!

A couple days later, on Saint Patrick's Day, Mike came into camp with a water chevrotain. This time it was my turn to be green with envy. The water chevrotain is actually a primitive deer, not an antelope; it is one of the fanged deer like muntjac and water deer. It has no antlers, and the males fight vicious territorial and mating battles with their teeth. I think they're cool, and I probably wanted one more than I wanted a zebra duiker. When I hunted a water chevrotain in 2013, I was hunting in an area off to the west, and there were probably more of them there, but I just didn't get one. In the area I was now in, the guides were running about 50 percent on this animal, so since Mike got one, I assumed I wouldn't.

The next evening, March 18, Tony and I got a black duiker not far from camp. Unfortunately, it wasn't a very big one—but it was a black duiker! We put it in his haversack and continued on. About nine o'clock, when the moon was low, Tony went "on point" and I saw the red eye—only the water chevrotain has a red eye. The red dot followed, and I shot the dot, seeing nothing after the flash.

We couldn't find him! Tony marked the spot and came back with a couple of the guys early the next morning. I should have gone with them—that animal was probably the farthest away from camp of anything I shot, but not all that far, and that didn't matter anyway—but Tony was confident, and I didn't want to get in the way. While they were gone, Mike and Franz and I worked on the skins, and I worried and fretted. About ten o'clock Tony and team came back with a big water chevrotain, the only animal among us that required next-day follow-up.

In between our amateur taxidermy we followed up some leads on both buffaloes and red river hogs. Early in the hunt we had seen fairly fresh tracks, just a day or so old, of both buffaloes and pigs not far from the nearest village, along a lovely swampy area about an hour from camp. Franz had the guys make salt licks, and we added palm nuts, often irresistible to pigs. They built a couple of machans and we checked the area frequently, but we never again saw fresh tracks. On the buffaloes I don't have a clue; they're there, but they wander around. On the pigs, those tracks were fresh and it was a big sounder. My guess is they were bedded close-by and we spooked them by setting baits and building machans. Who knows? Somebody will get lucky on these species, but it wasn't going to be us.

A few days later the moon was getting bright, but moonrise was a bit later every evening. Neither Mike nor I had anything happen while the moon was up and bright, but so long as it was before moonrise, or when the moon was too low to provide illumination in the trees, the moon phase didn't seem to matter. Mike and I were still seeing game just about every night, but neither of us had seen a zebra duiker.

It was just 7:30, a half-hour after dark and not a half-hour from camp, when Tony stopped, tense, and stared into thick bush to the right. He then took a couple of steps. I saw movement left to right, but I wasn't certain what it was, and then I saw Tony raise the laser. By now we were a pretty good team, but this time the light was bouncing on leaves, and I had extra red spots to choose from. I chose the last one, fired, and Tony dove into the darkness. A few seconds later he hollered: "You have the zebra duiker!" And I did.

Of course, Duiker King Mike got his the next night, bigger than mine, and that was pretty much the end of the story. Mike kept trying to get a black duiker, probably

On our last evening a local hunter brought in this monstrous zebra duiker, a fantastic animal. He took it just before dark on the road leading to camp. That's the way hunting luck goes!

the most common animal in the area, but that one animal eluded him. Failing to find any buffalo or pig tracks, Tony and I spent the last few evenings trying desperately to get a golden cat. We knew there was a golden cat in the area because someone had seen one on a previous safari, so we put a bait out—which wasn't hit. This sounds like a wild goose chase, and we knew it probably was—but since I had all the game I wanted in the salt and there was nothing else going on, it seemed logical to make the attempt.

We tried several calls near where the cat had been seen, and we were going down a steep ridge, intending to call along a little stream at the bottom when Tony froze. Instantly, he had the laser up. I'm going to give him the benefit of the doubt here. He knew I wasn't looking for bay or Maxwell duikers, and we already had a black duiker. So, since he's a good guy, let's go with his story: He said that he got a glimpse of this thing, and pointed instantly. I shot, as usual having no idea what I was shooting at, and Tony dashed down toward the creek. This was the first time I saw him get really excited. He started hollering, and I went in to help him haul out a huge black duiker, so old it was more gray than black, with horns that measured in the top ten even though one was broken.

This black duiker turned out to be my best animal, and between us Mike and I probably had the most successful safari since Liberia reopened. It wasn't perfect. We had issues with generators and ice makers and vehicles, and, honestly, there was no point in a two-week hunt because there was no realistic chance for a buffalo or a pig. On the other hand, it was clear that Morris and his team had found the right place for the small forest animals that most hunters go to Liberia to hunt. If the team is able to figure out where to find the bigger game, I'd try again. Mike Adams, the Duiker King, is already going back in April 2017—he really wants a black duiker.

Chapter Thirty

Caprivi Buffalo

In 2015, while hunting with Corné Kruger's Omujeve Safaris in Caprivi, I saw some really good buffalo bulls, good enough to convince me that the genetics in Caprivi were excellent. Also, the idea of hunting amid the islands and channels of the Caprivi looked interesting, reminding me of the buffalo hunting I did in Botswana in the 1980s. That was not only back when you could still hunt in the Okavango, but also when there were lots of buffaloes and a lot fewer elephants—before elephant overpopulation began to adversely impact all other species.

A challenge to hunting buffaloes in most of the conservancies in the Caprivi is that the quotas are extremely limited. Corné, for instance, had on quota more than twice as many elephants as buffaloes up through 2016. This may change as more buffaloes move north from Botswana to escape starvation from the plague of elephants, but for now, Caprivi buffaloes are pricey. That's perfectly OK if it's an extra-good buffalo

The year 2016 was exceptionally dry in Caprivi. Normally much of the area would be covered with water, leaving only islands, but everything was dry except for the deeper channels. Mobility was great, but game movement was not normal.

Although (or perhaps because) we weren't hunting elephants, we ran into several nice bulls. This is the best one, a huge-bodied "Botswana-type" elephant. His tusks are absolutely fifty pounds per side, and could go fifty-five.

hunt, but limited availability also means permits may be spoken for a long way out.

While buffalo permits are important to Caprivi outfitters, business up there has become an elephant-based economy. That's the numbers game in most areas—more elephant permits than anything else. And international politics have played right into the hands of Caprivi outfitters by allowing them to place a premium on their permits for their exportable trophy elephants.

At this writing in October 2016, things are looking a bit better on the elephant hunting scene for eventually getting Zimbabwe ivory back into the United States, and the CITES Conference of the Parties just concluded in Pretoria was the most positive for hunting in many years. While it was not stated publicly, it appeared that a lot of countries that are full-fledged parties to CITES—and "range states" (meaning hosts) to controversial species—have had a bellyful of U.S. Fish and Wildlife's heavy-handed environmental imperialism. However, at this writing it also remains a fact that, for the U.S. market, the largest hunting market in the world, the only two places where Americans can go elephant hunting and bring their trophies home are Namibia and South Africa. Thus, elephant hunting in Caprivi is really important right now. However, since it's also one of so few remaining options, those exportable Caprivi elephants have increased in value.

That's a boon to the outfitters, several of whom are good friends—but it's a bad deal for the average hunter who dreams of experiencing just one elephant safari. But here's how it really works: Namibia's Caprivi Strip, now formally called Zambezi Region, is chock-full of elephants right now, with Botswana's quarter-million overpopulated and increasingly undernourished elephants just to the south. Caprivi is better watered and isn't overgrazed, and trackless Angola lies just to the north. However, Namibia's CITES quota for exportable elephant trophies is limited, and based primarily on resident elephant numbers.

In addition to these permits, most conservancies also have "own use" permits, which gives the meat to the people and skin and ivory to the authorities. Obviously the exportable "trophy" permits have one value, while non-exportable "own use" permits have another, lesser value. The "own use" permits offer the opportunity to experience an elephant hunt at a greatly reduced cost. You just have to accept the fact that you aren't taking the ivory home. I did that in 2015, and shot a beautiful old bull that had been wounded by poachers. I have no regrets. Well, maybe just one: That ivory was stolen from the camp before it could be turned over to the authorities, so I guess the poachers had the last laugh after all.

As I wrote, a primary purpose for that hunt was to see Caprivi, and since elephant hunting is currently the most important activity for most Caprivi outfitters I decided it would be one last elephant hunt. I still regard it as my last elephant hunt and I'm happy to rest with that—but I didn't expect to be intrigued by Caprivi's buffaloes.

Namibia is a huge country, and most of it is too arid for buffaloes. Also, much of Namibia is ranch country, but because of bovine diseases, there has been no buffalo ranching. So, with relatively few buffaloes in a handful of enclaves including Caprivi, Namibia has always been very conservative with buffalo quotas. This has nothing to do with CITES, since the Cape buffalo isn't on anyone's list of threatened species. Rather,

This was our big problem. Since it was such a dry year, cattle were being grazed much farther out into the area than usual, on one side nearly to the park boundary. Buffalo don't like cattle, so despite the poor grazing, they were staying in the park more than usual.

After I shot my bull, his buddies didn't want to leave. This one looked aggressive for a brief moment, and I thought we might have a problem, but after a couple of minutes they all moved off.

it's a matter of the Namibian authorities being responsible and conservative with a scarce and valuable resource.

So "trophy" buffalo permits are limited and fairly costly, although the quality is good and worth the price. However, because of the elephant overpopulation in Botswana, more buffalo herds are stepping north across the Chobe River into Namibia. Some have probably come to stay, but many come and go. This changes the numbers game that wildlife managers must play. So, although you don't hear about this much, Namibia offers a few "own use" buffalo permits. It's the same deal as with elephants: These buffalo can't be exported. This is probably not of great interest if you're contemplating your one and only buffalo safari, but I really don't have a place for another buffalo shoulder mount. That doesn't mean I don't love to hunt them, and it doesn't mean that I don't target older bulls . . . it just means that I don't really care whether I can take the buffalo home.

I do catch some grief for this attitude; some hunters consider that the concept of full utilization and proper respect for the animal require the services of a taxidermist. I do not. I believe wild meat must be fully utilized—and it always is in Africa—and I believe I properly respect the animals I take whether I have the trophy mounted or not. I think that is my choice to make, and, realistically, I've never had the budget or space to mount *everything*. An "own use" buffalo sounded perfect!

Now Dawid Muller of Daggaboy Safaris enters the picture. You won't know the name from my writing because I'd never hunted with him before. We do have, however, a mutual friend in Dirk de Bod, so I suppose that was recommendation enough for both Dawid and me. Turns out that Dawid Muller, just a couple years younger than me, is another buffalo freak and one of Namibia's very few outfitters with serious buffalo experience. He's been hunting the Wuparo Conservancy in Caprivi for years—and it's one of the better buffalo areas in the country. He gets a dozen trophy bulls annually—in Namibia that's a huge buffalo quota—and a smaller (and irregular) number of "own use" permits.

Unusually for Caprivi today, in this area there are more buffalo permits than elephant permits. I think the concessionaire has something to do with that—Muller likes to hunt buffaloes, and although he's an extremely experienced and competent elephant hunter, this is not his passion. While I was there, we saw a lot of elephants, including several nice tuskers, and by chance I was also there when the annual quota-setting meetings were going on. It seemed to me that he probably could have gotten one or two more elephant permits if he'd lobbied for them—but he figured he had enough elephant permits and he'd rather spend the time hunting buffaloes. I suppose Dawid and I could agree on that!

I was there at the beginning of October in a year that was the driest Caprivi had been since about 1999. This was unfortunate. On the one hand, although there were still some deep channels, we could drive almost everywhere, so it was an easier hunt than it might have been, and we never even got our feet wet. On the other hand, cattle were grazing where their herdsmen normally couldn't get to, and buffaloes weren't coming out of the adjacent national park as much as they might in a normal year. So instead of being an Okavango-like experience, it was a park boundary hunt and like any other park boundary hunt anywhere in the world: Once the perimeters were checked to see if buffalo came in during the night, there wasn't much to do until late afternoon, when herds might be moving again.

Meat recovery and distribution is extremely important to the conservancies in the Caprivi. When everything is flooded, this process can be a nightmare, but this was the easiest buffalo recovery I've ever seen. We simply drove to the downed bull and hooked it up to the winch.

No worries—thanks to merciless and uncaring editors, I've always got plenty of work to do, and Dawid had a stack of South African hunting magazines, including quite a few issues I'd missed. The nights were cool, but middays were beastly

The Caprivi region doesn't have a profusion of plains game, but there are several interesting species. Southern roan are fairly plentiful, with a quota of two per year.

hot. Even so, as the days wore on, I took to walking or jogging for an hour or so during the heat of the day. With such a challenging daily schedule, the hard part was deciding whether I should do this before or after a long afternoon nap!

After numerous years hunting this area, Dawid had a good team and a good system. With us daily were Dawid's longtime tracker DaSilva and the conservancy's chief game guard, Brutus. Both were good guys, well-spoken, good senses of humor, and extremely tied in with the local community. So, if there was any major buffalo movement in our direction, we'd know about it. It was clearly in everyone's best interests for buffaloes to be shot, but there was absolutely no discussion of breaching any park or conservancy boundary to accomplish this.

And then there was Dawid's secret weapon, a fisherman (and probably poacher-come-to-Jesus) named Hendrik. Hendrik spent his days scouring the edges of reedbeds for buffalo tracks, where small bachelor groups or lone *dagga* bulls were likely to hole up. Per Dawid, Hendrik located about 50 percent of the bachelor bulls his clients harvested. As promised, Hendrik did, indeed, find fresh sign for me, two big tracks—but water conditions were such that the spoor led straight into reedbeds on the wrong side of the park boundary. We spent a couple of late evenings watching, hoping they might come out to feed on our side, but these buffaloes never showed themselves in daylight.

At the midpoint of the hunt, DaSilva—who has marvelous eyes—spotted three bulls in a grassy flat in our hunting area. *Game on!* The country looks open, but these guys know it very well, and also know almost imperceptible movement corridors that buffalo seem to use time and again. We made a couple of half-circles, using termite mounds, scant depressions, and occasional trees and bushes—and the buffaloes fed past us at forty yards, broadside, totally unaware. The problem is they were too young, all about seven or eight years old, bosses formed but not yet fully hard.

By definition the "own use" permit is supposed to be a nontrophy bull, age not specified, and none of these youngsters would ever be giants. But I don't shoot young buffalo bulls and, fortunately, neither does Dawid Muller. We were looking for an older bull, preferably with narrow spread or tips that were broken or worn. We let these young bulls pass and walked away, no regrets.

I had come to hunt with an "own use" permit, but when I arrived, Dawid told me he also had one unsold trophy permit and named a reasonable price. I suppose it was a cancellation—I didn't ask—but that gave us a lot of flexibility to hunt either a trophy or nontrophy buffalo.

The first morning we left camp at 6:15, probably a half-hour late. A very big herd had come in from the park, and we just missed them . . . they were moving out, scattered and feeding for several hundred yards beyond our boundary. Dawid and his team know this herd. They figured it held seven or eight hundred buffaloes, usually lots of bulls, and they tended to come in on about a week's rotation, graze for a couple of days, then go on. We had missed them by minutes, and we wouldn't see them again, but they'd left a couple of splinter groups behind.

DaSilva spotted a group of maybe twenty buffaloes, sort of a miniherd. They were drifting through fairly thick mopane, following in the wake of the big herd, but still within our area. We got ahead of them and worked them for an hour or so. As expected with a group trailing the herd, they were mostly bulls, but not a single one was even close to being a grown-up bull. Eventually they slipped past us and on toward the park, and as the morning heated up quickly, I figured their retreating dust would be the last sign of buffaloes we'd see that day.

Not exactly. Dawid and I tramped out to the road while Brutus and DaSilva cut across to get the Toyota. On the way DaSilva spotted four more bulls, so Brutus watched them while DaSilva hot-footed it out to find us. Here's where it gets odd. It would seem that these had to be another splinter group from the big herd, or at least satellite bulls—but they were moving west, directly away from the herd across the shorter axis of the concession. So maybe it was just coincidental that they happened to be in the same general area on the same day. Anyway, we caught up with Brutus watching them from a termite mound, and we watched them feed straight toward our

With Botswana now closed, Caprivi is the only place where free range/native range red lechwe can be hunted. We saw this young red lechwe bull as it wandered right by camp, and we glassed quite a few out in the swamp.

Land Cruiser. The vehicle spooked them a bit, so when last seen they were headed straight west into increasingly open ground.

I figured that was that—we hadn't even been close enough to look them over—but my team was pretty sure they'd soon calm down, and from this angle the boundaries were far away. So we hustled, walking hard in a big half-circle, not only not seeing but not even looking for the buffaloes. Well, it was a nice morning for a walk, but it all seemed pretty silly to me—until we ascended a small island and DaSilva pointed out four buffalo bulls, now about three hundred yards away but *behind us*—and *parallel to* our course. It wasn't magic; the buffaloes had simply worked their way along traditional movement corridors created by islands and flooded channels. Although it was now so dry the buffaloes could walk anywhere they chose, apparently out of habit they still tended to use familiar movement patterns.

The wind was fine, so I would have bent low and taken a straight diagonal to get ahead of them. Dawid must have thought similarly because he and I went one way, Brutus and DaSilva another, and after a few seconds Brutus whistled and motioned us in behind him, clearly admonishing his boss. We fell into line like good little soldiers, and our team took us on another half-circle that I thought quite unnecessary—except it did take us into low ground where we were completely hidden and could hustle along upright.

We finished our half-circle with a hook into a little patch of thornbush, no buffaloes in sight—and then, one after another, four bulls came around the corner of a little depression sixty yards in front of us and began feeding directly to us. Standing stock-still amid interlaced branches, we let them come.

Dawid whispered, "All of these are what I'd call 'trophy bulls,' if that's OK with you. I think they'll pass to our left, so let's pick out the best one."

It was the first day. This would probably be the expensive, "trophy" buffalo. Should we keep looking for a nontrophy bull, or seize the opportunity? I don't like to shoot on the first day, but I also know better than to kick sand in Mother Nature's face. I nodded to Dawid as the buffaloes continued to feed toward us.

These were all eleven-year-old bulls, operating as a bachelor group but none exactly what you'd think of as old *dagga* bulls. They were pretty much cookie-cutters of each other, one with a bit wider spread, another with a bit thicker bosses or longer tips. Mind you, judging them and picking the best bull was now Dawid's job, not mine, but I figured they were between 38 and 41 inches in spread, all with fully hard bosses, but not much wear on the horn tips. I was carrying a Krieghoff double .500, while DaSilva carried my scoped CZ .375 just in case. At this range there was no reason to switch. As they came near, I was focused on one bull—I'm not sure why—and Dawid switched me to another.

As predicted, they swerved to our left, the chosen bull broadside at not much more than twenty yards. I pressed the Krieghoff's cocking lever into the "fire" position, and then raised the rifle. We were so close that, of course, the buffaloes saw the movement, but it was too late. At that range it took only an instant to place the front bead on the shoulder, and the 570-grain DGX was on its way.

Outfitter and PH Dawid Muller is seen here relaxing at midday in the lapa *or lounge. Muller has been blessed with a fairly substantial buffalo quota for some years, and this has made him one of Namibia's more experienced buffalo hunters . . . and he loves it.*

The impact rocked the bull, but he immediately ran to my left where I was tied up in thorns and unable to swing the rifle. Dawid and I moved back to get clear, and by this time the four bulls were forty yards out and headed away, the stricken bull on the right and obviously struggling. I could have put in a going-away solid, but he went down and seemed anchored. We watched for a few minutes

Dawid and I took this very nice Caprivi buffalo at close range with a Krieghoff double in .500-3" Nitro Express. The bull went about thirty yards after receiving a 570-grain DGX to the center of its shoulder.

while his buddies stayed with him, and then we moved in and paid unnecessary insurance as the others reluctantly drifted away.

Dawid's buffalo hunts are normally ten days. I'd given him only a week. By the end of my hunt we knew where the big herd was, and if they held to form, they'd be in from the park within a day or two. So I missed out, but Dawid's next hunters were in good shape. No worries here. I'm going to try again when the water has returned and it's the kind of former-Okavango-now-Caprivi buffalo hunting experience it should be. Even so, to get within twenty-five yards of a buffalo with a double rifle in that seemingly wide-open ground was pretty cool.

Equally cool—perhaps because it was so dry—we saw a lot of game. In the far north of the concession we ran into roans and Chapman zebras. In reedbeds along the park boundary we saw plenty of red lechwes, which, with Okavango closed, is now a Caprivi-only species. Visible throughout were a lot of waterbucks, impalas, kudus, and reedbucks; hippos serenaded the camp every night. Quotas for plains game are small, probably as they should be, but this is actually a pretty good mixed-bag area—and we saw a lot of elephants.

Most were in cow herds with lots of youngsters, but through the week we saw several decent tuskers. In Caprivi this means around forty pounds; this region has never been known for heavy ivory. We saw one bull, however, that had broken tusks on *both* sides and, even broken, each tusk pushed fifty pounds. And we saw another beautiful bull with short, thick ivory that was probably fifty-five on one side and fifty the other. We approached to less than thirty yards and got some good photos, but I was not tempted . . . getting close to this lovely bull without wanting to shoot him convinced me once and for all: My elephant hunting days are over.

CHAPTER THIRTY-ONE

THE ZAMBEZI DELTA

The herd was a long black line on the horizon. It looked like a lot of buffaloes, but between patches of sawgrass and strands of papyrus you often don't see the whole herd until you're close . . . and that means you never know exactly how many buffaloes you're dealing with. This was a very big herd, certainly 1,500, probably 2,000 or more. It's a marvelous sight, and in Africa's hunting countries today, this is probably something to be seen and experienced only in the hunting areas surrounding Marromeu Reserve in the floodplains and swamps of the Zambezi Delta.

Although a magnificent spectacle, a herd this size creates challenges. At least in this area you know such a herd contains a number of mature bulls, most likely a few dozen, and probably several monsters. You also know that you will never penetrate such a herd well enough to look at all the bulls, and sorting just one for a shot takes

Our "class photo" from 2016, left to right: Tim and Riza Lesser, John Stucker, Donna and me, Joe Bishop, Paul Cestoni, Sara Bishop, and Julie and Dennis Hilling. Individual bags usually aren't large in the area, but in a ten-day hunt, most hunters take their most important trophies . . . and a couple of extras.

Kelly McMillan with a fine sable bull he took in 2012. The area has several thousand sables, probably the most common large antelope. Only rarely do they reach extreme size, but so far in my experience every hunter in the area who wanted a sable has taken a nice bull.

time, patience, and a bit of luck. As I write these lines in October 2016, this was just a few days ago and I was fortunate. It wasn't my shot or my problem, so I could sit back and enjoy the show.

As I've already written, there's no shade out there on the floodplains. It gets hot, and in most years and with most herds there's fetid swamp water and stinking boot-sucking mud to contend with. Bugs aren't bad, but the leeches are a nasty surprise. Even so, I like it out there because I've never found a better place to see so many buffaloes and close with them. So, on this day, with my own buffalo two days in the salt, I was accompanying friends Tim Lesser and John Stucker on their buffalo hunts and just along for the ride. No pressure on me!

At the outset we had two smaller herds in sight, so a normal plan would be to separate, Tim and his PH, Dylan Holmes, going for one herd while John and PH Poen van Zyl went for another. But this big herd was too enticing, almost certainly fresh out of the reserve, probably a temporary gathering of several smaller herds, and most likely containing some exceptional bulls. So we stayed together, hoping that we might take two bulls from a herd so large.

The accommodating sawgrass allowed us to get very close, less than fifty yards from the nearest buffalo, and with a strong wind in our faces. We found we were now too close, for we were unable to maneuver and able to see only a tiny fraction of the great black mass. So we were stuck, sweating, for a couple of hours, hoping the herd would move while the buffaloes, unaware of our presence and happy to be in a patch of good grass, stayed put, some feeding and many lying down. Eventually it became obvious the herd wasn't going anywhere, and equally obvious there were no mature bulls in our limited vista. After a quick PH conference, John and Poen crawled back into the sawgrass and circled to the right. Dylan and Tim stayed put, as did their coaches and observers, Tim's wife, Riza, and your humble correspondent.

A half-hour later, with us having no idea where John's team had gone, his shot rang out and his bull, hitherto unseen by us, ran along the edge of the herd and went down right in front of us. One would expect pandemonium in the herd, but not in a

Swift Bullets' Bill Hober took this really wide buffalo in 2014. He was using an original Rigby .416 built in 1929; I was using one of the brand-new English Rigby Big Game rifles, also in .416. I found the two rifles to be wonderfully similar.

herd this size. Most got to their feet and a few stampeded this way and that, but there was no mass panic. Our portion of the herd moved off a short distance, then calmed. Buffaloes know there is safety in numbers.

We were expecting John's shot to break the standoff, creating some shifting that might reveal a knot of bulls somewhere in that vast herd. Didn't happen. When the dust settled, we still had an impenetrable black mass in front of us, now a bit farther away. We could pick out any number of promising immature bulls, but the old boys that must be there—somewhere—were still invisible.

Dylan's tracker had been hauling a mysterious bundle, and I had passed it forward while we were crawling. I knew it was too light for water or food, but I had no idea what it was. Now he broke it out, and I saw that it was a drape of black mesh. He, Dylan, and Tim draped it over themselves and walked slowly toward the herd, looking like just one more black buffalo among a cast of thousands. On this day the wind was our friend, steady, increasingly strong, and in our favor. The buffaloes stood, staring, while the Trojan buffalo closed the gap and then paraded from one end of the herd to the other. When the buffaloes got nervous, the hunters went to ground; when they relaxed, the hunters got up and walked, a six-legged beast.

In fits and starts the herd had drifted away and was now probably four hundred yards from us—but Dylan and Tim appeared to be quite close to them. The scene was still clear in the binocular, and the buffaloes were starting to lie down again. By now I was pretty sure I'd seen a half-dozen hard-boss bulls in the press. The black drape stopped, and then I saw that Dylan had spread the sticks low and Tim's rifle barrel was peering out from under the black blind.

Following its direction, I was trying to guess which bull they'd targeted; after several minutes passed without a shot I guessed it to be a nice bull lying down on the edge of the herd. The herd had been disturbed enough that they wouldn't be stationary for long, so there was no reason to risk the chancy lying-down shot. Good guess. After an agonizing half-hour, the chosen bull rose, and Tim's shot followed in a few seconds. We'd been on the herd nearly five hours, but we had two good bulls. Both, I might add, a fair measure better than my own first buffalo taken nearly forty years earlier.

Africa has changed a lot in those forty years. Not all for the bad, but certainly not all for the good. Thanks to game ranching in Southern Africa, there is possibly, overall, more wildlife on the African continent today than there was in the late

Over the years both Donna and I have taken very good bushpigs. Although primarily a target of opportunity, bushpig sightings in daylight are common. Over the course of a ten-day hunt, most hunters will see bushpigs at least once or twice.

1970s and early 1980s. On the other hand, wild, unfenced African game country has shrunk. Lions, rhinos, elephants, and buffaloes have diminished as wild Africa has diminished. Of the traditional "Big Five," only the leopard, amazingly content in suburban environments, continues to prosper and expand.

As an example of this, the second "ten-year book" of my African odyssey was entitled *Where Lions Roar*. The regrettable inference is that it is a book about lion hunting, which it is not and which I will never write. That is partly because the market is too small but mostly because I don't know enough about lion hunting and, in today's Africa, cannot learn enough. My intent for that title phrase was to connote wild Africa, where lions still roar. Lions are in trouble in what remains of wild Africa, and while hunters and antihunters are in strong disagreement on the solution—if there is one—the places where lions still roar are diminishing.

So, as Africa has changed, I have changed as well. As I've already stated in this volume, I am reasonably confident I have taken my only rhino, my last lion, and my last elephant. In all three cases I no longer feel the need or the desire to pursue these animals again. I'm probably not quite done with leopard hunting—the chess game is just too interesting—and I am most certainly not done with buffalo hunting. From my first exposure forty years ago on Mount Kenya until today, I've accepted that hunting Africa's buffaloes is my special addiction.

Mind you, I have multiple African addictions. It's a big continent and nobody can ever see it all, but I've certainly tried to see as much as I could, and I've tried to hunt species unique to the various areas I've visited. You've seen a fair amount of that in this volume, which includes little-known hunting destinations such as Burkina Faso, Ghana, Liberia, and Tunisia. On the other hand, I've never lost my passion for Africa's spiral-horn antelopes, or for her big, black buffaloes.

As Africa has changed, my favorite places in Africa have changed. Namibia remains a favorite, likewise the Eastern Cape of South Africa, both well represented in this volume. A decade ago, at the start of this ten-year journey, Zimbabwe's Zambezi Valley would have been my clear-cut favorite, one of the best places to hunt buffaloes, always with a chance for a huge kudu . . . and yet affordable. Regrettably, the valley has changed. It still offers some of the best and most traditional tracking hunts for elephants. It still offers some of the very best leopard hunting, wild country where cats come onto the bait at last or first light. It remains a much under-rated "sleeper spot" for lions. Unfortunately, with the double hit of too many predators and a hunting quota that remained too high for too long, buffalo hunting isn't what it used to be. Bachelor groups—*dagga* bulls—are no longer easy to find, and too many herds have no mature bulls.

Depending on where you go, sometimes you return to camp for lunch, and other times you take your midday break in the field. When you go to the swamp for buffalo, count on a long, hot day—but the kitchen packs a good meal.

Also, I must admit that one of my favorite things about Africa isn't just the specific game being pursued, whether it be buffaloes, bushbucks, elephants, kudus, leopards, lions,

I took this fine suni in 2015. Although it's a fun hunt, I really don't have an excuse to take any more of the pygmy antelopes—but I brought along a Krieghoff with Hornady turkey loads to try out, and they worked wonderfully.

or whatever, but the variety and sheer randomness. The real charm of Africa for me is that you never know what you might see next! The Zambezi Valley is a wonderful dangerous-game area, but it's never been a good "mixed-bag" or "full-bag" area, and it's no longer what it was for hunting buffaloes.

Time marches on. I was fortunate to start my African odyssey in my twenties. I'm now sixty-something. I can't run like I could then, but I don't feel much different and, fortunately, haven't yet experienced major limitations. Surely they're coming, so I have no idea how much longer I can continue my African sojourns. As I said, this is my fourth "ten-year Africa" book, and that was something I didn't expect to write when I was first starting out. As much as I admire completeness and symmetry in both life and writing, I cannot predict there will be a fifth. If there is, then I don't know exactly what path(s) it might take.

I can certainly say, in late 2016, that I have future African hunts planned. As noted in the previous chapter, I am bemused and impressed by the buffalo hunting in Caprivi. It looks so open, but with long grass and small islands of cover, you can get *so close*! I'm certainly not done in Central Africa; I still need a meeting with the dwarf forest buffalo that has eluded me. I have a return to Uganda planned for 2017, and if I can find a way to afford it, I'd like to get back to Ethiopia. For that matter, if I could afford it—and I probably can't—I'd like to get back to Tanzania one more time. So, health and wealth permitting, there will be more African hunts and more fodder for writing in years to come. Never say never! Whether or not another African book might take shape, it's as certain as death and taxes that, if I'm able, in years to come I'll be spending more time in the Zambezi Delta.

The first three volumes in this series featured a chronological progression of the areas I visited as I continued my "hunt and peck" visits across Africa. This book required some exceptions, primarily to avoid undue length as well as some redundancy. At the beginning of this decade I was spending a lot of time in Zimbabwe's Zambezi Valley, so I made a conscious decision to combine several sojourns into one chapter; likewise, selectively, I combined multiple hunts in Namibia and South Africa. Here I must do it again, but certainly not for a dearth of material. I "discovered" the Zambezi Delta on a brief visit to Coutada 10 in 2006, then returned there for a "full hunt" in 2008. I first hunted in Coutada 11 in 2009, and I then hunted in Coutada 14 in 2010. These hunts are recorded in previous chapters. Since then I've returned to Coutada 11 every year, occasionally overlapping into adjoining Coutada 12.

This much time in one single area, year after year, is unprecedented in my African hunting experience. From a writing standpoint it is probably more difficult to pick out highlights than it would be to simply go back to my field notes and photo files and craft a chapter about each hunt. But even book manuscripts need to have some limits, so I decided on the former option.

In 2015 Mark Haldane and his team were just starting to experiment with man-made watering points for blue duiker and suni. By 2016 their use had produced several of the elusive blue duikers and had become a standard tactic.

First, however, it's important to me—if not to you—to explain why I, so often eclectic and peripatetic in my approach, have spent so much

Bushbucks are hard to hunt because they are thinly and widely dispersed, but the area grows very big Chobe bushbucks. Donna took this one in 2011, and between us, this is by far our best bushbuck.

time in coastal Mozambique. Obviously, to use the punchline from a favorite joke that can't be repeated here, it "ain't just for the huntin'." In 2006 the only two animals from the region that I hadn't hunted elsewhere were Natal red duiker and Livingstone's suni. As I wrote earlier, Mozambique's "native-range, free-range" nyalas offered a wonderful initial excuse, but that excuse is long since exhausted. Yet I keep returning.

I think it must be obvious that the Zambezi Delta has become one of my favorite places. There are multiple reasons for this. First, it's wild Africa, about two-and-a-half-million acres of wild Africa. Second, the most amazing thing is that, every year, I see it getting better. Mark Haldane's Zambeze Delta Safaris has managed Coutada 11 for about twenty-three years and neighboring Coutada 12 for most of the past decade and has invested heavily in both antipoaching and community programs, and I've been able to see the results. When I started hunting there, sables and buffaloes were in good shape, as were most species present. Today, however, I'm seeing exponential growth in Lichtenstein hartebeests, nyalas, waterbucks, and even common species such as reedbucks and warthogs.

Obviously this is a good outfit, well-managed and well-run, with a team that's an interesting mix of eager young PHs and experienced hands, the latter including Mark Haldane; his brother, Glen; and Mike Currie. The camps aren't fancy, but they're comfortable and clean—and the ZDS team makes it all *fun*, at prices that are still reasonable. The game is interesting. The current count of buffaloes in and around the Marromeu Reserve—not counting increasing numbers in the surrounding *miombo* woodland—was about twenty-five thousand in 2016, probably the greatest concentration on the African continent today. Good buffalo hunting is enough to keep me coming back, but I'm now seeing the quality improving annually, and swamp buffalo hunting is an altogether different experience from the tracking hunting I did so much of.

Plains game, too, is interesting. Nyala hunting is fascinating, Chobe bushbucks grow huge, and while eland numbers are still coming up, the area produces awesome Livingstone elands. The only real gap is I wish there were more greater kudus—but they're starting to work their way in from the west, and there's already a small quota. I may eventually see viable kudu hunting here.

For hunters interested in the "tiny ten," the place is a dream. Sunis, red duikers, and oribis are plentiful. The common (gray) duiker is not common, but is occasionally encountered. Sharpe grysboks occur but are extremely uncommon. Mixed into the suni forest with the sunis are surprising numbers of blue duikers—but, of some eighteen huntable species, the little blue duiker is probably the single most difficult animal to hunt. Joe Bishop got one in 2008 and Donna got one in 2016. In between, quite a few blue duikers have fallen, but I've never gotten one there.

Leopards are endemic, but difficult to bait. Most of the hunting to date for leopards has been done with hounds, which is legal in Mozambique. As with kudus, lions are surprisingly absent. There are a few; we see their tracks and sometimes hear them roar at night, but they are scarce—a fact that has helped the buffaloes prosper—and they are not on license. Elephants range in the forest, but the majority are out in the swamps. In recent years Mozambique has lost a lot of her elephants to poaching, but, in a recent count, the Marromeu complex was the only place in the country where elephants had increased.

Although almost uniformly flat, the country changes dramatically. The core is the Marromeu Reserve, floodplains of sawgrass and slightly higher savannas cut by deep papyrus channels. This is where the big numbers of buffaloes are found, and not much else. Then there's a broad belt of grassy floodplain studded with wooded islands. This is where the largest concentrations of waterbucks and hartebeests are found, as well as the attractive Selous zebras. No one really knows where the elands spend most of their year, but late in the season they come onto the floodplain in big herds.

Mark Haldane and I took this nyala bull in 2016. He's a beauty and those tips are really impressive. Only an idiot would pass on such a nyala and we didn't—but the initial flare is a bit too narrow for him to achieve the length he appears to have.

Beyond the floodplain, the *miombo* woodland starts, much of it relatively open sand forest. In certain areas, however, tall trees form a canopy forest, locally called suni forest. Scattered throughout the forest are slight depressions—pans—that collect water and grow the choicest grass. You never know what you might see at a pan, but a herd of sable antelopes is the most likely—and most nyalas and bushbucks are taken by sitting over pans or stalking into them. So how do I encapsulate a half-dozen safaris in this amazing place?

I'll start with the conditions, then move on to the people. Coastal Mozambique has a season that's a bit weird by Southern African standards. Rains are usually heavy and end late, so early hunts are hampered by deep water and long grass. In this area "early" means April through July. Buffalo hunting is fine, and elephant, leopard, and crocodile hunting is excellent, but plains-game hunting is difficult until things dry out a bit. So "peak season" starts in August and runs through October. Later is actually very good for game movement, the only trade-off being that it gets progressively hotter from late August onward. What all this means to the outfitters, however, is that the majority of a large quota must be harvested in the latter part of the season. There are smaller camps for smaller parties, but the main Mungari Camp is set up to handle larger groups of six or even ten hunters.

Waterbuck range in big herds far out on the floodplains, accessible only by Argo. This is the kind of waterbuck I had sought for a long time. It is thirty-one inches on both horns.

I appreciate this doesn't appeal to everyone, but in this situation it works. Mungari Camp is centrally located in the middle of a million acres of game country, so hunters and PHs can head out daily like spokes of a wheel. They have a system of "allocating" areas daily depending on game sought, so even when ten teams are out, it's unusual to encounter another vehicle, other than in passing on one of the main roads. Day schedules vary; part of the group may go to the swamp for buffaloes, others may stay out all day with a packed lunch, and some will return to camp for a midday meal and siesta. Swamp hunters will leave early and return late (sometimes very late), but generally the group gathers 'round the fire in the evening to swap stories.

With PHs and hunters, it can be a large gathering. One of the risks in such a situation is that, all too often, some hunters are charmed and others cursed, so success is uneven. That is certainly true on any given day, but this area is so game-rich that, across the board over those six safaris, *everyone* I've been in camp with on ten-day "buffalo and plains game" safaris has taken his or her primary animals.

On any safari we all have some days that are better than others, but on any given day there are plenty of stories to share around the fire, and I can honestly report that I've shared that fire with six wonderful groups. In 2012 I joined Kelly McMillan with several of his rifle clients, and in 2013 I shared camp with a group from Blaser Safaris. Mostly, though, we've picked a date a year ahead and filled the camp with friends and acquaintances. The former have stayed friends, the latter have become friends, and no one has gone away disappointed!

Over the course of six safaris there have been too many folks to mention everyone, but a few stand out. My English friend Christopher Cornell joined us in 2011. He took the sable he coveted and two very fine buffaloes—one in the forest and one in the swamp. Noted rifle collector Bill Jones was also there in 2011, of course with some cool rifles—including Fletcher Jamieson's famous .500 Jeffery. In 2014 we had the Legendary Arms Works folks, along with Bill Hober of Swift Bullets. Hober also took two buffaloes, both in the swamp. His second bull was a rare encounter with an unexpected *dagga* bull in the swamp. We darn near ran over it while traversing some sawgrass in the BV, and it instantly charged, crumpling the side of the vehicle right where Bill was sitting!

That year of 2014 included quite a star-studded cast. My old friend, fellow Marine, and Weatherby Award recipient Bruce Keller was in camp, along with his bride Jane (who shot her first buffalo). Larry Bucher and Buck Buckner, friends from Boone and Crockett Club, were also there. Larry has hunted in Africa more than anyone I know, and Buck is also an experienced African hand. All three of these guys have in-depth African experience that precedes mine. Fortunately, my judgment wasn't too far off, and all were impressed by the outfit, the area, and the amount of game. Later, in his laconic way, Buck remarked, "You know, that was a whole lot better hunt than I expected it to be." My only regret is that I was filming multiple projects and I wasn't able to spend nearly as much time with these guys as I wanted to.

In 2015 our camp included my friends from Georgia, Zack and Debbie Aultman, and Chad Allen and Rick Carrol (who I'd hunted with in the Zambezi Valley the year before). Also with us were J. C. Bell and Donna's friend Dr. Sadaf Khan. Sadaf, on her first African hunt, probably took the largest bag of anyone I've seen in the delta—darn near one of everything, including a blue duiker.

Due to a cancellation, our 2016 hunt just concluded was a smaller group: Joe and Sara Bishop, Tim and Riza Lesser, John Stucker, Paul Cestoni, and Canadians Dennis and Julie Hilling. The swamps were exceedingly dry, which for some reason seemed to congregate the buffaloes in big herds. As usual, everybody got a buffalo, and every single one was a really good bull. As usual, everyone who wanted a sable or nyala got one.

Luck is always a factor, but—aside from leopards, which I have no experience with in this area—it seems to me the three most difficult animals in the delta are the blue duiker, bushbuck, and crocodile. Blue duikers are plentiful, but skittish and hunted in thick cover. Julie got one, Donna got one, Sara didn't get one, and this time I didn't try. Bushbucks are difficult because bushbucks seem generally distributed rather than occupying specific habitats as they do in most areas. The Chobe bushbuck is extremely attractive with a lot of color, and the trophy fee is a bargain there. So I think most folks would take a good bushbuck if they saw one, but success on this animal is random. John Stucker got a monster and Sara Bishop got a good one. And, at last light on the last evening, I finished the safari with an old, heavy-horn ram.

Crocodiles are never easy, but timing is important. All of my hunts in this area have been late August through October, which is really past the time for the best crocodile hunting. This year the Zambezi was running too high and the swamps were too dry. Even so, Donna managed to take a nice croc.

Among the plains species the nyala is probably the most interesting to me. I don't have any reason to take another, but it's a challenging and interesting hunt, and, in my estimation, Africa's most beautiful and colorful antelope. In 2009 Mark and I "settled" for a nice nyala at the end of the safari—but the hunt isn't over, and we keep looking for a monster. In 2012 we got really serious about a huge nyala. Hey, everybody thinks I get special treatment because I usually hunt with Mark, but hunting with the boss isn't always the best deal in town. With a major operation to run, there will be days when he has affairs of state to tend to, so I'll go off with an apprentice, accompany a group to the swamp, or just spend a day in camp writing. Fortunately, we put up with each other very well.

Close to the Zambezi and right on the edge of the concession is the grave of David Livingstone's wife, Mary Moffat. She died there, probably from malaria, in 1862.

This is one of the only areas where Lichtenstein hartebeest occur south of the Zambezi, but they're doing well and now increasing rapidly. Hunting them on the open floodplains can mean long shooting; this monster was taken at 370 yards with a Blaser in .270.

So, a few days into the 2012 McMillan safari, I went off with an "appie" and we found a tall and extremely beautiful nyala that I couldn't resist. Nyalas, as I've learned, are very hard to judge. Height is impressive, but to get real length you need the "bell"—the out-and-in initial curve, and then you need the tips to flare back outward. So this was a good nyala, but not the thirty-inch Holy Grail we sought. Available quota is, of course, the outfitter's bible. Although the quota is large, available sables are always spoken for, likewise animals with small quotas such as elands and Selous zebras. The nyala is one quota that is never quite filled because sightings are uncommon until late in the season.

Not to be outdone, and with quota available, Mark and I kept looking. This hunt was late October, hot and dark of moon, and the nyalas were really hitting the pans. The problem is knowing *when* they're coming to water. Early morning? Late morning? Midday? Late afternoon? The latter is the most likely, but if nyalas are moving, the smart money is probably to pick a good pan and spend the day. Unfortunately, that's boring, and perhaps not the best use of a day in Africa. An alternative technique is to stalk multiple pans in succession. We did both.

Mark Haldane and I had to cover nearly 1,000 yards of open ground to get a shot at this Livingstone eland, and even then we had to take a 300-yard shot. Elands are increasing nicely, but the quota is small and that probably doesn't matter because they're rarely seen until very late in the season.

Again sitting with a young apprentice, I saw a group of a dozen nyala bulls come to a pan at midday. I was pretty sure the largest bull was "there," but having made one bad call, I was reluctant to make another. So, toward midday the next day Mark and I stalked that pan. We almost missed them; they'd already been to water and were departing as we approached. Mark led me on a quick stalk through the brush, and when we were about seventy yards from the group, he pointed out a nyala bull and set up the sticks. Counting that group of a dozen, by that time on that day we had looked at *thirty-five* different nyala bulls. This was the biggest of that day, and of that trip, but I don't think he was as big as the one I lost in 2008.

Depending on how tight or loose we held the tape, he was a sixteenth one way or the other of the magical thirty-inch mark. With that bull, our mission really was complete, but, after all, a hunter must have a goal, so we keep looking for big nyalas. The next year the Blaser safari was in late August, really too early for great nyala hunting, but toward the end, one of the PHs had seen a really big nyala at a pan, and that was a day that Mark needed to tend to business. So I sat there in the late afternoon, and just before sunset an amazing nyala stepped out of the forest. I crawled to a tree and took a rest, but the nyala had seen the movement and faced me. The shot was maybe a hundred and fifty yards, simple and doable, but as the trigger broke I knew the cross hairs had wobbled. I missed him clean as a whistle.

This past safari we had yet another report of a very big nyala. The place, not really a pan but a linear clearing, was far from water and seemed unlikely, but good intelligence is important. So we sat one evening with a strong wind and saw nothing. The next evening, far to our left, just at dark, we saw a procession of seven bulls. The last looked very big, perhaps the bull we'd been told about, so we made a quick march and in near-dark I took a shot I shouldn't have taken. Fortunately, I missed.

So we gave it a rest and came back a few nights later, this time setting up across the clearing from where that parade of bulls had appeared. It was early, just on five o'clock, when a bull stepped out of the forest directly across from us. His bell could have been wider, but the tips were fantastic, pinching in and then coming far out to obvious ivory tips. Staring at him, reluctant to move, I said to Mark, "Big nyala to our right."

No response. I tried again, "Tips are way out."

Calmly and flatly Mark replied, "Colonel, you're getting old and blind. Those tips are almost touching. Look again!"

My nyala was now stretching its neck upward to feed on a choice morsel, on the edge directly across from me. I risked a glance at Mark. He was intently glassing far to the left, at a nyala bull I'd not seen, and obviously wondering what I was seeing on that bull that he could not. "Not that one. Look to your *other* right."

He did, and immediately said, "Why don't you leopard-crawl to that tree and shoot him?"

So I did. It was another quartering-to shot, another wobble, but this time the bull was hit hard. We followed him into the darkening forest, almost like bongo hunting, and he was there at the end of the track. So I guess now we really are done with nyalas. Or are we?

The area is exceptional for warthogs and bushpigs. I'll never pass a good tusker, and Donna and I have taken several good ones of both species, but these animals are usually taken when encountered rather than hunted specifically. Reedbucks are abundant, easily the most plentiful antelopes, but trophy quality is average, so the reedbuck is primarily a "community quota" meat animal, and I've been happy to help. Sunis and red duikers are plentiful, and while the red duiker is primarily a target of opportunity, hunting the suni in the thick stuff with a shotgun is a specialized and interesting hunt. I've taken my share and probably won't hunt them again.

The short-quota specialized species have been sort of a one-time thing for me; I've taken just one sable, on eland, one waterbuck, etc. In 2012 Kelly McMillan and I both had permits for Selous zebras, a particularly beautiful race of zebras—pure black and white, no shadow stripes. Once widespread through much of Mozambique and on into Malawi, the delta is the only place this race of zebras is currently huntable, and their recovery is one of the area's numerous success stories. When Mark started hunting in Coutada 11 in 1994, he figures there may have been as few as just twenty. Today the population is approaching five hundred, but the quota is still just a handful a year.

They spend most of their time on the wide-open floodplains, so they are easy to find but the devil to approach. I suppose one might crawl—for miles—but it isn't necessary to get as close as one must for buffaloes, so what often works is to stroll along nonchalantly at a diagonal, gradually gaining ground. The herd will probably run short distances a few times, then stop to stare, and eventually—sometimes—you can get close enough.

Kelly was up first, shooting a .338, and I think we closed to a bit over three hundred yards when he shot a fine stallion. There was another male in the herd and they didn't go far, so with Kelly's zebra down, we continued on, and after a couple more approaches I was able to take a rest on a handy antheap and make a shot at four hundred yards.

Water levels vary from year to year, but in most seasons you can expect to get your feet wet hunting swamp buffalo. In some years you'll wade through channels in water up to your waist, and there will be times when you're gonna get stuck in the mud.

I've often written and said in seminars that shooting at such distances is unusual in Africa. It is, but there are times and places. On that hunt I was using one of McMillan's accurate bolt guns in .300 Winchester Magnum, set up with a big Nightforce scope and

This is not a giant crocodile as it is about a twelve-footer. A local fisherman had been taken from this hole, so this was a good croc to remove. I could only see the top half of its head, so I had no choice but to go for the brain shot, which is a very small target.

185-grain Berger bullets. Although a .300 magnum is always a good and versatile choice, that's really too much scope for thornbush hunting—but it's a fine rig for the delta's floodplains, and even for the wide-open pans. In 2015, when Donna had a turn for a zebra permit, she borrowed Mark's McMillan .300 with the big scope, and also used it for her hartebeest.

These days hartebeests are increasing so rapidly that they might be encountered almost anywhere, but the edges of the floodplains probably have the biggest numbers. With increased numbers, the quota has gone up, but when I started hunting in this area, the hartebeest quota was smaller, and it was 2013 before I had an opportunity to hunt one. To me these hartebeests are a total mystery. They are definitely Lichtenstein hartebeest, which I've hunted in Zambia and southern Tanzania. Think about what that means: The Marromeu area lies *south* of the Zambezi, an obvious barrier; to my knowledge only Kruger Park has Lichtenstein hartebeest south of the river. Go figure.

Anyway, when I had a permit, Mark and I headed out to the floodplain, and after some looking around, we spotted an unusually big hartebeest bull with a group of females. Using the diagonal approach, Mark and I walked for miles, but we weren't closing much distance. I was shooting a Blaser R8 in .270 Winchester, which is accurate and reliable—but these hartebeests are stout, and I was regretting Mark's offer of his .300. Finally, in wide-open grass with a bit of crosswind we had them at 370 yards. That's too far for shooting off sticks, at least for me, but there are some

Buffaloes love to graze and rest in short-grass savannas where there's almost no cover. It takes time and it's exhausting get . . . sometimes!

tricks. We had two sets of sticks, so we set one conventionally for the fore-end and the second under the butt, so I had sort of a standing benchrest. I held high for the distance and a bit into the wind, and the 130-grain Hornady landed perfectly. So far it's the biggest hartebeest taken in the area.

I can't say that about my waterbuck, but I can say that it's my best waterbuck! Donna got a good one back in 2011, by Argo out on the floodplains, but my turn didn't come until 2016. The waterbuck is a common and widespread animal and, as Ruark wrote, "there is no more ruggedly handsome animal in Africa." But although plentiful, really good ones are hard to come by and also hard to judge because the curve is critical to the total length.

I have shot some good ones, including elsewhere in this volume, but I always wanted to break the magical thirty-inch mark *just once*. So we put an Argo on a trailer and towed it out onto the floodplain as far as a Land Cruiser could go, then crossed the first papyrus channel, and immediately had waterbucks ahead of us.

There was nothing intriguing in the first group, nor in the second, nor in the third. (As I've said, there are lots of waterbucks out there, sometimes in bachelor groups into the dozens.) Ahead, through distance and heat waves, however, there was a lone bull that appeared wide, heavy, and marvelous. He was all of that, but with waterbucks it's essential they turn their heads so you can see the forward curve. Up close we decided his horns were too straight, but what about that one on beyond? Using the diagonal approach once again we closed to about two hundred yards, and this one seemed to have it all.

trying to get near enough for a shot, but with kneepads, gloves, and plenty of patience it's amazing how close you can

He did! I don't like to make a big thing about measurements, but over the years—starting in Kenya in 1977—I suppose I've taken at least a dozen waterbucks. Even discounting some of the smaller races that don't reach extreme length, I'd come close to that magical thirty-inch mark a few times, but never quite reached it. So that was our goal—and making that judgment, honestly, is asking a lot of a professional hunter. This one was thirty-one inches on both horns. Mission accomplished!

It's no great secret that I love all the spiral horns, but the elands are certainly among my favorites. The eland also offers Africa's very best wild meat, so if you're going to take an eland, make sure it's early in the safari. Although eland numbers are coming up, they don't seem to show up until the last few weeks of the season. This never mattered much to me because the few eland permits are generally spoken for—but in 2015 there was one available. Cool, except that the hunt was in late September.

No eland had yet appeared on the floodplain, but a decent bull had been seen along the edges of some big clearings about an hour from camp. I figured our chances were zilch, but Mark and I cruised the area both morning and evening, and I think it was just the third day of the safari—perfect timing to take an eland—when we spotted him far off across a huge clearing, probably a thousand yards away.

With eland there is no diagonal approach. The quartering wind wouldn't allow us to duck into the near tree line, and it was too far and too open to make the far tree line. A frontal approach was the only option. Using a few brushy termite mounds for cover, we hunkered low and butt-scooted when we had to. We had cut the distance in half when we ran out of cover, but we were still too far away for an eland and much too far for a .375. Now the bull was on the move. He crossed the end of the clearing and stood in a finger of trees, and a whole new set of termite mounds gave us options.

With more butt-scooting and a last termite mound, we were still a bit over three hundred yards away. That's far for a .375 with a 300-grain round-nose bullet, yet there was no way we were going to get closer. I was shooting the LAW rifle, extremely accurate, so if I could get steady enough, I thought I could pull it off. I crawled to the forward edge of the antheap, set the sticks low for a sitting position, and held a bit below the backline.

The first shot looked good and sounded good, but the eland turned away and began to run. I missed with the second shot, but the third shot, a solid, entered the right hip and exited the left shoulder. A few more steps and he piled up, a really nice eland bull—and some great eating for days to come.

In 2015 Donna put in quite a lot of time trying to get a croc and failed—but just now, in 2016, against all odds, when conditions were terrible, hunting with PH Gert Boosye, she shot one on an island in the Zambezi. The year for my Zambezi Delta croc was 2014. We tried the river a couple of times but, just as Donna experienced, the water level was too high. What this means is the sandbars aren't exposed, so there may be crocs lying up in the brush, but not where you can see them and plan a stalk. Our 2014 hunt was also in September, a bit late for ideal croc hunting, but water levels in the swamp were normal. Mark had a nice little pool where a couple of crocs were frequenting, so we anchored a warthog bait, built a blind, put in a trail camera, and a couple days later went out by Argo early in the morning.

The bait was on our side of the pool, thirty yards from the blind. The pool was rectangular, probably only another thirty yards across. About ten o'clock things got exciting. A crocodile cruised into view, and then hauled out on the opposite bank. This was a shootable distance and it was a shootable croc, but we were pretty sure it was a female. So we stayed really still, my buddy Conrad running the TV camera. Sure enough, an hour later the male came by. It wasn't clear if he wanted her, or just wanted her to move so he could have her perfect lying-up spot, but he climbed all over her. I couldn't shoot for fear of hitting both, and she never budged. After a while he gave up and slithered back into the water. I figured that was it for the day, but in just a couple of minutes the croc appeared on our side, just part of his head and the hump of his back visible.

There are three possible shots on a crocodile: brain, neck ("behind the smile"), and perhaps the base of the shoulder, although there is disagreement as to whether this

Meat drops are organized regularly, partly to deter poaching and partly because that's the right thing to do. The local chief does a dance to celebrate the bounty, and then each family will receive a share. In 2016 about eighteen tons of meat were distributed.

will anchor a croc. I have no opinion because I've never seen it used. The only option I had was the brain shot, the smallest target. I could see the eyes and I could see the "horns," and the distance was close. Holding behind the eyes and at a 45-degree angle down from the horns, I squeezed off as carefully as I could. The brain pan erupted, and that was the end of that crocodile. He was a solid twelve-footer, a nice crocodile but no monster. A local fisherman had been grabbed in this hole, so it was a good place to take one. Also, those few minutes of watching him wrestle with the female were some of the most exciting I've ever spent.

Of course, buffaloes are the big attraction, both for me and for most hunters who visit the Zambezi Delta. There are really two entirely different types of buffalo hunting: swamp and forest. Every year there are more buffaloes in the forest, and fresh tracks can be followed when you encounter them. This is difficult buffalo hunting because the forest is thick and noisy, but every season a few more are taken in the woodlands. I've never taken a forest buffalo there, although I've followed quite a few herds.

That said, however, I really like swamp hunting, and that's where the majority of buffaloes are taken. Argos are still used for hunting waterbucks and crocodiles on the edges, but swamp buffalo hunting is now done with the big Hägglund BV tracked vehicles, enabling full meat recovery. Buffalo hunters go to the swamps in rotation,

The big Hägglund BV tracked vehicles are a godsend—but they aren't infallible. It is possible to get extremely stuck, and breakdowns can occur. Zambeze Delta Safaris almost always sends two vehicles to the swamp in case something goes wrong.

usually two and sometimes three at a time. Depending on the herds spotted—and the size of the herds—they may split up, or if it's a really big herd they may stay together. Honestly, it's a very successful way to hunt buffalo. "Three-buffalo days" aren't common, but "two-buffalo days" aren't unusual, and it's pretty rare for a group to go into the swamp and come out without at least one buffalo.

This is not to say it's easy. Getting out to the herds means leaving long before dawn, and you will be clanking and bumping along for several hours. Then the real hunt begins when you see white egrets circling the herds. Then, well, who knows? There may be chest-deep channels and knee-deep mud to slog through, and there may be hundreds of yards of open ground to crawl across.

For sure it's going to be hot out there, and there is no shade. For safety the preference is to get back across the deepest channels before dark, but it isn't uncommon to rise at 3 A.M. and return to camp—with or without a buffalo—at midnight. Some folks hate it, most tolerate it because the buffaloes are out there, and a very few really sick people just love it. Count me in the latter group. Even the younger PHs aren't tough enough to go out there day after day—that's why it's done in relays. I'm certainly not, but in a ten-day hunt I'll usually go to the swamps three or four times.

Sometimes it's just for the ride, as it was with John Stucker and Tim Lesser. Sometimes it's Donna's turn and not mine, but I always take a turn for a buffalo, and if any quota is left over, I'll go for a second buffalo rather than repeat on plains game. So, all taken together, I've now done quite a lot of this swamp buffalo hunting.

There are some big differences between swamp hunting for buffalo and hunting for them in Tanzania, Zambia, and Zimbabwe. For one thing, we rarely track; instead, we follow the white egrets. For another, for reasons altogether mysterious, bachelor groups seem rare. The herds almost always contain fully mature breeding bulls—and often much older bulls that, elsewhere, we would call *dagga* boys and would find them on their own. Third, and extremely important, because the herds are big and the short-grass savannas where they often rest is *really* flat and open, shooting distances are longer on average than what is common in thornbush habitat. "Long" shots? *No*, nobody's crazy. But a hundred yards or so is a good, normal distance here. Half that is rare, and there are times when half again—a hundred and fifty yards—is practical.

So it's not "iron-sight country." The PHs mostly carry big doubles, and after you see the sawgrass where a wounded buffalo will invariably go, you'll understand why. I've used iron sights here (and will again), but I don't recommend them. A scoped rifle between .375 and .416 is the obvious solution, and a red-dot sight is another good option. There are just too many shots that are beyond certainty to use iron sights. There have been many times we've crawled close to herds, with the nearest buffalo just thirty or forty yards away, but Murphy's Law applies: The bull you want will not be the closest buffalo, and once you get in, it's hard to back off and start over.

I love seeing the big herds—and they can be really huge. A few years back Mark and I, hunting by ourselves, spotted a big herd on the horizon. We stopped the BV a kilometer or so out and began our approach—an amazingly foot-dry approach. As we neared, there appeared to be three or four hundred buffaloes on a short-grass savanna, many already lying down. This was clearly not the whole herd because there

That's a beautiful bull, about forty-five-inches wide, but he's too young. Give this one another three years and he's going to be a real monster! These days the average is coming up on the older bulls we're taking—but we're also seeing more big youngsters like this bull.

were scores of egrets circling and diving in sawgrass behind the animals we could see. At that moment we had plenty right in front of us.

The grass was short, but there were a few taller tufts here and there. So we started crawling from maybe two hundred fifty yards out, and since these buffaloes never even got nervous, we kept going until we had a half-circle of them arrayed around us, the closest less than fifty yards and the most distant barely over a hundred away. Perfect! The best bull we could see was lying down on the right side of the herd, a really fine old boy with extremely heavy bosses and worn tips. We crawled a few yards in his direction, set up, and waited, and when he stood, I took the shot. I think he ran a bit with the herd and then went down.

I really should remember because he was probably one of my best delta bulls—but what I remember most was that, after the shot, instead of retreating into the sawgrass, the buffaloes came out, and kept coming. They stretched out across the savanna for more than half a mile, too many to count, too many to even photograph. How many buffaloes are there when the herd is a thousand yards long and eight or ten animals deep? I said twenty-five hundred; Mark reckoned possibly three thousand.

This was the biggest gathering of buffaloes I've ever seen. Big herds are the norm out there, five hundred, six hundred, eight hundred . . . but nothing like that monstrous sea of buffaloes. My guess is it was a very temporary joining of several smaller herds because we tried to find them again the next day and could not—but there were lots of smaller herds in that part of the swamp. That was still the biggest herd I've ever seen, and the second-largest was probably the big group I got into this past hunt with John Stucker and Tim Lesser.

I've never had any real trouble with these swamp buffaloes, and although Mark's team now takes more than a hundred every season, nobody has yet gotten hurt—touch wood. Part of it is the open country; there's no bullet-eating brush. The open country does mean that shots aren't always as close as one might like, but in a near-absence of lions, these are calm buffaloes, and in big herds they seem to believe there's safety in numbers. It might take hours to sort through a herd, but there's usually plenty of time for the shot and to wait for good presentation for the shot. There's really no excuse for poor shot placement in a situation like this.

Of course it happens, and the sawgrass is never very far away. You do not want a wounded buffalo in sawgrass, and the papyrus channels are even worse. If a wounded buffalo gets into this stuff, we'll typically check the edges and maybe go in a few yards—but the vegetation is too tall and, on foot, you just can't see. So after a brief exploration we'll usually bring up the swamp vehicle, which is not only safer but also more effective because now you can see.

In my experience very few buffaloes are lost—honestly, a smaller percentage than when I was doing a lot of buffalo hunting in the Zambezi Valley. Using a vehicle for follow-up is not without hazard. Twice I've been in BVs that were hit by buffalo. The impact is horrendous, but it's better than taking a hit on foot. On the McMillan safari, I was with Kelly McMillan when he took a nice bull and got him down cleanly. We were trying to take two bulls from the same herd, but I didn't do quite so well. I got in what felt like a good shot with a McMillan in .404 Jeffery, but my bull ducked back into the herd, and we had a Mexican standoff for a little while.

During this impasse a bull detached from the herd and walked into the nearest sawgrass and vanished. Yes, chances were good that that was my bull—but he wasn't visibly limping and we couldn't see any blood on him, so we couldn't be sure. So we waited a bit, and when the herd finally started to move off, we were hoping they'd leave a downed buffalo behind them. No, there was no downed bull, and there was also no visibly hit buffalo trailing the herd. So the bull that walked into the sawgrass was my bull . . . or my bull was still able to keep up with the herd. Mark and I walked toward the edge of the sawgrass to look for blood.

Out in the swamps we see a lot of hippo tracks, but we don't often see hippos. Because of this, our impression is there aren't very many. Since 2016 was an exceptionally dry year, hippos congregated in a few pools. While hippos are no longer on license, obviously there are lots of them!

We were about ten feet away when my bull lurched to its feet from behind the first row of grass. He was facing right, quartering to us, and I assume he would have charged if he could have. Mark and I both shot, and this buffalo wasn't going anywhere. Remember, we'd *watched him walk into the sawgrass.* We had the spot mentally marked, but that stuff swallows buffalo so completely that we had no idea the bull had lain down right there at the edge.

As I said, we usually go to the swamps in teams, splitting up or staying together as the circumstances dictate. Last year I went out with Zack and Debbie Aultman—Debbie first, then Zack, and I'd bat cleanup if there was a chance.

Debbie got a lovely buffalo, but it took some time and the afternoon was getting on. Now, Zack Aultman is a real student of sporting rifles and a great shot—but the last couple of years he's been fighting serious eye problems. It isn't easy for *anyone* to pick the correct bull out of a shifting black throng. Now throw in some loss of vision! Anyway, PH Dylan Holmes found a gorgeous bull, but we couldn't make it work—and now we were getting to the witching hour, so we had, maybe, one more attempt before it was time to get out of Dodge.

We had already spotted another herd in a big opening just a kilometer or so away. We got around the wind, crept through some sawgrass, then crawled along the edge of the clearing, pitching up just over a hundred yards from the herd. So far so good, also quick and easy—but with the low sun now behind the herd, I think we all knew this was going to be a challenge for Zack. Then, just to our left, a magnificent buffalo bull stepped out of sawgrass we'd just traversed and started walking toward the herd. Big bosses, good shape, easily over forty inches wide.

Almost certainly having no idea how fantastic a bull this was, Zack got on the sticks, shot, and put him down . . . while the entire herd watched. Sometimes this happens. Buffaloes in herds feel secure. Lions are rare and poaching pressure is rarer, so the herds often stand or just run a short distance after a first bull is shot.

With Zack's bull down, PH Julian Moller immediately got me on the sticks and we started sorting through the herd. There were a bunch of bulls in this herd, but over on the right one appeared better than the rest. Julian saw him first, of course, and got me on him, so when he stepped clear, I was ready. I was shooting a LAW .375 with Hornady 300-grain DGX bullets. The shot was broadside, so I held on the shoulder, one-third of the way up. The herd stampeded to the left, and initially the bull was lost, but he came clear almost immediately, then stopped, head down. I would have shot again, but his rear was to me. So I hesitated, and as I was waiting for him to turn, he fell over, dead.

This is the most exciting part! The buffaloes are right there, and there are lots of them. The hard part is sorting through the herd to find a mature bull, and then getting him clear for a shot.

In 2016 Donna and I made a double play on two very nice buffaloes. That's not so rare in the delta, but it's unusual t Haldane—a great day in the swamp!

This year Donna and I went out to the swamps with Sara Bishop. Sara, of course, would shoot first, and I expected to bat cleanup again. This time Donna threw me a curve. She insisted I shoot before her. I argued only briefly—by this time we had about eight hundred buffaloes in sight, so it wasn't the time for lengthy discussion. This herd held a lot of bulls, and for once quite a few of them were visible—meaning on our side of the herd. Sara shot first, and here I think we made a bit of a tactical error. The shot looked good and sounded good, but her bull retreated into the pack and we didn't actually see it go down. When the herd finally moved off, an obviously injured bull trailed behind and was recovered, but it's probably better to be sure of the first one before proceeding, lest you have the nightmare of multiple wounded bulls to deal with.

Anyway, we didn't do this, but it all worked out. After Sara's shot, the herd drifted back a bit, and then a gorgeous bull stepped out over on the right-hand side. I think at 160 yards this was the longest shot I've ever made on a buffalo. I was very steady on good sticks and the bull was quartering toward me. I was shooting a .375 again, this time a CZ 550 with the stock I helped design for them. The shot felt great,

have them down so close together that you can get both in one photo. That's PH Gert Boosye, Donna, me, and Mark

right on the point of the shoulder, and the bull reared back and whirled, as they do. At that distance and in that press of buffaloes, there was no possibility for a second shot, but we could see the bull walk slowly into the herd—and then fall over, horns flat to the ground, nose straight in the air.

Now it was Donna's turn. She was shooting her Blaser R8 with a .375 barrel and with an Aimpoint red-dot sight. Wisely and correctly, she immediately said it was too far. But the herd was calm, so PH Gert Boosye and Donna started crawling to close some distance. I didn't really think they'd pull it off, but they had gained fifty or sixty yards when I saw Gert set the sticks low for a sitting position. From our angle, of course, it was pure guesswork as to which buffalo they were aiming at, but just left of center what appeared to be a very good bull had stepped to the edge and was quartering at nearly the same angle my bull had been. Yes, that one . . . he almost dropped to the shot, took a few steps forward, and went down—but he got back up and we watched as he paraded slowly along the near edge of the herd. Finally he stopped, clear, and she hit him again, this time broadside. He swung back into the herd, but went down almost immediately.

Dinners are a group event, usually presided over by Mark Haldane at the head of the table. The food is excellent, the camp is extremely well run, and the Zambeze Delta Safaris staff makes it fun—just like it's supposed to be.

When the herd finally moved off, we still had to recover Sara's bull, but Donna's buffalo and mine, both excellent bulls, lay about forty yards apart. Thanks to the BV, we were able to pull them together for a photo, a rare opportunity. That's the way it sometimes goes out there.

******

If there should be another ten-year book, completed in 2026, I have no idea what it might contain. My crystal ball ain't that good. I do know, right now, that as a slice of wild Africa the Zambezi Delta is pretty hard to beat. It's not that way because it was always so. Rather, it's that way because hunting outfitters, using funding from hunting, have protected and rebuilt the wildlife, effectively turning the clock back. I have no idea what this area might have been like in the 1960s before Mozambique's devastating civil war, but I know very little wildlife remained when the war ended. Today the area is as rich with wildlife as anything I saw in Botswana, Tanzania, or Zambia in the 1980s. That's why I keep going back, and if I'm privileged to hunt in Africa for a few more years, I'm sure I'll keep returning to the Zambezi Delta.